UBIQUITOUS LAW

Στην Αγγελική και τον Χάρη Μελισσάρη

Ubiquitous Law
Legal Theory and the Space for Legal Pluralism

EMMANUEL MELISSARIS
London School of Economics, UK

ASHGATE

Published by
Ashgate Publishing Limited
Wey Court East
Union Road
Farnham
Surrey, GU9 7PT
England

Ashgate Publishing Company
Suite 420
101 Cherry Street
Burlington
VT 05401-4405
USA

www.ashgate.com

British Library Cataloguing in Publication Data
Melissaris, Emmanuel
Ubiquitous law : legal theory and the space for legal pluralism. - (Law, justice and power series)
1. Legal polycentricity 2. Law - Methodology
I. Title
340.1'1

Library of Congress Cataloging-in-Publication Data
Melissaris, Emmanuel.
Ubiquitous law : legal theory and the space for legal pluralism / by Emmanuel Melissaris.
p. cm. -- (Law, justice, and power)
Includes bibliographical references and index.
ISBN 978-0-7546-2542-1
1. Legal polycentricity. 2. Law--Methodology. I. Title.

K236.M45 2009
340'.11--dc22

2008045428

ISBN 978 0 7546 2542 1

Mixed Sources
Product group from well-managed forests and other controlled sources
www.fsc.org Cert no. SA-COC-1565
© 1996 Forest Stewardship Council
FSC

Printed and bound in Great Britain by
MPG Books Ltd, Bodmin, Cornwall.

Contents

Acknowledgements

Over the years, many colleagues and friends read various parts and versions of this book. I am particularly indebted to Emilios Christodoulidis for patiently and generously following and supporting my work from the very beginning; Neil Duxbury for his attentiveness to my text and all his invaluable help; George Pavlakos for always being a strict but fair judge of my ideas. For their careful reading and valuable comments at various stages of development of this book, I am grateful to Neil MacCormick, Robert Alexy, Zenon Bankowski, Lindsay Farmer, Sean Coyle, Sylvie Delacroix, Peter Goodrich, Marie Fox, Niki Lacey, George Taylor, Mike Wilkinson and Lorenzo Zucca. Parts of the book were presented to audiences at Manchester, Keele, the London School of Economics, Leicester, Birmingham, the 2005 IVR Congress in Granada, and the 2008 Philosophy and Social Sciences conference in Prague. My thanks go to all those colleagues who attended the sessions and helped me rethink my arguments.

Parts of the book have appeared in a different form as articles: (2005b), 'The Limits of Institutionalised Legal Discourse', *Ratio Juris* 18:4, 464–83; (2004), 'The More the Merrier? A New Take on Legal Pluralism', *Social and Legal Studies* 13:1, 57–79; (2005a), 'The Chronology of the Legal', *McGill Law Journal* 50:4, 839–61; (2006b), 'Perspective, Critique, and Pluralism in Legal Theory', *Northern Ireland Legal Quarterly* 57:4, 597–609. I am grateful to the publishers for their kind permission to reprint parts of these papers here. I have since rethought and reshaped many of my ideas in these articles and they are now synthesized and enriched in this book.

Colleen Etheridge's friendship and administrative competence made my life much easier while completing this project. My thanks go to the staff at Ashgate for their efficiency and hard work in producing this book. I am also grateful to Alexandra Xanthaki, George Pavlakos, Aristotle Kallis, Pano Masti and Maria Voutsinou for always being there. Nothing would have been possible without Lindy Crewe. Finally, I would like to dedicate this book to my parents for their love and support, ubiquitous in time and space.

Introduction

During the final stages of writing this book, its subject matter hit the headlines in the UK. In an interview to the BBC, Dr Rowan Williams, the Archbishop of Canterbury, the Head of the Church of England, controversially argued that sooner or later Sharia law would become a recognized source of law for some people in the UK:

> It seems unavoidable and indeed as a matter of fact certain provisions of Sharia are already recognised in our society and under our law. So it's not as if we're bringing in an alien and rival system. We already have in this country a number of situations in which the law – the internal law of religious communities – is recognised by the law of the land as justifying conscientious objections in certain circumstances.[1]

At a time when the English media were admittedly struggling to find anything else of interest to keep them going for a while (perhaps with the exception of a destructive fire at Camden Locks Market in London), the reaction was immediate, widespread and, at times, angry. Conservative Shadow Community Cohesion Minister Baroness Warsi said: 'Dr Williams seems to be suggesting that there should be two systems of law, running alongside each other, almost parallel, and for people to be offered the choice of opting into one or the other. That is unacceptable.'[2]

David Cameron, the then leader of the Conservative Party, believed that 'state multiculturalism is a wrong-headed doctrine that has had disastrous results. It has fostered difference between communities and it has stopped us from strengthening our collective identity. Indeed it has deliberately weakened it.' He added that expansion of Sharia law was the 'logical endpoint of the now discredited doctrine of state multiculturalism, seeing people merely as followers of certain religions, rather than individuals in their own right within a common community'.[3] The Labour MP Geoff Hoon decided, rather patronizingly, that the Archbishop was

---

1 <http://news.bbc.co.uk/go/pr/fr/-/2/hi/uk_news/7239283.stm> (last accessed on 30 June 2008).

2 <http://news.bbc.co.uk/go/pr/fr/-/2/hi/uk_news/7239596.stm> (last accessed on 30 June 2008).

3 <http://news.bbc.co.uk/go/pr/fr/-/2/hi/uk_news/politics/7264740.stm> (last accessed on 30 June 2008).

punching above his weight and that he should not express opinions on 'complicated legal matters'.[4]

It is striking, though perhaps not surprising, that most people found it impossible to even conceive the law separately from the Leviathan State. But then again, why not? What is it about the State that allows it to claim exclusivity over the law? After all, that is what Sharia purports to be. Law! Is it then a different kind of law and, if yes, what kind and how does it differ to State law? And, as a graduate student once asked me, how come we have not devised some other word for it, a word like *shlaw*?

Once we start speaking of law outside the State, it would not take much for the floodgates to become wide open. Is Sharia the only such case of a different law? If yes, why? If not, what other cases are there out there? And if there are other such cases, are they so different to State law that we must come up with new words for them? But if we can all understand them as law, does this not mean that we are cognitively and conceptually prepared for that?

Things get even more complicated once one starts thinking about issues of rightness. 'Sharia law is unjust and cruel', some hastened to shout. 'It's eye for an eye and a tooth for a tooth and it has no respect for human rights, for women's dignity, for difference.' All this, in contrast to social contractarian State law, which most hold as not only the greatest achievement but also the continued embodiment of the great civic revolutions of the eighteenth and nineteenth centuries. State law is there to reduce pluralism and ensure fairness, certainty and peace. In response, others, Muslims and non-Muslim liberals alike, protested that judging the rightness and wrongness from the outside is typical of Western, European, paternalistic ethical imperialism. According to them, there is no such thing as objective rightness, although most would tone things down when faced with *some* practices.

But then we should stop and ask ourselves: what is it we do by asking whether Sharia should count as law or not in the first place? If we are saying what ought and ought not to be in the world, and whatever does not pass our test should somehow come out of circulation, is there not something suspiciously legal about this? Or are we simply saying what is in the world and what not? Can we do that though, especially in something like the law? If yes, under what conditions?

Finally, let us assume that we recognize the legality of orders outside the State. How is that to be managed? Dr Williams spoke of Sharia becoming *official* law. If this means sanctioned by the State, then the whole project seems rather self-defeating, as the very point is to reduce the State to another source of legality alongside innumerable others, if not questioning State law's claim to legality altogether. Then we would be faced with the even more difficult problem of how to manage all these legalities in a way that would prevent one of them from hegemonically dominating the rest while at the same time not allowing plurality

4 <http://news.bbc.co.uk/go/pr/fr/-/2/hi/uk_news/7239567.stm> (last accessed on 30 June 2008).

to regress into perpetual conflict and normative meaninglessness. In other words, the challenge is to reconcile diversity and order or, in the words of Boaventura de Sousa Santos, emancipation and regulation (de Sousa Santos 1995).

All this is of course familiar territory to legal theorists. The question concerning the sources of legality has always been central to legal philosophy. Two main attitudes to the question can be singled out. On the one hand, there are those who try theoretically to reduce complexity in the world of legality and refer all law to one single source. This strand accommodates the all too familiar distinction between conventionalist positivism, inaugurated and influenced by the work of H.L.A. Hart, and normativism, most notably Ronald Dworkin's interpretivism, at least in Anglo-American jurisprudence. The former remains faithful to the empiricism of David Hume, the political thought of Thomas Hobbes and Jeremy Bentham's vision about the law. Based on its moral scepticism, it reserves the claim to objectivity for the law alone. At the same time, motivated by the demand for political emancipation, it seeks to demystify the law and rid it of the unprovable claims from the religious or moral authority of the *ancien regime* by reducing the law to a social fact, which is sensibly identifiable and thus knowable and open to external critique. On the other hand, interpretivism takes issue with the rigidity of the positivist approach and tries to recover the law's flexibility by establishing its necessary connection with political morality. It takes a realist stance in relation to morality, maintaining its status and using constructive interpretation as the tool for arriving at conclusions about the right. So, despite their far from negligible differences, it appears that what these two strands have in common is their monism in relation to the legal and their yearning for an all-pervasive objectivity.

At the other end of the spectrum, unsurprisingly there are again various takes on the theme of the sources of legality and the singular/plural dilemma. This time, though, the differences are much less pronounced and the overlaps more frequent. Much of critical legal theory is concerned less with the source(s) of law than with what distorts normative meaning, rendering State law an apparatus of domination and the law's inherent inability to become co-extant with justice. So, although this kind of critical legal theory does not explicitly deal with legal polycentricity, the arguments from law's domination implicitly rest on the assumption that there are other normative orders outside the State, which are silenced by the latter and therefore done an injustice to. And there are of course theories of legal pluralism, which explicitly take on the task of proving that legality can be found inside and outside the State. The same idea has been treated in a variety of ways, ranging from the earlier sociological focus on 'law in the books' and the 'law of lawyers', the anthropological study of post-colonial contexts and the co-existence of local legalities with the law of the colonizing State, through to critical legal pluralism, which perceives of the law as radically diverse and dispersed, thus making it impossible, and perhaps even normatively undesirable, conceptually to pinpoint what the law exactly is. So, in terms of where law is to be found, what all these strands have in common is their tendency to decentralize the legal and, more often than not, criticize State law for violently standing in the way of this decentralization.

This book engages with these theoretical strands in order to explore the possibility of understanding the law in dissociation from the State while, at the same time, establishing the conditions of meaningful communication between various legalities. This task is partly methodological and partly substantive, although these two aspects are inevitably interlinked. It needs to be shown that the enquiry into the legal has been biased by the implicit or explicit presupposition of the State's exclusivity to a claim to legality as well as the tendency to make this enquiry the task of experts, who purport to be able to represent the legal community's commitments in a manner which is authoritative and, more worryingly, becomes constitutive of the law and parasitic to and distortive of people's commitments. But such a critique would not be sufficient in itself in the absence of some other way of exploring the legal, which will not be based on rigid epistemological and normative assumptions but rather on self-reflection and mutual understanding and critique, so as to establish acceptable differences on the basis of a commonality. Clearly, in order for this to be possible, a substantive theoretical basis is necessary. What needs to be established is the possibility of *some* degree of universal objectivity in relation to the law's existence and content, which will neither stifle and foreclose diversity nor radically under-prescribe and under-determine questions of law and rightness. This will not only inform the dialogue between legalities but also set the conditions of how and where this dialogue can be possible in a non-hegemonic manner.

Another central concern of this book has to do with the tension between the competing understandings of legal theory as, on the one hand, a philosophical venture and, on the other, as an instance of social theory. More often than not, these two approaches to legal theory are viewed as incompatible and antagonistic. To me, this makes very little sense. Any social theory needs some philosophical grounding in order for it to get off the ground at all. Every enquiry into the world is inevitably based on certain non-empirical presuppositions that one needs to be aware of and be prepared to revise at all times. But such a philosophical substratum is not sufficient, when it comes to the law, which is firmly placed in context and rests on the way those participating in it experience legality. So, one of the aims of this book is to combine the philosophical with the socio-theoretical in a productive way. Therefore, it is neither a work in pure legal philosophy nor one in empirical sociology. It is rather an attempt to provide a philosophical grounding of a socio-theoretical approach to the law. Not, though, by reaching a conclusion once and for all concerning the concept of the law, which socio-legal theory can then adopt and go on to apply in empirical work, but rather, and reflecting my view of the legal, by grounding the constant interlinking and mutual redeemability of philosophical and socio-theoretical claims through which the sense of law will emerge and remain under continuous critical review.

In Chapter 1 I discuss some of the most influential theorizations of the law, namely Hartian positivism, Dworkinian interpretivism and critical legal theory, and critique them on the grounds of their implicit adherence to an image of the law either as necessarily associated with the State or, especially in the case of critical legal theory, as necessarily a power relation between addressors and addressees of normative statements. Legal pluralism seems like a promising alternative to this monistic and necessarily hegemonic view of the law. In Chapter 2 I survey the ways in which legal pluralism has been theorized, in order to see whether they do justice to the pluralistic and emancipatory potential of the law. I conclude that what I term positivistic legal pluralism, that is early sociological and anthropological accounts, falls prey to the same methodological and substantive shortcomings of their monistic counterparts by applying too rigid epistemological criteria from an external perspective in order to conceptualize and recognize legality. On the other hand, post-modern, critical legal pluralism comes much closer to realizing the emancipatory potential of law, but I argue that it is undermined by its refusal to provide anything more than a vague and wholly indeterminate conception of legality. In Chapter 3 I work with Robert Cover's account of nomic diversity, in order to arrive at an understanding of the law, which will be able to accommodate pluralism without giving up on the possibility of a meaningful order. I argue that it is possible to formulate a universal sense of law, understood as the combination of the law's normative and factual aspects, which is thin enough not to over-prescribe, but also not completely vacuous. I propose that the law should be understood in terms of the shared normative experiences of people in various contexts. Therefore the content of this sense of law can only be fleshed out and determined in specific contexts. Such an understanding of legality will serve both to kickstart the enquiry into the legal and ground the communication between diverse *nomoi*.

In Chapter 4 I turn back to the methodological question by giving a critical account of legal theory as an expert culture, which substitutes the commitments of participants in legality with its own perspective, thus inevitably objectivating the law. In a programmatic fashion, I then suggest that legal theory should take an interperspectival, critical turn, democratize itself and become the forum in which various legalities can communicate in a self-reflective and mutually critical manner. In Chapter 5 I begin to develop a suggestion for a universal sense of law, which can guide interperspectival, critical enquiry. Kicking off from a discussion of the pragmatics of State legal discourse, I conclude that in law the constative and the performative are inseparable. It is precisely this which leads to the conception of the law in terms of what I have already called shared normative experiences. I also show how State law remains insensitive to this, because of its specific remit of reducing moral and political complexity and the historical circumstances which shaped and determined it. In Chapter 6 I explain shared normative experiences further and suggest how making sense of the law in such terms can serve the project of a legal pluralism, which aims at reconciling emancipation and regulation, diversity and order. Finally, in Chapter 7 I suggest that shared normative experiences are framed by conceptions of time and space and that legal theory should become more mindful of the close interplay of the experience of these dimensions and people's normative commitments.

The idea of ubiquitous law may scare off the traditionally liberal-minded, both those who wish to see the law shrinking and carve out a larger space for the private, and those who want to further the reach of the law but in the light of universal all-pervasive principles of justice. My hope is to help rethink and resolve this antinomy by relieving the law of the fear of domination and restoring its critical and emancipatory potential. The law's ubiquity will then mean polycentricity of authorship and control over it, and hopefully this can at least be used as a critical tool in the first instance.

London, 3 February 2009

Chapter 1
Perspective, Critique and Pluralism in Legal Theory

Introduction

The task I set for myself in this book is, first, to show how mainstream legal theories rely on the association of the law with the State as a methodological and substantive presupposition and, secondly, to point towards a reconceptualization of the law as well as a rethinking of the research programme of legal theory. This new research programme will make the best of the pluralistic potential of both, as well as reconcile the philosophical with the social theoretical study of the legal. The aim of this first chapter is to highlight a methodological shortcoming of some of the most influential legal theories and show that there is a need for an alternative way of theorizing about the law. My main targets are conventionalist positivism, epitomized by the work of H.L.A. Hart, and Ronald Dworkin's interpretivist substantivism, which have dominated legal philosophical debate over the past few decades, at least in the English-speaking world. I shall begin by arguing that the Hartian version of positivism cannot back both its twin claims to neutrality and generality at the same time, or at least not in the way that it goes about doing so. Dworkinian interpretivism may be better equipped for avoiding the same errors but, at the same time and because of its aversion towards conceptual analysis (at least of the positivistic kind), it wrongly rests on the presupposition that the institutional framework of law is of secondary significance but also given as a matter of general, albeit tacit, consensus. Thus not only does conceptual analysis (precisely of the positivistic kind) creep in theorizing about the law, but interpretivism also loses sight of its pluralistic and critical aims, which are purportedly central to it. Finally, although it is not my primary target, I will show that critical legal theory, in the broadest possible sense, is also found wanting because it is either not interested in questioning the exclusivity of State law, or at least a vision of the law as a one-way relationship of domination, or does not manage to criticize that with any conceptual clarity. In the next chapter I shall discuss whether theories of legal pluralism have managed to reclaim that pluralistic potential. The analysis here cannot but be rather cursory and selective, but I should emphasize that I am not interested in exposing all the methodological failures of all legal theories, but rather select some of the most influential ones[1] and bring to light their tacit, unjustified, and unexplained reliance on the assumption that the law is necessarily associated with the State.

1 I will make special mention of Hans Kelsen in Chapter 6.

Methodology in Legal Theory

Conventionalist Positivism

There is little doubt that contemporary legal theory owes much to and has been greatly influenced by the philosophy of H.L.A. Hart. Anxious to stick to his analytical guns and locate meaning in use and context, Hart argued that it is only through observation of how participants in the law speak and communicate about the latter that we can arrive at conclusions as to what the law is or, rather, what the law *is held* to be.[2] As is well known, a key distinction in Hart's theory is that between the internal and the external points of view. The crux of his legal theory is the thesis that the theorist observes the practices of the participants in a legal system and then qualifies, systematizes and generalizes those practices so as to formulate a context-transcendent and axiologically neutral concept of law, which will reduce the latter to a set of other concepts of lower degree of complexity. So, presumably after observing *prima facie* legal practices, Hart came to the conclusion that the law consists in the combination of a set of primary and a set of secondary rules. Among those secondary rules, the rule of recognition occupies a central place, for it provides the criterion for the identification of rules *qua* legal.

One problem with Hartian methodology that was quickly identified pertains to the nature of the external point of view. Hart suggested that the theorist observes, or ought to observe, *from the external point of view* what participants do and what meaning they attribute to their practices *from the internal point of view*. But if the external perspective is truly and fully external, the theorist will be unable to make any sense of participants' practices. All she will be able to see, as Hart himself argues in the context of discussing John Austin's idea of law-following as habit, are some regularities, which are either meaningless or meaningful with reference to the conceptual scheme of the observer rather than that of the participants. MacCormick came to the rescue by qualifying the distinction between internal and external. He addressed the fact that Hart failed to consider the possibility of understanding social behaviour through a process of *Verstehen*. Thus he distinguished between the hermeneutic and volitional aspects of the internal point of view. The former is assumed by the observer, the social scientist, who understands what participants in a legal system do but does not share their commitment (MacCormick 1981, 32–40).

This is admittedly a, perhaps unfairly, rough and brief reminder of the parameters of Hart's social-scientific/philosophical methodology. Nevertheless, it already shows that the Hartian project can be understood in terms of a set of

---

2 I am conscious of the fact that positivists, including Hart, have vehemently denied the charge of semanticism. Their defences are not entirely convincing, not least because they have not yet told us what exactly their methodology is and to what extent they rely on (criterial) semantics, in order to 'describe' the law. However, this is not a debate I want to enter in this context. I simply take as uncontroversial that positivism offers a description of paradigmatic cases of law from the external point of view (see Endicott 2001; Stavropoulos 2001).

couplings and distinctions relating both to the perspective of the participants in a legal system and the theorist, who seeks to conceptualize the law by observing it in action. Hart's positivism purports to be a *neutral* and, at the same time, *general* account of the structure of legal thought. But it also goes further than that by arguing that only such an uncommitted and universal account can be philosophically interesting. At the same time, Hart sends confusing signals as to how he goes about conceptualizing the law in such a neutral and general way. On the one hand, he claims to be offering a theory of law firmly embedded in the social by describing the book as an essay in *descriptive sociology*. On the other hand, and rather confusingly, he claims to be engaging in *general conceptual analysis*. This dual character strikes one as rather odd from the outset, as it seems impossible for conceptual analysis raising claims to universality and descriptive sociology to be reconciled in that way. All the more so, when we consider that they are coupled with the claims to generality and neutrality. In what follows I shall try to highlight some points of stress between all those claims.

Starting with description and generality, the problem is that the former cannot square with the latter, if the claim raised is an *a priori* one. Sociological description cannot help being both selective and context-bound. All a sociologist aiming at description can do is observe and record regularities, which she will have already picked out by employing a pre-selected concept, which will already have *some* content. This concept will serve as the criterion of inclusion (and exclusion) of the observed communities. In turn, observation will help clarify and refine the concept, which, though, has always already been guiding sociological enquiry. Thus a descriptive sociologist will be able to raise rather modest, context-bound and indexical claims. This, however, does not seem to have been Hart's or other analytical positivists' aim. The adage is that the only legal *philosophical* project worth pursuing is the effort to account for *the* concept of law in an a-historical, *a priori* manner. But it appears that this is not possible by way of description and then abstraction.

Seen from a different angle, in Hartian methodology the perspective of the participant seems to be conflated with that of the observer. In order to draw his image of law as the union of primary and secondary rules, Hart focuses on Western legal systems or, in any case, legal systems structurally resembling the one he was participating in as a former practising lawyer, and a teacher and researcher in legal academia. Perhaps it would be too much to expect Hart to sever his theorization entirely from his intellectual environment, which was marked by an adherence to 'black letter law', despite his hard efforts (Lacey 2004). After all, the discipline of law had not quite awoken from a 150-year-long lethargy (Duxbury 2005). The teaching of law was still vocational in orientation and focused exclusively on the systematic and largely uncritical study of statute and precedent (Lacey 2004). Or perhaps it would be unfair to ask Hart to provide anything other than 'armchair sociology' (Penner 2002, 442).

Irrespective of how much weight we place on historical and biographical explanations, Hart's 'sociological' method cannot be defended theoretically. In assuming the external-hermeneutic point of view, Hart plays down the fact that he *was* a participant in a legal system and makes very little, if any, effort to address the difficulty and complexity of the project of assuming the external perspective. His analysis seems to be kicking off from the assumption of the universality of the form that the legal has taken in specific cultural and political contexts (Coyle 2002). His point of departure is thus necessarily *a posteriori*, as he seems to have already tacitly or unconsciously selected the cohort of legal systems which qualify as such, and then goes on to single out their commonalities and conceptualize the law in an abstract manner. Thus, first, his 'descriptive sociology' becomes very much prescriptive, to the extent that it forms the criteria of inclusion in the concept of law from an epistemic, third-person perspective, which is merged with the first-person point of view; secondly, it does not describe but one form of law rather than paradigmatic cases of the *concept* of law.[3]

MacCormick's appeal to *Verstehen*, a suggestion which Hart accepted (Hart 1994, 243), does not provide a way out. The trouble is that *Verstehen*, especially if it is coupled with Hartian conventionalism, which MacCormick tried to refine rather than question, meets an insurmountable limitation. Namely, the observer, who assumes the standpoint of participants, can only learn what she already knows (Abel 1977). The hermeneutic attitude still maintains the distance between observer and observed and relies on the assumption that the states of the two parties are parallel, symmetrical and commensurable. For a Hartian legal sociologist to recognize legality when she sees it, she will have to refer to those paradigmatic cases in order to see whether the *prima facie* normative phenomena that she observes fall under the core meaning of law or they occupy some place in the conceptual penumbra. But this method is bound to leave out a number of phenomena, which, seen from a different perspective, could be of a legal nature.

Raz offers a rejoinder to this objection: 'There is nothing wrong in interpreting the institutions of other societies in terms of our typologies. This is an inevitable part of any intelligent attempt to understand other cultures' (Raz 1979, 50). This is indeed true and, in fact, it underpins some of my central arguments in this book. However, the problem with conventionalist positivist methodology is that the claims to generality and conclusiveness are raised too soon, when it is not even certain that they can be raised at all. As various theories of legal pluralism have pointed out, it is this philosophical imperialism, the delusion that our thick and conclusive concept of law can be imported into different contexts without losing any of its explanatory force and without doing injustice to these other contexts, that consolidates and lends legitimacy to State law perpetuating its domination. To be sure, one must start from somewhere and the best place to start from seems to be the familiar concepts available at home, but this is precisely that: a starting

3 This point is made very convincingly by Brian Tamanaha, who tries to disentangle conventionalism, functionalism and essentialism in Hartian jurisprudence, in order to formulate a project of positivist socio-legal theory (Tamanaha 2001). Tamanaha's suggestions are extremely insightful and important, so more on them in Chapter 2.

point and not 'the final arbiter' (J.L. Austin [1956] 1979, 8). First impressions must be put to further tests, which might even prove to be endless. The problem with Hartian positivism is that, although it is correct in trying to establish the possibility of saying something about the law in an a-contextual manner, not least because we seem to be referring to the legal as a distinct normative order rather consistently through time, it does not set the right conditions for the discourse through which this concept will be discovered and formulated. In order for an observer to be able to draw any conclusions as to what it is that a specific group of people has been 'recognizing' as law, she must engage with that community, in order to achieve a richer understanding of its normative commitments and, at the same time, enter a process of self-reflection about her own preconceptions of legality and instigate self-reflection on the part of that community as well. Moreover, Hartian legal theory does not seem aware of or allow any space for the falsifiability of its specific, context-bound conceptualization of the law, nor does it offer any way of gaining such awareness. And I would argue that central to the task of legal theory is precisely the awareness of its limitations and the effort to overcome them, seeking help from outside rather than barricading itself within its conceptual schemes. But I will have much more to say on these questions later on in this book.

The tension between description and generality is related to a second point of stress in Hartian methodology, namely the tension between conceptual analysis and neutrality.[4] It is true that the most charitable reading of Hartian legal philosophy would treat it as an exercise in conceptual analysis rather than descriptive sociology, despite Hart's confusing declarations. Hart's aim seems to have been to observe how the concept of law is employed and then to engage in analysis, which would sharpen our awareness of the term, to allude to Hart's Austinian influence, correct mistakes, deduct any contingencies and formulate a universal and context-transcendent concept of law. But can this ever be neutral? Can the recognition of the law *qua* law, that is as a source of normativity, ever be uncommitted?

Stephen Perry argues, correctly I think, that it cannot (Perry 2001). He distinguishes between Hart's substantive and methodological positivism. The former consists in the separation and sources theses. The latter has to do with the nature of legal theory, which for Hart is uncommitted and external. But Hart also purports to explain legal normativity and obligation as conceptual parts of the law. And here is where Perry's critique kicks in. It is impossible, he argues, to explain and clarify the concept of obligation from the external or hermeneutic point of view. Hart tells us that officials and other participants in a legal system regard themselves as obligated by the rules that the system consists in. He also famously refused to give an account of the reasons why participants experience this obligation. Perry argues that this does not sufficiently explain and clarify the concept of legal obligation. At the core of Hart's analysis of obligation:

---

4 In fact, what I have said about descriptiveness and generality holds for analysis as well.

> is simply a descriptive statement that (a certain proportion of) members of the relevant group regard themselves and all others in the group as obligated to conform to some general practice. This statement uses rather than analyses the concept of obligation. In the original text of *The Concept of Law* Hart in effect maintains that officials regard themselves and all other officials as obligated, in that unanalysed sense, by the general practice that constitutes the rule of recognition. To those who so regard themselves, this presumably does not come as news. If they or others want to know whether they are in fact under such an obligation, and if so shy, enlightenment is not forthcoming. Precisely because Hart's account of obligation is descriptive and external, it cannot be said to have succeeded in clarifying or elucidating the concept in any significant way. (Perry 2001, 334–5)

Perry is right in pointing out that a robust legal theory must provide an account of what makes widespread acceptance of norms stemming from a particular source obligatory. The fact that people do accept the law as a source of rules capable of guiding their action (let alone widespread acceptance of the content of specific rules) is surely more than just a happy coincidence and calls for an explanation richer than the assumption that people, almost unreflectively, obey the law because everyone else does so or the circular argument that the sense of obligation is to be understood in terms of the justified criticism for breaking the rules.

Hart's pursuit of neutrality in legal conceptual analysis accounts not only for the explanatory incompleteness of his positivism but is also, crucially, responsible for the critical inertia of his jurisprudence. Precisely because it is incapable of accounting for obligation and is happy to treat recognition of the law *qua* law as a mechanical and unreflective convention, this version of hermeneutic legal theory is stripped of any critical force in two senses. First, it is normatively inert. Positivists often reiterate the Benthamite argument that it is only prior knowledge of the law that can make law reform possible. Hart too was a value pluralist (Lacey 2004, 221) and much of his theoretical work on the law is informed by the Humean belief that the law is the only objectively and publicly identifiable crucible of integration of diverse and often contradictory moral attitudes. So, it is only in the presence of a common point of reference, laying the law with all its problems in plain sight, that axiological discourse about the merit or demerit of the law can become possible. In other words, if you do not know what needs fixing, how can you fix it or even want to fix it in the first place?

This Benthamite argument rests on at least two fundamental presuppositions. First, it assumes that it is possible to conceptualize the law without reference to its substantive normative content. Otherwise, it would be paradoxical from the outset to speak of good or bad law. Secondly, it presupposes that the law is imposed from above and beyond the community of people, which consider it law. If the normative character of the law is content- and reason-independent in the sense that the only reason behind it is the contingent and fragile fact of common acceptance of or simple compliance with a source of norms as legal on the part of the participants, without there being any commonly held reasons for this acceptance, those participants become simply legal *subjects*, while legal authority/authorship is deferred to those with specific institutional roles or plainly raw power. Thus, legal practice, and by this I mean all instances of legal rule-following, irrespective of whether it is put to the test in an institutionalized trial environment or not, becomes depoliticized and unreflective. For conventionalist positivism the law stands in the way, or, at least, outside, of politics and becomes the subject matter of technical expertise in the hands of the privileged few. This dichotomy is spelled out by J. Austin, and, with a careful reading, it does not seem to have been abandoned by Hart (J. Austin 1996). Despite the fact that Hart located meaning in use and rules in the fact of convergence of behaviour, when it came to conceptualizing the law, he shifted the focus from the community of participants to the officials of a legal system. The participants in a legal community accept as such what officials consider law but they do not also have to accept it as morally sound law. It is thus that, on a normative level, law reform becomes always external to the life of the law itself.

So what is left for the legal theorist to do? The critical toolbox available to the Hartian legal philosopher is depleted and she falls in a trap set by none other than herself. She is reduced to recording linguistic usage, turning a blind eye to the substantive charge of the concepts which she deals with. She thus becomes the spokesperson for those with authority to enact the law. For Hartian positivists the point of legal theory is to map the world of legality, to picture it in an uncommitted, shallow way, to offer a neutral conceptual analysis. The dangers in that are great, as Marcuse forcefully points out:

> Austin's contemptuous treatment of the alternatives to the common usage of words, and his defamation of what we 'think up in our armchairs of an afternoon'; Wittgenstein's assurance that 'philosophy leaves everything as it is' – such statements exhibit, to my mind, academic sado-masochism, self-humiliation, and self-denunciation of the intellectual whose labor does not issue in scientific, technical or like achievements. (Marcuse 1991, 173)

And elsewhere:

> In the totalitarian era, the therapeutic task of philosophy would be a political task, since the established universe of ordinary language tends to coagulate into a totally manipulated and indoctrinated universe. Then politics would appear in philosophy, not as a special political philosophy, but as the intent of its concepts to comprehend the unmutilated reality. If linguistic analysis does not contribute to such understanding; if, instead it contributes to enclosing thought in the circle of the mutilated universe of ordinary discourse, it is at best entirely inconsequential. And, at worst, it is an escape into the non-controversial, the unreal, into that which is only academically controversial. (Marcuse 1991, 199)

Marcuse warns us against the tendency of analytical linguistic philosophy to treat concepts such as freedom, equality, justice and, I would add, obligation and law as akin to terms such as broom and pineapple, the true meaning of which can be ascertained simply by paying close attention to the use of words. The aim of philosophical enquiry is not simply to draw the horizon of meaning but to extend and move beyond it, to expose the distance between actuality and potentiality by unpacking the mystifications consolidated in ordinary speech. The Hartian legal philosopher is unable to be critical in any sense. She must give up on her ability to make any meaningful comments *as a legal philosopher* about the content of the law. In order for her to be able to raise claims of law reform, she will have to switch the hat of the legal theorist for that of the political or moral philosopher or simply that of an informed citizen, running, of course, the risk of not being taken seriously as either a legal or a political philosopher. As Marcuse again points out, the contingent fact of academic division of labour becomes an overarching methodological principle, thus politically disabling the philosopher and subordinating her to the imperatives of particularization and expertise and facilitating the radical separation of philosophical reflection from political involvement (Marcuse 1991).

It is striking how the stark dichotomy between those employing the term 'law', and those whose opinion concerning its real meaning counts, is now transposed from the level of practice to that of knowledge. In exactly the same way that officials in a legal system determine the law through their practices, on an epistemic level it is the professional legal philosopher who is deemed enlightened enough to discern and describe the meaning of the terms employed by that community of officials. This blatantly consolidates the power relation between law-givers and legal subjects by mediating in a way which arbitrarily represents, therefore necessarily *mis*represents, the normative commitments of the participants in that community and, at the same time, vests with epistemological authority the arbitrary selection of a certain source of norms as legal. The Hartian positivist simply reconstructs the official's use of the concept of law and arbitrarily projects it as the belief of those experiencing the law and on whose normative commitments its true meaning depends. The latter are thus unjustly sidelined both practically and epistemically. With its insistence on neutrality, Hartian positivism aptly reveals the dangerousness of the culture of expertise, especially when the latter colonizes a lived environment such as the law.[5] The expert legal philosopher substitutes others in their experience of the law. Thus, not only does she silence those who can meaningfully speak of law, but, at the same time, the poverty of her philosophy is revealed: she can learn nothing from anyone, as she is not interested in so doing, and she cannot teach anything to anyone other than by violently imposing meaning on their practices.[6]

5 Surprisingly, Marcuse reserves a special role for the expert philosopher, whom he considers to be in a privileged position in unpacking the complexity and mystification of beliefs and critically and actively intervening in the world. I will have more to say on expertise in legal theory in Chapter 4.

6 I expand more on the critique of Hartian positivism as an expert culture in Chapter 4. See also Goodrich 1990.

And yet, Hart leaves the back door open for another sort of critique. There is a normative undertone in Hart's account of the transition from pre-legal normative orders comprising only primary rules to fully fledged legal orders of primary and secondary rules (Perry 2001; Finnis 2007). The latter are *better* because they provide a solution to the problems of uncertainty, ineffectiveness and rigidity. Therefore normative orders not displaying the characteristics of modern State law are implicitly inferior. As a historical observation this may seem rather innocuous. After all, regulation of complexity is generally regarded as a good thing. However, Hart's thesis cannot be simply a historical observation as this would presuppose a counterfactual sharp distinction between pre-modernity and modernity as historical periods alone, rather than as analytical and normative tools supervening on a historical process. Hart's argument inevitably leads to the conclusion that contemporary normative orders with pre-modern features, which managed to survive the transition to modernity, are already demoted to second-class normative orders, for they cannot guarantee certainty, effectiveness and flexibility. This, in combination with the sense that these three State law features are higher values, already provides a sufficient reason for intervening in order to change such orders and bring them in line with modern State legality. Similarly, since it turns out that the core sense of law is the core sense of good normative ordering, those legalities placed by Hart in the penumbra of conceptual doubt, because they do not display the full range of secondary rules, are salvageable because they are of legal quality but still in urgent need of reform in order to catch up with the paradigmatic cases of legality. It therefore appears that not only is Hart's conceptual monism not neutral but it is also rather dangerous because of its implicit but strong normative foundations.

Interpretivism

Dworkin has taken issue with some of those shortcomings of Hartian positivism and especially the uncommitted nature of the positivist method. He criticizes positivism, along with all theories claiming to be *meta*-ethical, precisely for being disengaged and claiming to assume the external, Archimedean point of view (Dworkin 2004). This, he argues, is, first, impossible, because when entering a theoretical discourse about concepts such as law, equality, liberty and so forth, one inevitably raises substantive claims as to the content of those concepts. Secondly, it is an unattractive alternative, as the Archimedean attitude makes for a legal theory, which is morally and politically impoverished and, therefore, undesirable.

Thus, Dworkin opts for a different methodology. He collapses conceptual into normative analysis and argues that every legal theory cannot help being substantively engaged with its object of study and offer interpretations which will shed the best possible light on the law. And through that interpretation, the concept of law, which is inextricably linked to its content, will be continuously revisited and clarified. Dworkin accepts that there is *some* differentiation between the law and other normative orders, even in the very weak sense that we refer to some normative phenomena as law, whereas to others we do not. To the positivist objection that if there are no criteria that need to be satisfied in order for something to count as law in the pre-interpretive stage, then we would be led to indeterminacy as *anything* could pass as law (Raz 1986), the interpretivist response is that all we need to look for in the first instance is widespread *prima facie* consensus as to what constitutes law (Stavropoulos 1996). But what this response leaves unanswered is the logically prior question of why such consensus is present in the first place. Why does the linguistic category of law exist? It is only by asking those questions that we will be able to ascertain whether there is such a consensus at all.

Look at Dworkin's purportedly uncontroversial thin concept of law as the justification of prior coercive political decisions (Dworkin 1986, 110). Despite the fact that interpretivists play down the importance of this *prima facie* concept of law, it is of paramount importance and inevitably taints the rest of their analysis. As Frank Jackson points out, conceptual analysis is necessary at this very first stage, in order for us to single out the subject matter of our enquiry (Jackson 1998). It is conceptual analysis which will clarify our intuitions and folk theories. Dworkin, however, skips this necessary part of enquiry, indeed rejects it as irrelevant and even politically dangerous, and moves on to ask the normative, substantive questions about the content of the law. But has he really done away with the need for conceptual analysis? Veronica Rodriguez-Blanco (2005; 2006) suggests that the answer to that would be yes, if the only conceptual analysis available would be the one resting on the discredited distinction between the analytic and the synthetic (see Quine 1951; Kripke 1972; Putnam 1973), that is the distinction between what can be known simply by way of analysis and understanding and what requires empirical work in order for it to be known.[7] Jackson terms this kind of analysis ambitious and contradistinguishes it to modest or non-ambitious conceptual analysis, which abandons the analytic-synthetic distinction and reacts to the unnecessary proliferation of the kinds of necessity. If concepts are identified with their place and function in the actual world and their relationships rather than their relations with other concepts, it is revealed that the necessary *a posteriori* differs only superficially to the necessary *a priori*, but they ultimately refer to the same thing. Thus:

> the idea that fallibility can be reconciled with the a priori and […] conceptual analysis should be practised in its modest or non-ambitious role. In other words, the analysis of possibilities should not play a major role in determining what the world is like, and thus conceptual analysis cannot determine the fundamental nature of our world. Indeed, on the contrary, conceptual analysis is the activity of describing in less fundamental terms, given an account of the world stated in more fundamental terms. (Rodriguez-Blanco 2006, 41)

7 Although I agree with Rodriguez-Blanco's conclusion as to the need for conceptual analysis, I am sceptical as to whether this is what Hartian positivists have actually been doing. As I argued earlier on in this chapter, awareness of the fallibility of one's *a priori* conclusions and the modesty of conceptual analysis requires devising ways of facilitating falsification. Positivism, it seems to me, has not shown an interest in doing this.

Here is where the inconsistencies and problems of the interpretivist project are revealed. Interpretivism is meant to be essentially pluralistic. Every interpretation is acceptable but only the one which will pass the relevant tests set by the political community will prevail. But this pluralistic attitude offers too little too late. Dworkin seems happy to open up the dialogue on the law's content but plays down the conceptual discussion as devoid of any content and therefore a waste of time. And yet, this has deeply substantive consequences, as the *prima facie* conceptualization of the law over which there is presumably a general, loose consensus, is *all but neutral*. It is the product of a very specific understanding of the law, which is, as Dworkin correctly intuits, inevitably shot through with normative meaning and not just a question of neutral, detached analysis. This is not only an image of the law as inextricably linked to the State but also an image of the law as the relationship of domination between addressor and addressee, those equipped to discover an a-historical justification of coercion and those who need to be coerced because of the instability of their ability to exercise their autonomy or to recognize rightness when they see it. Thus the horizon of normative meaning is fixed long before the process of interpretation kicks off.[8]

Moreover, interpretivism problematically rests on the assumption of the co-originality of the political community with State law. Dworkin is happy to allow State law to become an empire, to assimilate all other discourses, to subordinate everything to the history of the institution. By promoting the internal point of view as the only possible vantage point for observing the law, the interpretivist precludes the possibility of there existing other conceptual schemes, in the light of which the same data about the world of concepts and objects might be ascribed different meaning without this entailing that all but one will be *necessarily* and *objectively* wrong. Dworkin takes a rather robust tack on metaphysical and moral realism in assuming that *all* beliefs about the world are commensurable on *all* levels, simply because there are *some* things, the meaning of which is determined by themselves alone rather than by our mental states in relation to them. Such a strongly realist methodology would perhaps be adequate from *within* a conceptual scheme, but it would certainly not allow us to even begin to examine whether there are other conceptual schemes out there. In the context of a social science such as legal theory, this can be crippling and have far-reaching consequences. Whereas the Hartian objectivist claims to take the hermeneutic point of view and goes on to raise context-transcendent claims about the concept of law without realizing that she merely projects her experience and beliefs about the legal onto other phenomena, the interpretivist opts for the internal perspective and assumes that it is all-inclusive. Thus, it loses sight of any alternatives.[9] Either way, the result is the same: interpretivism, in much the same way as conventionalist positivism, marks the end of politics and the hopeless normative impoverishment of legal theory, only

8 For an institutional theory of law, see MacCormick and Weinberger 1986.

9 For a powerful critique of Dworkinian law-as-integrity in the context of the profoundly morally unsound context of apartheid South Africa, see Christodoulidis 2004.

this time not by denying the relevance of politics in legal analysis, as positivism does, but rather by subsuming all discourses under the legal institution. The legal theorist becomes an apologist of that institution being blind to the fact that what she tries to lend principled coherence to is already subordinated to institutional imperatives, which cannot themselves be subject to thematization and critique.

Unless, of course, the interpretivist method is one of conceptual analysis *pace* Jackson. In that case, there would be very little to differentiate interpretivism from analytical positivism. If interpretivists start from the internal point of view and then go on to raise a claim to universality both as to the concept of law and its content (or even if these two are merged), they would be committing the same fallacy as the positivists, who oscillate from the local to the universal without allowing other localities to have a say in what counts as paradigmatic and universal. In fact, the interpretivist fallacy would be even more grave, as substantive and essentially contested judgements would be elevated to the plane of universality and objectivity, again almost foreclosing pluralism and precluding falsifiability.

Critical Legal Theory

This section should begin with two caveats. First, as I mentioned in the introduction, it should be emphasized that critical legal theory (CLT) is not my target in this book. The reason I am taking this detour here is to show how the internalism/externalism, law/morality, ideal/real antinomies have dominated legal philosophical debate to the point of even stifling or misdirecting any attempts at critically re-theorizing the legal. Secondly, I should admit from the outset that it is probably unfair and inaccurate to lump together all the variations and kinds of CLT. There are so many differences between various strands of CLT as there are common concerns and aims, so as to make it impossible to speak of a school or even a tradition. It is indeed questionable whether ways of thinking about the law so diverse as feminist legal theory, critical race theory, the 'trashing' project of American critical legal studies, deconstructive attitudes to the legal text, the Foucauldian reduction of law to discipline and power and so forth form a family of scholarship. I will, however, dare to talk about them in conjunction, not simply because of the pragmatic reason of lack of time and space. It is also because not only do critical legal theorists already refer to CLT as a distinct philosophical strand, but the genealogical relation of those diverse strands and the common aim of or claim to critique provide a common ground, which does not make it entirely unwarranted to speak of CLT as a kind of thought and scholarship.

I will use as an usher into the discussion of CLT an article by Costas Douzinas, arguably one of the pioneers of CLT in the UK. The article is entitled *Oubliez Critique* (Douzinas 2005) and I believe that it succinctly highlights and subconsciously reveals the shortcomings of CLT. In part the article is a philosophical and historical retrospective. Douzinas uses Gillian Rose's idea of the trinitarian nature of critique. In the Kantian legacy critique is the tribunal of reason. Emancipation is about law-giving, autonomy is both about the self and the *nomos*. The Kantian critic's aim is to liberate herself from the constraints of nature and make humanity and reason sovereign from outside the utter reality of history. Hegel transformed the critic into a litigant/witness and critique into the tribunal of history. The critic became embedded in the here and now, occupied the internal perspective and critique became immanent. The Hegelian tradition is based on the impossibility of uncommitted critique. And, finally, there is the critic as clerk, who records and seeks law in truth, thus denying the former its independent existence. The clerk collapses the *ought* into the *is* and legalizes reality. All three kinds, Douzinas goes on to argue, reveal that law and critique are inseparable. There is critique in law and law in critique. Modernity is marked by *nomophilia*; Douzinas tells us that 'critique is immanent to law and the more the critic denies and decries the law, the more he expresses his subjection and love for the law. I am not saying much more here than modernity can be described as the era of *nomophilia*' (Douzinas 2005, 52).

And, according to Douzinas, even CLT never managed to shake off this *nomophilia*, despite its hard efforts to expose the pretensions of objectivity of mainstream legal theory, as well as the inability of the law to see the crippling effect of its institutional structures. American critical legal studies failed to form an agenda and a distinct politics; the BritCrits were either assimilated by the 'establishment' (Goodrich 1999) or failed to live up to their critical agenda in their institutional roles as teachers and administrators in law departments. Inevitably, much of critical legal scholarship, even that inspired by deconstruction and the Derridean idea of justice as *avenir* (Derrida 1992) has been consumed by exegesis of the new holy (critical) scriptures, as these fall in and out of fashion. To this I would add that it can, no doubt, be understood as a side-effect of the professionalization of scholarship, the obsession with citations, which has transformed originality into a cause for fear rather than an aspiration and an aim. So, a new *nomos* is set for CLT. Not the one set by the State any longer but rather the one set by CLT itself as transformed through its assimilation by the institutional apparatus reproducing trends and schools, learning and reiteration and keeping the market going.

Douzinas then turns from the retrospective to the programmatic. He seeks a way out of this *nomophilic* vicious circle; he wants to try to interrupt the *nomothetic* process in which even CLT has been entangled. In what he calls the New Times, which are marked by the 'mass exportation of democracy', the 'gradual weakening of sovereignty and its replacement by international organisations under the control of the Major Powers', and the 'ubiquity of murky and intertwined financial military and technological networks' (Douzinas 2005, 66), critique has ceased to be immanent or threatening, the critic has been tamed, and even what at some point seemed emancipatory about the law, such as human rights, has been hijacked and employed by the new international economic powers, which have become the new sovereign. In times like that, when domination is masked as liberation and imperialism as the spreading of the democratic word, Douzinas argues that critique ought to turn to *polemos*, it ought to recover or reinvent its antagonistic streak and become conflictual: 'This would not be critique as judgment within or without history but acts of cutting neither applying the law nor hoping for a redemptive epiphany' (Douzinas 2005, 68).

Douzinas is right, I think, to be critical of critique, despite the obvious self-reflexivity and circularity of this task. From the outset, the CLT project focused on disclosing the falsity of the claims of objectivity and justice that the law raised and highlighted the inability of the law to reconcile with justice. Derrida famously declared this shortcoming of the law, arguing that, while it rests on the finality of decisions and finitude of reasons, justice requires a constant deconstruction of meaning, the awareness of our fallibility and the never-ending revisiting of the question calling for a just answer. Justice is always *á venir*; no decision can ever be said to be just, Derrida has taught us, whereas legality is bound to the here and now (Derrida 1992). This fear, yet fear not divorced from hope, of the impossibility of justice in the law has underlined, whether directly influenced by Derrida or not, the work of many critical authors. Feminists have always taken issue with the male bias of the law and the inability of the latter to do justice to the female particular, and one of the big internal debates is whether law reform will make any difference and whether it is worth struggling for the betterment of the law, or assume a radically external point of view; American critical legal studies tried to discredit the law on grounds of its political bias; psychoanalytic theories of law sit it on the therapist's couch and hypnotize its true traumas out of it.

But the law does not raise and defend claims in and by itself, so CLT also chose to target those legal theories which took on the task of defending the law on its behalf. The attack focused on orthodox, for lack of a better word, legal theories for failing to see or admit the stark opposition between law and justice or by being too preoccupied with their analytical project of description and conceptual tidiness instead of taking the normative perspective and taking a stance in matters of injustice. Thus, critique of the law turned into a sectarian war of legal philosophical factions. Theoretical blows started being exchanged, a little too often below the belt, and quickly the two camps found it difficult to remain on speaking terms or even face each other. And one would hardly be able to argue that this is a productive intellectual mitosis rather than petty feuds within the same caste.

In setting those targets, CLT already unconsciously makes two substantive and, at the same time, strategic errors. First, it is mistaken to underplay the significance of the ontological question of law. Anxious to criticize the *prima facie* law, that is the law of the State, for being radically dissociated from justice, CLT already endorses one of the main assumptions of orthodox legal theory, namely that there is no disagreement as to the *phenomenology* of the law and what remains to be discussed is how to organize that tentative knowledge of ours in concepts so that we are able to say something meaningful about the *concept* of law rather than just the observed empirical reality. CLT rejects the second leg of that project by denying the relevance and significance of legal metaphysics or, indeed, the possibility of a general theory of law, and focuses instead on the law–justice antinomy. But it seldom addresses the first leg of the orthodox project and never notices that the whole thing should be inversed. In other words, it tacitly accepts the premise that there is something that we all recognize as law, even though it is impossible to form a theory about it, instead of attending to the fact that conceptual clarity may prove the most powerful critical tool in the effort to question those *prima facie* intuitions, which orthodox legal theory tends to present as a coherent conceptual framework. Even those critical legal projects that stretch the understanding of the legal and refuse to differentiate between the law and apparatuses, institutions, and practices of social control, still leave unquestioned the legal status of law, so to speak. Their aim is to play down the uniqueness and functional, if not ontological, privileges of the law, but this is undermined by the obvious disregard for the conceptual differentiation of the latter, which is always used as the most disarming argument by orthodox legal theories.

Secondly, its obsession with the law–justice antinomy reveals not only the disappointed *nomophilia* of CLT but also its self-contradictory unconscious embracing of the firm distinction between ideal and real. Thus, even in cases in which critique starts precisely from questioning this distinction by placing itself in the Hegelian tradition of locating the critic and her object of study in history, if the conclusion is that law and justice are drastically divorced then the thesis is tantamount to accepting that the two universes of word and deed can never meet. There is something almost theological in this *ad infinitum* asymptoton between justice and law, ideas and matter: the two perennially converge but never coincide, because it is only fragments and intuitions of justice that we can access until we can make sense of the infinity to which the two curves stretch. And we can only make sense of this infinity by way of revelation. Thus, post-modern critique seems to regress to pre-modernism by deferring the most important questions of human co-existence to the unknown and, indeed, unknowable. But this leaves CLT defenceless to the allegation that it is incapable of uttering anything meaningful about the here and now and making a difference, which after all goes part and parcel with critique, instead of simultaneously lamenting and rejoicing for the always-to-come nature of justice. The conclusion that our institutional arrangements never have been and never will be just debilitates not only the law and legal theory but also politics, by removing the emancipatory potential from any political struggle that aims at institutional reform, no matter how radical that may be. But the point of critique ought to be precisely the opposite, namely to explore whether and how this emancipatory potential can be accommodated in an institutional structure by pluralizing, diversifying and politicizing the latter, which may require a radical rethinking, both metaphysical and moral, of our concepts and practices.

So, does the solution lie in turning from *krisis* into *polemos*, as Douzinas suggests? As I have already implied, not only would I not take that view, but I also believe that it is another symptom of the problems of CLT. According to my reading of Douzinas' programmatic ideas, he seeks to replace sovereign (legal, uncritical) reason by a new sovereign ideal, which has not yet been formulated or even conceived but will hopefully become apparent in the course of the subversive struggle against the universalizing, imperialistic tendencies and practices of the law, its masters and its apologists. It seems to me that Douzinas' 'tentative, and probably wild, suggestions' seem like a return to Marxist perfectionism without the Marxian descriptive and normative clarity on human nature, history and their synchronization.

The problem, I would suggest, lies in the original premise, namely that the critic is a judge, a witness or a clerk. Accurately as this imagery may capture the historical phases of critique and the transformations it has undergone, when it is ascribed a quasi-conceptual or even normative content, it merely serves to reproduce the image of the critic as the detached enlightened observer, whose role is to cure the *lumpen* from their false consciousness, while he remains safe within the academic haven, where the virus of ideology does not reach. And it is difficult to see how such a critic will be able to engage in any sort of *polemos*.

Critique is not the caricature of a tribunal, in which the robed and bewigged judge passes sentences on the hapless, muzzled accused. Critique is indeed a tribunal in that it must grapple with questions of right and wrong, which urgently call for answers. But, although critical theory must enlighten us by providing alternatives, it must do so in a modest and non-ambitious manner, which requires it to have reconciled with its fallibility. And this cannot be achieved by the Hartian or Razian observer, who describes what he experiences from the internal point of view and then goes on to pretend it was all done from outside; the Dworkinian interpreter, who tacitly accepts the positivists' description of law as that normative order which derives from the State; or, finally, the critical legal theorist's external critique of the ideology of law and orthodox legal theory, which ends up endorsing most of the latter's assumptions and concerns, including the identification of the law with the State, and finds itself in the uncomfortable position of not being able to make something better of those assumptions. I will argue in Chapter 4 that, in order for it to achieve the dual aim of conceptual accuracy and critique, legal theory must become pluralistic itself by cancelling the distinction between observer and observed and thus the quasi-legislative task that it has set for itself by assuming that it is better placed to understand practices and concepts than the very participants in those practices. Instead, it ought to see itself as part of and, perhaps, the instigator of a discursive procedure, in which conceptual and normative assumptions and intuitions will be put to the test, with the aim being not the formulation of universal concepts or principles but a thin groundwork of consensus, upon which pluralism can flourish. But this, of course, means entering this discourse with a suggestion as to what this thin conceptual and normative basis may be, which in turn requires going one step back and rethinking the concept of law stripped of historical contingencies such as its association with the State.

Conclusion

In this chapter I hope to have set the tone of the book by highlighting the methodological deficiencies of some of the most influential contemporary legal theories; deficiencies which entangle those theories in dilemmas and antinomies perpetuating the assumption that the law is conceptually (and morally) inextricably linked to the State. The problem is that this assumption is foundational to mainstream legal theories and thus makes them insensitive to the intuition that law is to be found in non-State contexts. At the same time it disables the critical and pluralistic potential of legal theory. In the next chapter, I survey some central theories of legal pluralism to see whether they are more successful in making the best of this critical, pluralistic potential.

Chapter 2
Orthodoxies and Heterodoxies of Legal Pluralism

Introduction

Chapter 1 was devoted to a critique of some of the most influential legal philosophical strands on two grounds: first, on their implicit or explicit methodological and substantive reliance on the assumption that the law is necessarily connected to the modern State either as its only source or the only forum in which plurality of worldviews can be meaningfully reduced; secondly, on their adherence to a view of the law necessarily as a power relation between addressors and addressees. I said in the introduction that the challenge is to reconcile emancipation *and* regulation, plurality *and* unity. It appears that the tradition of monism cannot live up to this challenge. This is why I will now turn to theories of legal pluralism and explore their potential in seeing through the task of decentring the law without giving up on the possibility of all transcontextual normative meaning.

There is something very intriguing about the idea of legal pluralism. It can be *legal theory*, for it is discourse about the law, it looks for an answer to the question of what the law *is*. To the extent that it deals with law substantively by making normative claims concerning the right, it is also *jurisprudence*, it sets itself a positive, normative, quasi-legal task. At the same time though, and it is here that the intriguing idiosyncrasy mainly lies, legal pluralism is the study of other legalities and subsequently legal theories. Thus it becomes *meta-theory*, that is a discourse on other discourses on the legal and, to the extent that it implicitly or explicitly sets substantive criteria for hierarchizing legal orders, it is also potentially *meta-jurisprudence* as well (which legal order ought to prevail?). So, legal pluralism means being attentive both to the plurality of norms but also to the ways in which they are organized in and around practices. This multiple task of legal pluralism is what differentiates it from any other kind of legal theory and to what it owes its exceptional value. It comes with the promise that it will enable us to form a spherical view of the legal universe, and, unlike other approaches to the legal as I argued in Chapter 1, help us achieve a multiplicity of points of view and legitimately oscillate between them, thus maintaining conceptual clarity without giving up on mutual critique. But great expectations can lead to great disappointments. The question that I am tackling in the next three chapters is how and to what extent these attractive promises of legal pluralism can be realized.

I start the exploration of the idea of legal pluralism with a discussion of some of the most prominent legal pluralistic accounts and examine whether they manage to achieve the full potential of legal pluralism and, at the same time, overcome the methodological and substantive problems generated by the implicit or explicit monism of mainstream legal theory.[1] I argue that theories which have tried to make sense of legal pluralism have not yet managed to wed its theoretical, meta-theoretical, jurisprudential and meta-jurisprudential aspects. I classify those theories into two broad strands that I name *empirical-positivistic* and *theories of diverse, dispersed legality*, and come to the conclusion that, despite the great differences between them, they all share a basic shortcoming: they overemphasize one aspect of legal pluralism over the others, thus reducing themselves to either a legal theory that views the law from well within a legal system or just a sociological, external recording of legal phenomena. I shall argue that the reason why these theories have fallen short of the full potential of legal pluralism is that they have been thinking about the latter in the wrong terms. Their aim has been to form one uniform theory with a diverse research object and either a normative or an explanatory value. But by doing so, they already fail to recognize the crucial fact that legal pluralism as a way of theorizing the legal *must itself be pluralistic*, that it cannot be contained in the form of a one-dimensional legal theory. In other words, they fail to make the best of the concurrent diverse natures of legal pluralism. In the next chapter I will argue that, because of its inherent diversity, legal pluralism must be approached not as another legal theory but as *a radicalization of the way we think about the law, which must permeate and inform all our thinking about the law*. This means shifting the focus from strictly defined and hermetically closed legal *systems* to all manifestations of people's shared normative commitments. It also means giving participants in such legal discourses a voice in order for them to explain themselves without the distorting interference of a distant observer. At the same time, what must be established is the possibility of communication between those legal discourses, a possibility which rests on two necessary requirements: first, that there be a universal sense of law, however thin. This must include an account of both the factual and the normative sides of the coin, enabling mutual recognition between dispersed legal discourses but also mutual critique. In Chapter 4 I shall show that these requirements can be satisfied and argue that, at least in the first instance, the only available forum for the development of the project of legal pluralism is legal theory, which must detach itself from State law and provide a forum in which the dispersed legal discourses and theories can reveal themselves as such and communicate with each other.

1 The list of versions of legal pluralism surveyed here is of course not exhaustive of all those available. See, for example, the classic accounts of Geertz (1983), Arthurs (1985) and Pospisil (1971) as well as the very important contributions of Menski (2006). In fact, literature on legal pluralism seems to be steadily proliferating. However, I choose to focus on these few specific accounts, which I hold as paradigmatic of the two main strands, which I single out in this chapter.

A Survey of Theories of Legal Pluralism

Classifying theories of legal pluralism is a methodologically fraught task from the outset. Masaji Chiba attempts to address the problems of theories of legal pluralism, which he attributes to the lack of an operational definition of legal pluralism. He defines legal pluralism as 'the coexisting structure of different legal systems under the identity postulate of legal culture in which three combinations of official law and unofficial law, indigenous and transplanted law, and legal rules and legal postulates are conglomerated into a whole by the choice of a socio-legal entity' (Chiba 1998, 242). He sees the value of that definition in that it combines all the central features of most theories of legal pluralism, thus making them comparable, and in that it provides an operational framework. It seems to me that this definition does not go far enough, firstly precisely because it is a *definition*, which introduces rigid criteria of recognition, thus narrowing down the scope of legal pluralism; secondly, because it still relies heavily on categories such as 'legal structures', 'official' and 'unofficial' law and so on, that are neither descriptively not normatively useful.

The most prevalent distinction of theories of legal pluralism is that introduced by J. Griffiths (1986) between weak, juristic or classic legal pluralism on one hand and strong or new legal pluralism on the other. The former approaches legal pluralism always in the light of State law, whereas the latter focuses on social groups developing their own legal systems within the boundaries of a State. This distinction is often referred to as more or less authoritative both by authors who want to argue with it (see, for instance, the comprehensive account of theories of legal pluralism by A. Griffiths 2002) and against it (Tamanaha 1993). I choose not to follow that model for the simple reason that I do not think it really is a distinction. Many of the presumably 'strong' theories of legal pluralism are as weak as their classical counterparts in that they seek to discover and describe legal orders with the application of predetermined criteria. This shared empirical approach is a much stronger criterion to go by than the rather contingent association with State law.

The following taxonomy of theories of legal pluralism is based mainly on their methodological choices and it aims simply at mapping the territory. I am conscious of the fact that no map and no representation is normatively neutral. However, I hope that the classification itself is not over-prescriptive and that it does not prejudice my critical remarks on the theories I discuss.

Empiricism-Positivism

Traditional sociological and anthropological legal pluralism Early theoretical endeavours in legal pluralism concentrated on the ability of the law to be responsive to the community by acknowledging its actual needs. It was the study of the tension between formal law and the ways in which social co-existence was regulated in actuality. These attempts range from sociological critiques of formal law to the legal anthropological study of the effects of colonization and the imposition of colonialist law upon colonized peoples. Despite their methodological and substantive differences, what all these versions of legal pluralism have in common is their empiricist-positivistic approach to law, as they apply formal criteria in order to identify non-State legal orders and their relationship with State legal orders.

Georges Gurvitch argued early on that judicial monism corresponded to a contingent political situation, namely the creation of large modern States between the sixteenth and nineteenth centuries (Gurvitch 1935; Carbonnier 1983). Eugen Ehrlich was one of the first to contribute a great deal to the sociological turn of the debate by pointing out that in many cases the legislators were totally unaware of the social needs and the normative orders that various communities were developing and that very often there was a conflict between the latter and State law (Ehrlich 1936). He argued that the major legal codifications outrageously ignored the 'living law', which he saw as the concrete as opposed to the abstract expressed in legal texts (Ehrlich 1936, 501). He sought to demonstrate that every official legal ordering must be based upon the actual social reality and that the law cannot remain isolated and alienated from the people. Unrefined as that argument may sound, it was a very important first step, because it actually proposed a socially oriented legal pluralism distinguishing between the 'law of the lawyers', the technical concept of law void of social or moral meaning and relevance, or at least unaware of it, and the self-regulating capacities of social formations. Thus it overcame the fixed instrumentalist notion of law, which portrayed it as a means in the hands of the power centres (Cotterrell, 1995). Ehrlich emphasized that purpose-oriented effectiveness and formalization of the law can no longer be incompatible. The only way to achieve that would be to use living law as a source for State legislation. According to Ehrlich, State law has mainly a dispute-resolving function. What makes 'living law' unique is the fact that it prevents people from appealing to State law, since it provides them with more flexible and, importantly, more uncontroversial ways of resolving disputes. Social relations emerge mainly within associations, which have their own regulatory functions (Ehrlich 1936, 58; Cotterrell 1984, 32). What binds the person to the association and in the second instance to society as a whole is the fear of exclusion, since this is usually the sanction for violating a norm of most social groups. Ehrlich's analysis is valuable to the extent that it brings to the fore social formations with self-regulating mechanisms, which are independent from the law of the State, and in that it suggests that this 'living law', being much more direct, is subsequently genuinely binding for people. This explicitly questions the exclusivity of State law and clearly broadens the horizons of the study of the legal. However, despite Ehrlich's attempt to redefine the concept of legality by extending it, he remains well within positivism to the extent that he understands law exclusively as a formal order. Moreover, he tends to understand phenomena of self-regulation in the terms of and in opposition to State law. Gurvitch was among those who accused him of broadening the concept of the legal too much and hence neglecting the 'spiritual elements' in social relations (Cotterrell, 1984). Finally, Ehrlich's insistence on sanctions, however informal, reveals his adherence to an image of the law as *necessarily* heteronomous and based on a conception of the application of force as normal rather than exceptional. It is, however, very important to trace the seeds of the possibility of an emancipatory theory of legal pluralism already in that early stage.

Carbonnier's tack on legal pluralism (1983) is similar to Ehrlich's. He imagines it as a conflict between different normative orders of structurally complete social formations such as the State and the Church, or as a conflict between the *loi nouvelle*, the *droit actuel* on the one hand and the *droit ancien* on the other. This conflict is generated by the fact that juridical abrogation does not coincide necessarily with sociological abrogation, which leaves a void to be filled by the public conscience.

Anthropological legal pluralism takes the same basic idea a step further. John Griffiths (1986) defines legal pluralism as 'that state of affairs, for any social field, in which behaviour pursuant to more than one legal orders occurs' (Griffiths 1986, 2). Although there is a tendency to emphasize the continuity of the legal phenomenon, and indeed anthropologists are very reluctant clearly to conceptualize or define the law,[2] more often than not there is talk of 'central and peripheral' laws, indigenous and folk law, and so on. Although there is no theory determining the criterial definition of the various legal orders, the point of departure of research is the assumption that there *are* such legal orders, institutionalized and closed, which clash with State law. This is evident even in the most careful anthropological-ethnographic studies of legal pluralism, such as Sally Falk Moore's and her concept of semi-autonomous social fields (Falk Moore 1973).

This anxiety to look for empirically identifiable laws is evident in von Benda-Beckmann's comment (1988) on Merry's impressively comprehensive article of legal pluralistic theories (1988). Von Benda-Beckmann believes that there is an analytical question which must be answered first, namely the one concerning the essential qualities of the law. The main argument is that, although there are so many descriptive theories of legal plurality, 'little conceptual progress has been made' (von Benda-Beckmann 1988, 897); that 'talking of intertwining, interaction or mutual constitution presupposes distinguishing what is being intertwined' (von Benda-Beckmann 1988, 898).

Those theories of legal pluralism, which I have called 'empirical-positivistic', seem to presuppose a rather straightforward picture of the world in which law is what meets certain criteria such as the existence of a system of rules, institutionalization, enforcement of these rules with sanctions and the like. By applying these formal criteria to *prima facie* regulatory orders, positivism draws conclusions as to whether they are legal or not. If so, then State law has to recognize them as such, they have to be respected and not interfered with. But who is to judge the legal nature of these orders? Whence are the criteria drawn? There are at least two possible answers here:

2 See Allott and Woodman (1985) and Griffiths (1986) regarding Galanter's (1981) notion concerning the decentred application of norms.

a) We draw the criteria from our experience of the law We all live by and in the law; we can all tell the difference between the law and other normative orders. There are some features which recur in various contexts. Therefore, they are designated as the conceptual core of the law and, every time their combination is traced, we can safely claim that there is law. But this line of reasoning undermines what legal pluralism seeks to establish in the first place. If there are self-regulated groups, which are colonized by the dominant legality, classifying their form of regulation in the terms of the dominant legality has an equally colonizing effect. It is a form of epistemological heteronomy, which is bound to prove detrimental for the substantive autonomy of the group in question; it is an attempt to impose externally a meaning which has been formed under different material and normative conditions. That amounts to projecting *our* internal point of view to a different context, thus inevitably misinterpreting the object of our study. A kind of injustice is done here as a final judgement *is* imposed in the absence of the interested party in the guise of descriptive objectivity. The parallel with mainstream analytical positivism here is evident.[3] The fallacy lies in mistaking and misrepresenting the internal point of view as capable of achieving generality and neutrality.[4]

b) Law is what its subjects designate as law At first sight, this way of understanding the law and thus setting the agenda of legal pluralism is a much more promising path to take, not least because it seems more consistent with the very aims of the research programme of legal pluralism. Brian Tamanaha has put forward such a version of legal pluralism and his suggestions deserve to be discussed at length.

Tamanaha offers an insightful reworking of positivism as a conventionalist socio-legal theory. One of his initial premises is that positivist legal theory has not managed to shake off its essentialism as to the concept of law. This essentialism sets a yardstick of measuring the legal nature of various practices of rule-following, thus potentially leaving out of the picture other instances of legality understood and referred to as such by participants in them. Natural law (in all its manifestations), on the other hand, disregards the fact that the law is a social construction constituted by linguistic practices, which ascribe the world of institutional facts their meaning. Once Tamanaha has laid out his critique of mainstream legal theory on the grounds of its methodology, he goes on to propose a way of capturing the concept of law by wedding conceptual and sociological analysis. He subscribes to the two main positivist theses, namely the *separation* and *social sources* theses, but qualifies them

---

3 See Chapter 1.

4 For an account of how this has been the 'Western' approach to Chinese law, see Ruskola 2002. Although I find the critique of such approaches convincing, I would take issue with its fundamental theoretical premise that '[u]ltimately, the answer to the question whether or not there is law in China is always embedded in the premises of the questioner: it necessarily depends on the observer's definition of law' (Ruskola 2002, 183), to the extent that it rests on the assumption that it is impossible to have and, at the same time, strive towards *some* universal sense of law.

substantially and substantively. He extends the former so as to cover functionality as well as morality and modifies the latter as follows:

> Instead of applying this thesis only to state law, it will be applied to all manifestations and kinds of law, including customary law, international law, transnational law, religious law, and natural law. Their specific shapes and features will not be the same as those discerned by Hart for state law, but whatever distinctive features they do have will be amenable to observation through careful attention to the social practices which constitute them. All of these manifestations and kinds of law are social products. The existence of each is a matter of social fact. (Tamanaha 2001, 159)

It is on that basis that Tamanaha formulates his conventionalist social theory of law. His fundamental thesis is that the attention of the socio-legal theorist (indeed, any legal theorist, as the sociological cannot be divorced from the philosophical in this scheme of things) should be turned to the way people speak about the law. Tamanaha explicitly privileges the external point of view as the appropriate one and argues that whenever a *sufficient number of people* (and anyone is a candidate here, not just those assigned with an institutional task, like Hart's officials) with *sufficient conviction* refer to a social practice as law, that practice automatically becomes an object of enquiry for the social theory of law. He acknowledges that this is a rather broad understanding of the law, which will probably upset mainstream legal theorists, but this, he argues, does not reveal a problem with his suggestion but rather the inability of such theorists to abandon the colonizing method of essentialism, which has haunted legal theory for a very long time. Finally, a conventionalist social theory of law is essentially and substantively pluralistic. Tamanaha argues that it addresses the problems of early sociological and contemporary anthropological theories of legal pluralism, as well as the reductionism of functionalism and the vagueness of post-modern theories, by abandoning the essentialism that haunts the former while still dissociating the concept of law from the State and by offering a criterion for differentiating the law from other non-legal social norms.

Tamanaha is certainly right to reject essentialism as methodologically and substantively flawed and, as I shall argue in more detail later, he is also right in trying to redress the problem of vagueness of post-modern legal pluralistic theories. I would also agree with him on a number of other points. First, that legal pluralism is a project of reconceptualizing the law and that it cannot be accommodated in and by the existing models of theorizing the latter. Secondly, that the way linguistic communities speak about the law should be taken seriously, in order for legal theory to be able to overcome its patronizing and colonizing tendencies. Thirdly, Tamanaha is right in suggesting that sociological enquiry should not be kept separate from the philosophical study of the law.

So, Tamanaha convincingly addresses most of the problems of mainstream legal theory, which I singled out in the first chapter. However, two interrelated problems persist and do not allow his 'social theory of law' to get off the ground. First, it is not clear what the aim of that social theory of law is. Tamanaha subscribes to a pragmatist approach to social enquiry and states the objectives of the social theory of law as follows:

> to keep a close eye on what people – legal actors and non-legal actors – are actually doing relative to law, and to discover and pay attention to the ideas that inform their actions. These ideas, beliefs, and actions give rise to law, determine the uses to which law is put, and constitute the reactions to, and consequences of, law. (Tamanaha 2001, 165–6)

At the same time, he insists that the law has no essence beyond the linguistic conventions and practices constituting it. Still, he argues that it is of course possible and, indeed, necessary to differentiate between uses of the term 'law' which are relevant for a general jurisprudence and those which are not, such as law of nature, laws of grammar and so forth. The criteria of the distinction, however, are loose and intuitive rather than strict rules of usage, which raises the suspicion that the law has some essence beyond our mental states in relation to it. But that aside, any other use of the word law meeting a minimum of semantic conditions, in which Tamanaha controversially includes authority, are acceptable as proper uses of the word law. And such criteria he implicitly treats as universal but also largely uncontroversial.

What is not clear from Tamanaha's social theory of law is what the socio-legal theorist may gain from that enquiry. At worst, she will be engaging in a rather unsophisticated exercise in semantics. At best, she will have some more rough information as to what various communities refer to as law, which she will map in an inevitably inconclusive and indeterminate manner. But, if she has already given up on the possibility of there being a trans-contextual sense of law, one that can be formulated and grasped irrespective of the instances of its application, there is little point in engaging in that enquiry, as there seems to be very little to be learned from cataloguing. In fact, it seems hardly possible to kick off the enquiry in the first place, as the socio-legal theorist will be inescapably trapped within her own closed conceptual scheme. Moreover, it is difficult to see what the place of philosophy is in this exercise, which seems purely and solely sociological in nature.

It is telling how a kind of conceptual universalism creeps into Tamanaha's argument. He implicitly sets a conceptual threshold, beyond which certain practices count as law-relevant-for-jurisprudence. He already concedes that there are *some* criteria which pre-exist and, indeed, guide social enquiry into the legal phenomenon but then goes on unconvincingly to attempt to play down those criteria by arguing that they only reveal a very loose and vague *prima facie* content of 'law', making a substantive and contested suggestion as to what the minimum content of law is by including authority in it. And the implicit bias in Tamanaha's analysis is not only conceptual but also normative in that the 'sufficient number' of people with 'sufficient conviction', which set the threshold of legality, already introduce substantive criteria concerning the inclusiveness of law as well as the quality of the commitments of participants in it. But in view of the fact that, for Tamanaha, these are best observed externally, his pluralistic conventionalism already potentially both over-prescribes and misrepresents the attitudes of participants in a law. The only way to avoid such tacit but overly prescriptive presuppositions is, first, to be clearer about that universal sense of law, which can make possible, inform and help kick-start and guide socio-legal enquiry; secondly, to make enquiry itself open and inclusive and move towards cancelling its separation from substance; thirdly, one must be clear as to how that claim to an a-contextual sense of law can be constantly testable and revisable so that it does not undermine the point of legal pluralism.

This brings me to another aspect of the same problem. If there can be no sense of law, all the various phenomena, which are experienced and referred to as legal by the participants in the respective communities, can only be normatively and ontologically incommensurable with each other. This means that the socio-legal theorist will not be able to question the legal nature of the practices which she observes. With no yardstick available to her, she will have to accept the beliefs of the observed as true knowledge. Similarly, she should be unable to use that new data, in order to question her own beliefs about *her* concept of law. In other words, the socio-legal theorist is deprived of any critical faculty. Any attempt at criticizing a conception of law will in turn always be open to the critique of essentialism and paternalism. This is what Tamanaha's pragmatism is inevitably led to, as it explicitly rejects any kind of transcendentalism, moral or conceptual:

> First, it [pragmatism] insists that any normative arguments based upon an alleged special insight into the Absolute are based on a false claim; secondly, it suggests that what counts when determining which normative assertions we should accept is whether, when acted upon, the assertions result in consequences we find desirable; thirdly, it reminds us that the best way to determine whether the consequences are desirable is to play close attention to the facts of the matter. (Tamanaha 1997, 246)

Although context-sensitive pragmatism is a promising path to take, one needs to be more careful in setting the conditions of enquiry into the existence and function of the legal. This not only puts the possibility of such an enquiry in question but it also potentially compromises its impartiality, thus undermining the very point of legal pluralism. In Chapter 4 I will make some programmatic suggestions as to how these problems can be addressed.

The Other Legal Pluralism: In Search of a Diverse, Dispersed Legality

Setting the agenda In a seminal article on legal pluralism, Merry diagnoses a transition in the way legal pluralism is approached by theory (Merry 1988). After discussing a large number of legal pluralistic theories, she formulates some suggestions, which should guide legal theory in the light of the recognition of the dispersal of the legal phenomenon:

- Theory must move away from the ideology of legal centralism, that is the assumption that the only legitimate legal order is the one applied and enforced by the State.
- In order for that to be achieved, the law must be understood historically rather than purely conceptually: 'Defining the essence of law or custom is less valuable than situating these concepts in particular sets of relations between particular legal orders in particular historical contexts' (Merry 1988, 889).
- Moreover, the law ought to cease to be understood as merely a set of rules and start being perceived more spherically as a system of thought: law is not simply a set of rules exercising coercive power, but a system of thought by which certain forms of relations come to seem natural and taken for granted, modes of thought that are inscribed in institutions that exercise some coercion in support of their categories and theories of explanation (Merry 1988, 889).
- Legal pluralistic thinking in the above terms also facilitates the study of social ordering in non-dispute situations.
- Finally, comprehending the interconnectedness of various legal orders offers a new way of thinking about social relations of domination.

Over the last two decades, various theories of legal pluralism, which very often style themselves as post-modern or critical, have taken up those challenges, seeking to reconceptualize legal pluralism both as a state of affairs and as a theoretical discourse. These newer and theoretically more refined and self-conscious approaches differ from one another. Still, the commonalities are such that it seems legitimate to talk about a uniform new tendency in legal pluralism. This 'new' legal pluralism moves beyond the post-colonial project of discovering and giving voice to legal institutions that exist in the margins of State law. Instead, it looks for legal orders dispersed across the social spectrum within the boundaries of a specific jurisdiction. The focal point is thus shifted from seemingly coherent and insular self-regulating communities such as indigenous peoples, upon whom the law of a colonizing State has been imposed, to groups existing within an established and 'homogeneous' polity. The bond between the members of such groups may still be ethnic (for example, the travellers) or religious (for example, the Amish and the Mennonites or Islamic communities practising Sharia law). But the new legal pluralism goes further than this. It tries to locate the legal in all those forms of regulation that are not sanctioned by the law of the State. Moreover, it does not specify ethnic or religious homogeneity or any other all-encompassing link as a necessary prerequisite of the legal. This approach yields striking results. For 'laws' exist, so the thesis goes, in financial associations, groups of people sharing a lifestyle or participating in a common activity, and so forth. Margaret Davies lists some examples drawn from the Australian context, making a reference to Robert Cover:

> In contemporary Australia … we could note that distinct sites of jurisgenesis can be found in Indigenous communities, in religious associations, in feminist groups, in prison populations, among law enforcers, small business people, executives in large corporations and among ethnic minorities. (Davies 2005, 109)

In what follows I shall devote some time to some theorists who, in one way or another, have taken on the task of legal pluralism as envisaged by Merry and have offered alternative theories of legal pluralism. Namely, I shall refer to Günther Teubner's (1992) systems theoretical approach to pluralism from the point of view of structural coupling; Boaventura de Sousa Santos' (1995) account of intertwined legalities; and some more post-modern or critical accounts of legal pluralism such as the ones offered by Desmond Manderson (1996), Margaret Davies (2005), and Martha-Marie Kleinhans and Roderick MacDonald (1998). I shall also refer specifically to Robert Cover's account of the utterly real commitments that give rise to legal universes and the violence that State law does to these other legal orders. Using Cover's work as a starting point and drawing on all those theories of legal pluralism, I shall build my meta-theoretical argument about law and legal pluralism in the next chapter.

Günther Teubner and a Systems-Theoretical Legal Pluralism Teubner (1992) subscribes to the programme of the new legal pluralism described by Merry and tries to qualify it from a systems-theoretical point of view. His point of departure is the closure of legal systems and their inability to make sense of other discourses in their terms. Drawing on the notion of reflexivity, Teubner's aim (1983) is to propose a new way of theorizing legal pluralism so that it becomes helpful in the project of making the law as responsive as possible to other discourses.

Teubner asks the fundamental question of what is to count as distinctively legal and how State and other laws are to be interrelated. Unlike anthropological and early sociological legal pluralistic theories, Teubner does not apply empirical criteria. His aim is to clarify what makes communication between State and other law both possible and, secondly, fruitful. Moreover, his understanding of the legal *proprium* has a different and distinct basis. Teubner rejects theories that set normativity as the ultimate criterion for the recognition of a legal order (Teubner 1992, 1449), according to which legal pluralism consists in normative expectations and excludes cognitive and behavioural ones. He finds this solution inadequate, firstly because it regresses into the debate concerning how legal and non-legal are to be distinguished and, secondly, because it does not grasp the processual and dynamic character of legal pluralism. Similarly, functionalist theories, which promote *social control* as the ultimate criterion, are not adequate either (Teubner 1992, 1450). They are too inclusive and, although they might be useful in pointing out functional equivalents of the law, they are not especially helpful in distinguishing between legal and non-legal norms.

Teubner counterproposes an understanding of legal pluralism in the vein of the systems-theoretical take on the linguistic turn: 'Legal pluralism is then defined not as a set of conflicting social norms in a given social field but as a multiplicity of diverse communicative processes that observe social action under the binary code legal/illegal' (Teubner 1992, 1451). This understanding of the legal is essentially positivistic to the extent that it focuses on demarcation of the law from its environment but, crucially, it differs from ordinary positivism in that it leaves it up to legal discourse itself to delineate its boundaries in relation to its environment. If the legal seals itself from its environment in such a way, communication between legal orders becomes rather improbable. This is what Teubner tries to make sense of. He is very sceptical about the use of terms such as 'interdiscursivity'. He points out that communication between legal orders is inevitably distorted. He explains this in terms of what he calls 'productive misreading'. When norms transcend the boundaries of a discourse and enter a new one, their meaning undergoes a critical shift. They either cease to be read in the light of the binary code 'legal–illegal' and therefore lose their legality altogether, or they are adapted to the programme of the discourse which they have become part of, and change their meaning although they are still classified under the code 'legal–illegal'.[5] So, meaning cannot be imported or exported unaltered. For that reason Teubner prefers the term 'mutual constitution' coined by Fitzpatrick (1984) to describe the way that State and non-State legal orders make sense of each other. However, he sets three necessary conditions:

> First, against all recent assertions on blurring the 'law/society' distinction, the boundaries of meaning that separate closed discourses need to be recognized. Second, mutual constitution cannot be understood as a transfer of meaning from one field to the other but needs to be seen as an internal reconstruction process. Third, the internal constraints that render the mutual constitution highly selective must be taken seriously. (Teubner, 1992: 1456)

If the binary code 'legal–illegal' is promoted as the element which crucially determines the legality of regulatory phenomena, legal pluralism shifts its emphasis from the study of *social groups* developing legal orders to *self-regulating discourses* and the legalization of various language games. In this process linkage institutions (Teubner 1992, 1457) change character as well. Linkage institutions are those essentially contested concepts, such as *bona fides*, the meaning of which varies depending on the context in which they are placed.

In the new project of legal pluralism, these adaptable linkage institutions facilitate the connection of the law with social processes. Thus, a new channel of communication is established that prevents the law from colonizing its environment and instead enables the productive misreading of the latter by the former. When

5 For the groundwork of a systems theory of law, see Luhmann 1985, 1988a and b, 1995a and b.

the law is structurally coupled with society *informed by legal pluralistic critique*, it becomes more responsive as it co-evolves with regulatory discourses dispersed in society. Understanding legal pluralism as the law's tacit knowledge of its social ecology (Teubner 1992, 1461) will relieve socio-legal theory from the constant anxious concern to import the knowledge of politics or that of social sciences so as to make it more responsive, both of which end up juridifying politics and science without guaranteeing the responsiveness of the law.

Boaventura de Sousa Santos and the Emergence of New Subjectivities The fundamental question concerning legal pluralism, which de Sousa Santos (1995)[6] tries to answer, is how the apparently mutually excluding pillars of regulation and emancipation can be made compatible. Legal pluralism is for him the new reality in which we develop new ways of understanding the world and therefore new ways of regulating our lives. However, this regulation is not static, it cannot and does not claim finality. It is an ongoing process of rediscovering and regulating the world.

De Sousa Santos distinguishes between three phases in the debate about legal pluralism: the colonial period; the post-colonial period in capitalist modern societies; and post-modern legal plurality, which includes transnational, suprastate orders. He claims that what makes the third period exceptionally post-modern is the fact that there is a shift from definitions of law to the identification of three distinct levels of analysis which correspond to the three time-spaces of the legal phenomenon: the local, the national and the transnational (de Sousa Santos 1995, 117). The third stage is marked or preceded by an epistemological transition, a new form of knowledge and understanding of the world. Instead of modern knowledge, which is an aggregate of unquestionable truth claims making sense of our world with a claim to coherence, rightness and certainty, he suggests that it is a different kind of knowledge we should be pursuing, namely, what he terms 'a prudent knowledge for a decent life' (de Sousa Santos 1995, 489). This emergent epistemological paradigm weds science and society. Unlike modern knowledge, which claims exclusivity, post-modern knowledge is knowledge of the self and the community. It does not offer tools for explaining the world and to which the world must fit; it is an ongoing process of understanding and revising our explanatory tools.[7]

In the discussion about the ways to identify the various normative orders, de Sousa Santos begins with the remark that it is not enough to acknowledge their plurality

---

6 *Toward a New Common Sense* (de Sousa Santos 1995) is a very complex work and it is not without great difficulty that one can put a finger on what exactly it is about. As Twining puts it: 'The result is rather like a gigantic sandwich containing a variety of succulent ingredients held together by a less appealing outer casing' (2000, 197). Although the analogy to a sandwich is not entirely happy, Twining does have a point about the internal coherence of de Sousa Santos' book.

7 Another theory of legal pluralism that focuses on epistemology and the law as the integrative medium of different perceptions of reality is that offered by Warwick Tie (1999).

but it is necessary to also ground it theoretically (de Sousa Santos 1995, 403), thus pointing to the shortcoming of empirical-positivistic legal pluralism that is content to simply observe from a distance. De Sousa Santos then tries to do so by isolating social configurations, that is, six-dimensional and thus complex structures, and by observing which kind of law they are regulated by, which kind of power relations one can trace in them and which epistemological form permeates them. At the same time he examines which institutions guarantee the regularization of patterns of social relations, the social agencies, and the developmental dynamics, which basically are the factors that perpetuate their existence and can be both aims and means of reproduction. The six structural places are the householdplace, the workplace, the marketplace, the communityplace, the citizenplace and the worldplace. He argues that these structural places always remain stable and hence reliable as social 'topoi' and observational standpoints. According to de Sousa Santos, what makes those places unique is the fact that they are both social and geographical constellations and that their specific spatiality makes locational and temporal reference always possible. The clue as to what each of these structures represents is more or less in their name. Nevertheless some points of the typology and the argument seem a little vague. What appears to be the cohesive element of each of these structural places is the specific form of social relations that are being developed within them. These social relations constitute a web around a basic element, which imbues them and determines their development and appearance. This element, as de Sousa Santos perceives it, varies from one structural place to the other and is associated with the functions of each of the latter. Thus, for instance, the communityplace is 'clustered around the production and reproduction of physical and symbolic territories and communal identities' (de Sousa Santos 1995, 421), whereas the workplace is 'the set of social relations clustered around the production of economic exchange values and of labour processes, relations of production stricto sensu … and relations in production …' (de Sousa Santos 1995, 421). The worldplace, a concept that sounds rather broad and somewhat obscure, is defined as 'the sum total of the internal pertinent effects of the social relations through which a global division of labour is produced and reproduced' (de Sousa Santos 1995, 421). It constitutes a universal umbrella for all the other structural places. Comprising both social and political spheres (namely nation-States), the worldplace provides the necessary universal framework and the organizing pattern for their development and reproduction.

It is also useful to see how de Sousa Santos understands the law in the first place. He identifies three distinctive features, three structural components of the legal phenomenon, which characterize every normative order and not just State law. These three characteristics are rhetoric, violence and bureaucracy (de Sousa Santos 1995, 112). Rhetoric, as the art of persuasion by argumentation, is both a communication form and a decision-making strategy. So are violence and bureaucracy, the former implying and involving the use or threat of physical force and the latter referring to the regularization of procedures. These three structural components have no stable form but function in mutual articulations within each normative order. The way in which they are combined determines the final form of the legal order and its functional pattern. It must be noted that de Sousa Santos does not use these three features as strict criteria in order to identify legal orders. Rather, he detects normative phenomena in various social fields, then tries to apply rhetoric, violence and bureaucracy and comments on the form of interpenetration of the three structural components.

The synthesis of the above forms de Sousa Santos' picture of legal pluralism. He imagines it as a cluster of interpenetrating legalities, which regulate all instances of our whole lives and correspond to our knowledge of the world. As this knowledge changes, so do the forms of regulation we experience. He uses three telling metaphors to describe the new epistemological and legal paradigm. The *frontier* means we never belong fully to one or the other side. We do and do not have the internal point of view at the same time, to borrow a Hartian image. Living on the frontier enables us to perceive the centre as oppression rather than emancipatory regulation. Achieving a *baroque* subjectivity means that order is always suspended. The baroque is always suspicious of totalities, it is extreme and does not subscribe to rational calculations. Finally, the South must recover its voice. We must rediscover the *colonized different*, only not in an imperialistic manner, which purports to be scientifically universalistic. It must reclaim its voice and language and the North must be prepared to listen to it carefully.

Variations on the theme of critical legal pluralism Desmond Manderson goes further than de Sousa Santos and describes pluralism in even looser terms (Manderson 1996). He, correctly I think, accuses modernist legal theories (including positivism, theories advocating the connection of law with morality, as well as the critical legal studies movement, and most versions of legal pluralism) of reifying notions of order and coherence. But even when those theories depart from the conception of the law as tied to a State or a State-like formation, Manderson reproaches them for still adhering to the spatial metaphor and speaking of overlapping territories or normative geographies. Instead, he argues, legal theory ought to endorse and combine the research projects of critical legal studies and the thesis from the indeterminacy of meaning on the one hand and legal pluralism and its central tenet of the proliferation of legal sources on the other. This will, in Manderson's view, enable us to move towards a new legal aesthetics, which will represent the legal as rhythm instead of time, as chaos instead of order. This new 'legal chaotics', as Manderson terms it, will allow space for turbulence, incoherence and uncertainty. And thus, he adds, fear will be replaced by hope, as it is only uncertainty that makes hope possible.

Margaret Davies makes a more modest but similar suggestion when she argues that legal pluralism should be seen as an 'ethos' rather than a specific theory defining the law in a rigid, criteriological fashion (Davies 2005). She distinguishes between two branches of legal pluralistic thought. On the one hand, there are theories that look for a plurality of laws as autonomous and defined institutions and, on the other, those that see plurality in law as the proliferation of interpretive communities and attitudes. This tendency towards the pluralization of the legal is evident, Davies argues, even outwith theories that place themselves under the canopy of legal pluralism. She concludes that the shift from monism and singularity to plurality is not only possible but also normatively desirable, and it calls for the adoption of an open concept of law – a concept that will abandon the modern claims to totality.

Finally, Kleinhans and MacDonald argue that it is necessary to radicalize the project of legal pluralism as *critical* legal pluralism, rejecting the traditional social scientific way of distinguishing the legal as impoverished (Kleinhans and MacDonald 1998). It therefore departs from the conception of law as social fact and locates the legal within the subjectivity of legal subjects. This has a number of consequences. The legal defies objectivity and authoritative interpretation; the relation of control between law and subject has a two-way character; the metaphysical differences between various normative orders collapse, because 'these normative orders cannot exist outside the creative capacity of their subjects' (Kleinhans and MacDonald 1998, 40). Kleinhans and MacDonald respond to the obvious criticism that the law is essentially social and cannot be reduced to the individual by arguing that:

> Critical legal pluralism makes no appeal to some 'essential' or 'anthropomorphic' individual, but rather to the way the modern self perceives itself to be individualistic. The modern self is a construct, but this construct has itself a constructive capacity, and it is upon this constructive capacity that the internormative character of legal pluralism must be focused. (Kleinhans and MacDonald 1998, 44)

Robert Cover and the Plurality of Jurisgenerative Commitments Cover never subscribed explicitly to a legal pluralistic research programme. He targeted primarily theories of law as literature and abstract legal interpretation. As a result, he is seldom referred to as a 'legal pluralist' nor his work indexed as an account of legal pluralism. However, his work is marked by his strong anti-State thought and very clear pluralistic tendencies. It is in his 'Nomos and Narrative' (1983) and 'Violence and the Word' (1986) that Cover tries to establish the inherent connection between State law and violence. The pivot of his argument is that State law operates with violence in order to establish itself as the sole legitimate normative system, in contrast to other normative orders that develop within communities in the margins of State law. In addition to that he gives his account of how the State institutionally and hierarchically organizes its violence. His final argument is that legal interpretation and the enrichment of legal meaning meet an insurmountable barrier raised by the State with the use of violence. In 'Nomos and Narrative', Cover begins by establishing that the *nomos* we all inhabit is unavoidably related to a narrative in which it is embodied: narratives are models through which we study and experience the transformations taking place when a given simplified state of affairs is made to pass through the force field of a similarly simplified set of norms (Cover 1983, 10). The normative world which determines our lives is created by predominantly cultural means and is constituted by a bulk of symbols: rituals, traditions, texts and objects. Therefore, the richness of legal meaning is inevitable. Cover makes clear that he is interested neither in the legal, technical term of legal meaning nor the distinction between living law and law in action. What he argues is that within the same legal universe there is room to accommodate an enormous number of experienced interpretations, *nomoi* and narratives seemingly incompatible with each other, as one of them is bound to be predominant by the use of means other than interpretation and commitment, namely by violence.

Cover distinguishes between two types of law, the 'paideic' and the 'imperial'. His intention is not so much to form a typology that could accommodate all the historical legal paradigms but rather to comment upon two fundamental functions of the legal, that is, the world-creating and world-maintaining functions, that can co-exist, as indeed they do, even in late modern legal systems of advanced capitalist States. Paideic law is world-creating. It implies the existence of a community, the members of which acknowledge a set of common needs and obligations, base their life and worldviews upon these and their 'obedience is correlative to understanding' (Cover 1983, 13). On the other hand, in the model of imperial law 'norms are universal and enforced by institutions. They need not be taught as well, as long as they are effective' (Cover, 1983). In this paradigm, social relations are not determined by the commonality of needs and obligations and the unity that this commonality establishes, but rather by the principle of peaceful co-existence set up by the aforementioned institutionally enforced norms.

The ever-expanding social differentiation and the subsequent proliferation of various kinds of social bonds, groups and discourses lead inevitably to the proliferation of interpretations and legal meanings. Different communities share different narratives, which are the outcome, to a great extent, of the materiality of the bonds holding communities together. What safeguards these narratives and at the same time consecrates them are their objectification and the degree of personal commitment to them (Cover 1983, 45). 'To know the law – and certainly to live the law – is to know not only the objectified dimension of validation but also the commitments that warrant interpretations' (Cover 1983, 46). The reality that the law creates and the alternatives to reality it offers would simply exist in the world of ideas, if it were not for the personal commitment of those who share the *nomos*. It is the strength of that commitment that determines the extent of law's hegemony. 'Law is the projection of an imagined future upon reality' (Cover 1986, 1604). This alternity designed by the law is being substantiated through the transformation of word into action on behalf of the people. 'Law' is never just a mental or spiritual act. A legal world is built only to the extent that there are commitments that place bodies on the line (Cover 1986, 1605). At the stage of jurisgenesis, that is at the stage of the creation of a *nomos*, commitment is a *sine qua non* condition of the outset of the new normative world. Social bonds, common beliefs and cultural possessions are embodied in the commitment to the common objectified value, that will become the fundamental norm of the new *nomos*. Commitment can urge people to shield their normative universe with their own bodies; it makes martyrs of the community or the individual and murderers at the same time. The importance of commitment is not exhausted in the jurisgenerative stage. Normative world-maintaining would not be feasible without acts of commitment. But this time the commitment is towards the normative word instead of the law-generating idea. As long as there are distinct cultural media generating common worlds shared by a number of people, who subsequently form communities, where they share beliefs, shrines and weapons and are prepared to defend them irrespective of the undesirable consequences of their struggle, there will be a plethora of legal interpretations, and legal meaning will have a bulk of different properties.[8]

The question then is how State law responds to this plurality of legal meaning. Cover argues that State law, being the only interpretation that can establish itself with institutionalized means, resorts to violence. He does not seem to accept that sanctions, violence and the law are internalized. What he argues is that communities are seeking either to maintain their own normative world, like, for instance, communities living in insular autonomy such as the Amish and the Mennonites (Cover 1983, 26), or, in the case of more politicized communities, to struggle against the State and question the legal interpretation of the latter (a project which Cover terms 'redemptive constitutionalism'), for example, the civil rights movement (Cover 1983, 31). But the State and its institutions overlook this multiplicity of legal meanings by usually stating 'the problem not as one of too much law, but as one of unclear law'. In this way the State denies the legitimacy of any other interpretation, *nomos* and narrative. Therefore, from a number of equally legitimate legal meanings, State law is bound to prevail. An already established *nomos*, a normative world that managed to impose itself after the clash of the multiple interpretative communities and assumes universal legitimacy, does not need acts of commitment for its maintenance and perpetuation. What substitutes commitment is institutionalization and the formulation of hierarchical structures. An institutionalized normative order protects itself by hiding behind the legal meaning, to which it has attributed the privilege of exclusivity in legitimation and behind its apparatuses and institutions. When the judge resolves disputes by silencing one of the demands produced before her or when she deals with pain and death as, for instance, in the course of a criminal trial (Cover 1986), she is never alone. She shares the responsibility of her actions and words with a number of people. The legal system invents its mechanisms of depersonifying its operations and thus making them more flexible and effective. These operations sit comfortably with legitimacy, because they are carried out with the vocabulary formed in reference to the predominant legal meaning.

---

8 It seems to me that Rodolfo Sacco's 'mute law' refers to much the same idea, namely that the law is experienced and generated through participants' commitments rather than (simply) by its sytematization in linguistic tokens, which separate themselves from and then authoritatively address those from whose normative commitments the emergence of law depends (Sacco 1995).

Conclusion

This foray in theories of legal pluralism aimed at clarifying and re-framing the law question. In the first chapter I argued that one of the shortcomings of mainstream legal philosophy, including critical legal theory, is that it remains monistic by elevating context-specific conceptions of the legal to a higher degree of abstraction, thus raising claims to universal validity. The same error is committed by empiricist-positivistic theories of legal pluralism. Although they are correct in trying to dissociate the law from the State and look for instances of legality in the margins, as it were, of State law, they use context-specific conceptions of the legal as criteria for the identification of legal systems. Critical, post-modern theories of legal pluralism reverse the whole enquiry. Namely, they deny the possibility of saying anything meaningful about the concept of law and collapse the latter into all other kinds of normativity as well as forms of social control. This is a thesis that needs to be examined carefully and this is what I shall do in the following chapter, while in Chapter 4 I shall go on to make a suggestion as to the methodology of legal pluralism.

Chapter 3
On the Theoretical Groundwork of Legal Pluralism

Introduction

This is what I have argued so far: in Chapter 1, I reviewed some influential legal theoretical strands and highlighted a methodological shortcoming, namely their heavy reliance on the contested presupposition that the law is necessarily associated with the State, as well as their vision of the law as coercively addressed by a small part of the population to others. With these assumptions in place they go on to conceptualize the law purporting that this conceptualization is either neutral and general (in the case of positivism) or obvious and uncontroversial but, at the same time, unnecessary, as it is either in the light of its content that the law ought to be understood (in the case of Dworkinian interpretivism) or as the target of critique (in the case of CLT). In Chapter 2 I visited some central theories of legal pluralism, precisely because their initial premise is that there is no necessary connection between the law and the State and because legal pluralism seems a promising path to take in trying to reconceptualize the law in an emancipatory manner. I criticized classical legal pluralistic theories on the same grounds as orthodox legal positivism, that is for importing a tacitly pre-formulated concept of law in different contexts and conceptual schemes and using that as a criterion for the identification of the legal. I also explored Brian Tamanaha's conventionalist approach to legal pluralism and, promising as I found this to be, I pointed out that it is still in need of qualification. Finally, I gave an exposition of post-modern theories of legal pluralism (and I shall use this term as a shorthand for those specific theories hereafter) as well as Robert Cover's essentially legal pluralistic thought. In this chapter, I start by assessing post-modern legal pluralism and support my conclusion that the question of legal pluralism comes down to the question of whether it is possible to formulate or even aspire to formulate a trans-contextual, trans-epochal sense of law, while being fully aware of its fallibility, and what this sense may include. I believe that this starting point will enable legal theory to pluralize the concept of the law as well as its very own research programme. In what follows, I shall explore the substantive issue of whether it is possible to conceptualize the law in an *a priori* but still pluralistic manner. In Chapter 4, I shall return to legal theory and the methodological question and suggest a way in which legal theory can make the best of the legal pluralistic potential.

On the Possibility of a Plural and Yet Universal Sense of Law

A pressing question arising from post-modern theories of legal pluralism concerns the conditions of existence of the legal. Post-modern legal pluralist theories seem to discard the possibility of grasping the concept of law and forming a-contextual knowledge of it. They do so by conflating various normative orders and placing them all under the canopy of the law. But this is puzzling for at least two reasons. First, in doing so, post-modern theories of legal pluralism do not account for a fundamental intuition manifested in our linguistic practices. We *do* refer to some normative phenomena as distinct and recognizable in one way or another, whereas we reserve other terms or qualified uses of the word 'law' for other types of norms. We differentiate (although, to be sure, the parameters of the differentiation are contested) between moral and legal norms, habits and formal prescriptions. We intuit a difference between the statements 'You must brush your teeth before going to bed' or 'You must not write your name on the essay before submitting it' on the one hand, and, on the other, statements such as 'It is an offence for a man to rape another man or a woman'.[1] In other words, we can intuitively tell the difference between normative utterances of a *legal* nature, as opposed to utterances which can be ascribed a prescriptive value but do not count as law. Kleinhans and MacDonald respond to this point by saying that the contrast noted here reveals the limitations of language. Moreover, they maintain that there is no *a priori* difference between legal and other normative orders and that the word 'law' is mistakenly associated with official or State law and that this use is the result of the differentiation and autonomization of the legal profession and official legal practices (Kleinhans and MacDonald 1998, 41).

A basic assumption in this book is that there is nothing in the meaning of law that implies, presupposes or entails its necessary connection with the State. Such an association seems to be a purely contingent historical fact. MacCormick makes this point when he argues that:

> The state cannot live without some minimal law and minimal respect for it, and it cannot thrive without a considerable body of law and considerable respect for it. But straightforward identification of the state with the law is erroneous. This is true even though it is the case that we must look to a constitution to find out whose actions are the ones that can be imputed to the state as its acts for one or another purpose.[2] (MacCormick 1999, 25)

However, what the conditions and rules of use of the word 'law' hint at is the connection of the word to a *linguistic practice* at the very least, albeit not *necessarily* one that has any relation to the practices of officials working within the law of the

1 England and Wales Sexual Offences Act 2003, s. 1.

2 Roderick MacDonald makes the same argument in MacDonald 1998. For a string of conceptual arguments against legal centralism, see Davies 2005.

State and those institutions associated with it. Laden with ideology as normative language may be, the intuitive differentiation between various instances and employments of it deserves closer attention at the very least, in order to determine whether there is anything undiluted by ideology that we refer to and, if yes, what its properties and what the right way of disclosing it may be.

Secondly, to the extent that they collapse different sorts of normative orders into each other, post-modern legal pluralist theses seem to contradict themselves. They often purport to be giving a descriptive account of the fact of legal pluralism. But, on other occasions, they carefully avoid claiming that their description is strictly *a posteriori* and synthetic, thus creating the impression that they indeed work with an *a priori* concept of law. Therefore, they already seem to use the language game of the law (on language games, see Wittgenstein 1967) and, indeed, rely on it in order to articulate a theory of *legal* pluralism as opposed to general value pluralism[3] while, at the same time, denying the distinctiveness of the legal.

But perhaps I am doing an injustice to legal pluralist theses (according to which the concept of law is indeterminate and vague) by accusing them of not taking into account a self-evident truth about the way we speak. Perhaps what lies beneath the arguments from legal chaotics (Manderson 1996), new subjectivities (Kleinhans and MacDonald 1998) and pluralism as ethos (Davies 2005) is a more robust theory of pluralism. Maybe the argument is not that 'there is no such thing as law' or that 'every kind of normativity can be classed as law' but, rather more modestly and plausibly, that 'there is a plethora of seemingly incompatible things that can count as law'. But in order for such an argument to be sustained it is necessary to unpack the conditions under which it can be true. In addressing this issue we will also be asking whether it is possible to acquire some objective knowledge of what counts as law without, at the same time, abandoning the project of legal pluralism. In what follows I shall discuss this and argue that it is indeed possible to offer an account of the law that is both universal and pluralistic. I will also try to demonstrate that, in order to sustain this position, it is necessary to subscribe to a contextualist understanding of law, which entails not giving up altogether on the possibility of saying something about the law in an a-contextual, universal manner.

Metaphysical and cognitive pluralism comes in many forms. Nicholas Rescher has offered a comprehensive and careful categorization (Rescher 1993), which will prove very useful for the purposes of this chapter, although my aim is not to advance a theory of alethic pluralism. Rescher distinguishes between four kinds of pluralism: *scepticism*, *syncretism*, *indifferentist relativism* and *contextualism*. The sceptic rejects all competing views as indefensible. When two views on truth or rightness are mutually contradictory, then neither can be true. This position is rejected by syncretism. On this latter analysis, all contradictory views are equally true. Indifferentist relativism accepts that it is possible to choose between

3 Though it must be emphasized that, even in order to articulate a theory of value pluralism, it seems equally necessary to have an *a priori* sense of value.

competing views. But any choices made will be arbitrary since they will be based on preferences, habits and other considerations that do not yield the basis of a rational justification. Finally, contextualism is a perspectivalist-cum-objectivist position according to which: '[O]nly one alternative should be accepted, and this acceptance has a [rational] basis …, albeit this basis may differ … from group to group, era to era, school to school' (Rescher 1993, 80).

Scepticism is probably the easiest version of pluralism to deal with. I believe that one argument suffices to strike a decisive blow against it. What the sceptic does not seem to take into account is the problem of self-reference. The statement that 'anything that can be said about anything can never be true' necessarily includes this specific statement itself. Scepticism cannot exclude its main tenet from the totality of propositions to which it relates. But this leads to the paradox of the sceptic denying the possibility of her own proposition being true, thus rendering it meaningless. So, if the sceptic were right, she would be committing not only a logical but also a performative contradiction, for she would refute her own claim along the lines of 'X is Y but this is not true'. Moreover, as Rescher points out (Rescher 1993, 86), the sceptical thesis is based on a misapprehension of our cognitive endeavours. We inquire about the world and ask ourselves practical questions because we want to acquire true information about the way things are and arrive at correct answers able to inform and guide our actions. And when we do arrive at these answers, we raise claims to truth and rightness that we are prepared to defend against rival views.

Syncretism will prove a little more difficult to rebut. At first sight, the analytic principle of non-contradiction compels us to reject the thesis that contradictory statements can all be true at the same time. But there is a possible counterargument here. The syncretist could argue that contradictory statements can all be true simultaneously. This could be said to be the case to the extent that all relevant statements are relative to a conceptual scheme that is determined by the specific context in which they emerge. Implicit in this is a refutation of the distinction between analytic statements (that is statements which are true with reference to their meaning alone) and synthetic ones (the truth of which can only be tested with reference to experience). On this latter view, no proposition can be true transcendentally and absolutely. Truth is always relative to experience. So, as concepts are relative to the actual world and the relationships of people to it, even the non-contradiction principle only becomes meaningful within a specific conceptual scheme. But, while this thesis is more powerful than scepticism, it still does not deal convincingly with the problem of self-reference. In order for the syncretist to raise a claim to truth with her central tenet, she must be prepared to accept that there are at least *some* statements, such as the syncretist thesis, that are, if not absolute, then true in all conceptual schemes, or else be led to the paradoxical and untenable conclusion that all communication is impossible.[4]

4 For a classic argument against conceptual schemes, see Davidson 1973. See also Hacker 1996.

Let me try to see how this would translate in a legal context. Post-modern legal pluralist theories could be interpreted as advancing a thesis akin to Tamanaha's conventionalism, namely that law is whatever a community, however defined, decides is law. The argument is purportedly neutral in that it does not prescribe the preferences of communities and makes the concept of law strictly contingent upon specific conceptual schemes. But it soon becomes clear that this claim cannot be sustained. A syncretist legal pluralist would have to concede that she is unable to recognize a legal conceptual scheme when she sees one. But this already means that she will be unable to see the boundaries of her own conceptual scheme and grasp what differentiates it from others, as she will have already given up on *any* criteria of sameness and difference. And yet, the purportedly neutral syncretist thesis rests on the possibility of such criteria existing to the extent that it must presuppose that legal conceptual schemes emerge and develop in distinct ways, which are somehow cognizable. This is tantamount to implicitly accepting that it *is* possible to make a-contextual true statements about what the concept of law entails. However, syncretism shies away from such an admission, thus being reduced to the paradox that 'there are other legal conceptual schemes out there but we have no way of knowing that they exist', which is just short of saying that the only conceptual scheme that exists is the one in which we are placed. So it becomes clear that the question then turns from whether it is possible to say anything about the law from an a-contextual vantage point to what we can say and how thick and pervasive it will be. And answers to those questions are provided more convincingly, I believe, by contextualism.

But before moving on to contextualism, let me make a very brief note on indifferentist relativism. This position is marked by one fundamental shortcoming that does not allow it to get off the ground. As I have already said, indifferentist relativism accepts that more than one version of the truth can be valid but the choice between them can only be an arbitrary one, based on preferences that cannot be justified and so on. I believe that the following argument by Rescher suffices to disprove this thesis:

> one cannot consistently both stake a claim to the rational validity of one's views and at the same time reject all commerce with rational standards and criteria. In this regard, our commitment to our own cognitive position is (or should be) unalloyed. We can and should see our own (rationally adopted) standards as superior to the available alternatives – and are, presumably, rationally entitled to do so by seeing them as *deserving* of preference on the basis of the cognitive considerations we ourselves can rationally endorse. (Rescher 1993, 102)

Put simply, the central contextualist claim is that there can be various attitudes to truth that are determined by the experiential background of individual agents or communities. From the point of view of cognition, it is perfectly rational for one to show a commitment to what she holds as true, while at the same time acknowledging the possibility of the eventual falsification of her belief. From a metaphysical point of view, this means that truth is *to a certain extent* relative to conceptual schemes that are determined by experiential background and other pragmatic factors. But this does not imply that there is no truth independent of our ability to experience the world and make sense of it. Contextualism can be understood as the reconciliation of metaphysical pluralism with realism about truth. Michael Lynch suggests that we understand conceptual schemes as *networks* of concepts that are structurally foundational (therefore not absolutely so), and compatible with a fuzzy distinction (therefore *still* a distinction) between analytic and synthetic statements (Lynch 1998). It follows from this that conceptual schemes are not (as other radical forms of pluralism would have to concede) incommensurable. But the existence of conceptual schemes and the dependence of truth upon them do not preclude some degree of realism about truth. Lynch subscribes to Alston's theory of minimal realism, which rests on the distinction between concepts and properties (Alston 1996). On this view, it is possible to have concepts that are thin and underdetermined and are only fleshed out with specific properties within specific, context-bound conceptual schemes.

The distinction between concepts and conceptions is of course familiar to legal philosophers. Influenced by Rawls' use of the distinction (Rawls 1971), Dworkin relies heavily on the idea that there is an objective concept of law of which there are many competing conceptions. However, note the difference between the contextualist understanding of truth and the implicit strong realism in Dworkin's account. As I noted in Chapter 1, Dworkin subscribes to an all-pervasive realism, which necessarily holds all alternative interpretations of law (or the value of 'legality' which underpins the practice of law) *bar one* as mistaken. On the other hand, contextualism sees such alternatives as *true* with reference both to a universal sense of law and the specific context, in which they develop. The former opens up the space for mutual understanding *and* critique and the latter for difference.

It may have been noticed that I have been reluctant to speak of a universal concept of law. The reason for that is that I do not want to make any strong realist claims, which would inevitably involve the argument in analytical nitpicking. In fact I do not think it necessary to pick between a robust externalist and an internalist account of the law. Whether it refers to something which somehow exists in the world or a universally shared concept, what I call the universal sense of law is a universalist claim raised in the course of the enquiry into the legal. At the same time, though, and very importantly, it is constitutive of the possibility of discourse about the law. No sooner does such a discourse begin than the presence of an underlying universal sense of law making it possible is revealed. The question then is how exactly to articulate this sense. Consistent with meaningful contextualism, such a universal sense cannot exhaust all instances and manifestations of legality. Rather, it can and should be a thin theory of law determined in context by being attributed specific properties in light of the experiential background of those who share them. Thus, the *a priori* association of the concept of the legal with the concept of the State is contingent and cannot be backed by any robust conceptual argument. It might well be the case that, in certain conceptual schemes, the law is attributed the property of emanating from the State or some State-like political formation, without this counting as an absolute truth about the concept of law. But this does not mean that we must throw the baby out with the bath water. Dissociating the law from the State or, indeed, from the properties that our conceptual schemes and legal cultures attribute to the concept of law (an error often committed by sociological and anthropological legal pluralism, as I showed in Chapter 2) does not presuppose or entail abandoning the possibility of forming *any* a-contextual knowledge of the law. On the contrary, having a thin sense of law seems indispensable for a theory of legal pluralism. Pluralism after all can only predicate a common point of reference. And, as I have already noted, this is precisely what post-modern theories of legal pluralism do not take sufficiently seriously. They already purport to be theories of legal pluralism while at the same time they deny the possibility of speaking about the law in a way that will be meaningful across all conceptual schemes or legal cultures.

Cover's Contextualist Legal Pluralism

Having set out a taxonomy of metaphysical and cognitive pluralism and applied it in the context of the law, it is now time to try to unpack the kind of legal pluralism that Cover seems to be describing in 'Nomos and Narrative'. It is very easy to misunderstand Cover as taking a syncretist approach to the concept of law and legal pluralism. The fact that he seems to merge narrative with normativity, interpretation and commitment with the law's existence, can be interpreted as a relativistic argument, akin to the common thesis of post-modern legal theories, according to which the concept of law differs *essentially* from context to context. But, as I shall argue in this section, a closer reading of 'Nomos and Narrative' reveals that Cover's central thesis is by and large contextualist in orientation. Cover accepts that there is an objective sense of law, albeit a thin and under-prescriptive one. This, after all, is what allows him to theorize about the law in the first place. At the same time, Cover maintains that the law can only be determined and developed against the shared background and commitment of a specific community.

Cover is often understood as simply emphasizing the plurality of interpretive attitudes to 'official' law. For instance, Davies regards the idea of 'jurisgenesis' as the ascription of alternative meaning to the same legal text by communities that are partly integrated into the mainstream. These alternative interpretations compete with the official interpretation in the courts. But alternative interpretations are doomed to failure when set alongside mainstream views. This is because judges adhere to the official and conclusive legal meaning (Davies 2005, 109). If that were the case though, if Cover only spoke of competing interpretations, his argument would stand indefensible against theories that describe the law as an integrative medium. And the most powerful ones here are, I believe, those put forward by Dworkin and Alexy. In the Dworkinian scheme of things, with its reliance on a robust moral realism (Dworkin 1986; 1996; 2004; Stavropoulos

1996), every interpretive attitude is *prima facie* admissible in the pre-interpretive stage. But, in order for these interpretations to acquire legitimation and to count as law, they must be subjected to the tests of fit and justification and successfully pass them. Once all the competing interpretive attitudes have been sieved through the integrity test, then the correct meaning of law, the right answer, the answer that ought to win universal acceptance, will emerge. Alexy tells us that legal discourse is open to all communicative offers as to the content and meaning of the law (Alexy 1989a). Albeit subject to certain real, institutional constraints, legal discourse is still regulated by the rules of general practical discourse, which establish the connection of the legal with the moral and the testability of the former in the light of the requirements of justice. These (and other such) conceptions of the law as a concept (the real content of which is revealed in and through the practice of applying it) allow for a plurality of interpretive approaches to manifest themselves. Moreover, these approaches compete with one another – each claiming to offer a correct account of law.

To the extent that the legal institution provides the necessary framework for these competing voices to be heard, there is no room for *legal* pluralism – that is, for a plurality of distinct, autonomous and, relatively or absolutely, closed conceptions of legality. In that (legal pluralist) image of the world, the law is still singular and stems from a single source, whether it be an elected body of representatives, the courts or any other 'forum of principle'. What *is* pluralistic is the process of exchange of interpretive takes, through which the final, official 'right answer' will emerge. To that extent, Davies' distinction between legal pluralism as the theory of autonomous institutions, on the one hand, and legal pluralism as the plurality of interpretive approaches, on the other, ceases to be meaningful, as those two pluralisms refer to two different things.

If Cover were an interpretive pluralist, he would not be able to speak of *too much law* but rather only articulate the much more modest claim that State law as we know it, whether it be the product of tradition, civic revolutions or colonization, does not in fact provide the appropriate framework for free and uncoerced communication because of its inherent political biases. Useful and enlightening as it may be, this kind of sociological, historical critique can add very little to our knowledge of the concept of law, cannot explain the plurality of legal phenomena and, in any case, it is being carried out much more efficiently and convincingly by critical readings of modern law,[5] which do not, and do not need to, categorize themselves as pluralistic.

But Cover goes one step further. Yes, he speaks of interpretation and meaning. He tells us explicitly that alternative interpretations (in his example, the Mennonite interpretation of the first amendment of the US constitution) assume 'a status equal (or superior) to that accorded to the understanding of the Justices of the Supreme Court' (Cover 1983, 28). At the same time, though, he insists on

5 The most prominent examples here would be the critical legal studies movement, feminist and critical race theory, and post-modern jurisprudence.

drawing the outer limits of interpretation, which are marked by the commitment of individuals and communities. He tells us that 'creation of meaning entails … subjective commitment to an objectified understanding of a demand' (Cover 1983, 45) and that 'the range of meaning that may be given to every norm – the norm's interpretability – is defined, therefore, both by a legal text, which objectifies the demand, and by the multiplicity of implicit and explicit commitments that go with it' (Cover 1983, 46). Law emerges as a result of this commitment, the acts that it motivates and the narratives in which it is represented.[6] The conflict between instances of jurisgenesis does not reveal merely a semantic disagreement. On this point, I am prepared to concede ground to Ronald Dworkin on the meaning of words in legal texts.[7] Disagreement concerns the content and the properties that the concept of law possesses for particular communities. 'To inhabit a *nomos* is to know how to *live* in it', Cover tells us (Cover 1983, 6). And '[legal precepts] are also signs by which each of us communicates with others' (Cover 1983, 8). In light of these points and the earlier analysis, communities form their meaning schemes through the intertwining of their shared experiential data. It is within such schemes that the legal is interpreted and determined as a result of being ascribed specific properties. What emerges from processes of this sort is an enriched, thick and particular understanding of law that is meaningful to those in the relevant community. But what is enriched and fleshed out in particular contexts is a trans-contextual sense of law. And this sense can be recognized as such from within any conceptual scheme or community. This is how Cover's analysis of interpretive conflicts differs from theories of law as an integrative medium. Cover sees such conflicts as irresolvable from within a *nomos*, whether that be the official one of the State or not, because the dispute is not played out on the minimalist level of the trans-contextual sense of law but on the maximalist level; on the level in which legal communities determine the content of the law through their normative commitments. The particularity of this thickened account of law is what explains the incommensurability of various systems of law on *some* levels.

As I mentioned earlier, how to articulate this trans-contextual sense of law remains an open question. However, a couple of things already become clear. The thin sense of law will have to move beyond the internalist/externalist as well as the normative/social binaries. Recasting Cover's tack on the law in terminology

6 It is not entirely clear to me what role Cover reserves for narratives in a *nomos*. At times he seems to be suggesting that narratives *are* the *nomos* in question: 'the very imposition of a normative force upon a state of affairs, real or imagined, is the act of creating narrative' (Cover 1983, 10). But later on he confuses things by saying that narratives 'create and reveal the patterns of commitment, resistance and understanding' (Cover 1983, 17). Whether narratives reveal or create law is, indeed, an important question, although not one that must be urgently addressed in this context. However, let me say in passing that I would be inclined to argue that narratives *embody* and *reveal* the commitment of participants in a *nomos* rather than creating the latter.

7 I am referring to Dworkin's 'semantic sting' argument (Dworkin 1986).

introduced by Sally Haslanger, such a sense must be sensitive to its manifest, operative and ameliorative or target aspects (Haslanger 2005; see also Haslanger 2006). These respectively refer to the way concepts are employed, the work they do in specific contexts and the work we would like them to do. In their combination, the manifest, operative and ameliorative aspects yield the meaning of a concept. Thus, the clarification of concepts entails more than just a semantic inquiry, an exploration of the social construction of concepts through practices (in other words, ideology) or normative argument alone. It contains all three. Although Haslanger speaks about concepts, the argument can be legitimately adapted to fit the terminology used in this book. A universal sense of law (as well as the specific understandings of it in particular contexts) must be attentive to its manifest, operative and ameliorative aspects, in order for it to be both faithful to the real context in which the law develops as well as flexible enough to allow for critique and change.

Although at this stage the discussion of the universal sense of the law is still formal and has not been fleshed out with any content, it already becomes clear that it has *some* substantive repercussions. Namely, it puts into question preconceptions of law as necessarily associated with authority, inscription, the existence of a system of rules, institutional structures with legislators, adjudicators and law enforcement agencies, and so forth. In other words, it requires us to take a step back, urging us to start thinking about the law afresh in a way that will restrict the horizon of possibility as little as possible.

Cover offers us a promising starting point in giving this sense of law some content by speaking about the law in terms of the commitment of participants in a *nomos* and, more importantly, his idea of alternity. For Cover, the law is the bridge between the ideal and the real, the present and an imagined future state of affairs, which can be arrived at through the mediation of normative commitments from participants and their determination to act upon their commitments. 'A *nomos*, as a world of law, entails the application of human will to an extant state of affairs as well as toward our visions of alternative futures. A *nomos* is a present world constituted by a system of tension between reality and vision' (Cover 1983, 9).

And in a rather Kelsenian vein, Cover adds:

> Law is what licences in blood certain transformations while authorizing others only by unanimous consent. Law is a force, like gravity, through which our worlds exercise an influence upon one another, a force that affects the courses of these worlds through normative space. And law is what holds our reality apart from our visions and rescues us from the eschatology that is the collision in this material social world of the constructions of our minds. (Cover 1983, 9–10)

Of course, Cover (like Kelsen) is not suggesting that the law stands in a causal relation to the consequences of its application. But he insightfully points to a quasi-causal connection between the way the members of a legal community understand the world as well as the way they want to and can transform it in common through the spectrum of their normative commitments, their *nomos*. The under-prescriptive sense of law, which as I have argued ought to be the object of study of a theory of legal pluralism and, indeed, legal theory as a whole, would consist in the symmetry between reality, law and alternity, the dimensions of the connection between word and deed, and the parameters of the correspondence between the law and the world. In Chapters 5 and 6 I rethink the law along these lines. First, though, it is necessary to examine in which forum this universal sense of law can be employed and serve as the starting point of enquiry and discourse.

Accommodating Normative Diversity: Cover's Political Liberalism

I said by way of introduction that, at first sight, Cover's reluctance to give up entirely on a normative meta-order, which will lend coherence to the legal universe, is puzzling. On the one hand, he exposes the jurispathic nature of State law, of a tainted narrative that purports to speak to all normative communities, despite their differences and the acts of commitment constituting them. On the other hand, he is anxious to maintain the significance and possibility of a bedrock – a bedrock that will not only prevent a dominant legality from colonizing and doing violence to other legal orders but also, and perhaps more importantly, prevent those dominant legal orders from heteronomously and violently imposing themselves on those participating in them. Cover realizes that his argument from legal polyphony itself has normative undertones. He also realizes that this argument must have some objective and a-contextual foothold. Indeed, modern and post-modern legal pluralisms alike admit as much, albeit implicitly, when they advance the thesis that the law of the State ought to be more attentive to and accommodating of alternative legalities. But what else can this argument be but a universalizable moral argument from diversity and self-determination as values? This is how Cover puts the point in a much quoted passage from 'Nomos and Narrative':

> It is the problem of multiplicity of meaning – the fact that never only one but always many worlds are created by the too fertile forces of jurisgenesis – that leads at once to the imperial virtues and the imperial mode of world maintenance. Maintaining the world is no small matter and requires no less energy than creating it. Let loose, unfettered, the worlds created would be unstable and sectarian in their social organization, dissociative and incoherent in their discourse, wary and violent in their interactions. The sober imperial mode of world maintenance holds the mirror of critical objectivity to meaning, imposes the discipline of institutional justice upon norms, and places the constraint of peace on the void at which strong bonds cease. (Cover 1983, 16)

At the same time, and even more puzzlingly, Cover does not discard the possibility of judges suspending their jurispathic function, assisting other *nomoi* to flourish rather than stifling them, but also keep under control the jurispathic tendencies of other interpretive communities in light of some constitutional, hence universal, values.

Many analysts of Cover's work find it difficult to justify his faith in the world-maintaining function of an essentially jursipathic law. Likewise, they find it difficult to explain the way he deals with the inescapable tragedy of having to resort to violence in order to avoid violence (Sarat and Kearns 1992; Ryan 1995). To a certain extent, this puzzlement is not only understandable but also justified. As soon as a normative order is institutionalized as law and consolidates its content and boundaries through the participants' commitment, as well as the narratives in which these norms and acts are synthesized, meaning meets its limits. This, after all, is the most powerful insight in Cover's work. How can a judge transcend those boundaries of meaning and be able to claim that she delivers justice, that she can make sense of all the arguments laid out before her fairly from an external point of view? How can anarchism and liberalism be embraced at the same time without losing something from both?

I would suggest that the problem does not have to do with Cover's admission that there is room for some degree of trans-contextuality. This is inevitably implicit in every argument concerning the value in diversity, tolerance and mutual respect. Not only that but *some* degree of objective rightness is built in the very sense of law. In Chapter 6 I will say more on how I believe that the fundamental principles of Kantian liberalism (stemming from the norm of autonomy and respect for every moral agent) provide the starting point that makes all practical reason and communication possible (see Pavlakos 2005). It is upon this basis that dispersed, non-State legal orders will avoid turning 'wary and violent' and regressing into incoherence in their discourse. On this level the plural legal orders can communicate meaningfully and be criticized from a universal viewpoint. Therefore, it is not possible to say that everything or nothing goes, or that the selection between different moral attitudes is arbitrary and based on contingent and subject-dependent preferences. Moreover, it is imperative that meaningful communication and the possibility of critique are maintained.

The real question then is how this discourse is to be operationalized so that the tension between diversity and order can be relieved and the paradox of the transformation of violence into peace can be resolved. What is at stake here is the ability of non-State legal orders to determine themselves by attributing specific content to the ideas of law and justice. Also at stake is the right of participants in those orders to opt out of them. And so too is peaceful co-existence and communication between legal orders. Moreover, a prime concern of a theory of legal pluralism ought to be the exploration of the conditions under which this communication can be transferred from the realm of an institutionalized and therefore closed legality onto the political sphere. Perhaps this is where 'Nomos and Narrative' must be read rather creatively. Despite the law's jurispathic tendencies, Cover still seems to believe in some form of constitutionalism. Although he tells us explicitly that he has little faith in judges and courts, he still believes in an instant of revolutionary jurisgenesis which he hopes will awaken judges to the dynamism of constitutional meaning (Cover 1983, 67). And he ends 'Nomos and Narrative' with the following lines:

> It is not the romance of rebellion that should lead us to look to the law evolved by social movements and communities. Quite the opposite. Just as it is our distrust for and recognition of the state as reality that leads us to be constitutionalists with regard to the state, so it ought to be our recognition of and distrust for the reality of the power of social movements that leads us to examine the nomian worlds they create. And just as constitutionalism is part of what may legitimize the state, so constitutionalism may legitimize, within a different framework, communities and movements. Legal meaning is a challenging enrichment of social life, a potential restraint on arbitrary power and violence. We ought to stop circumscribing the *nomos*; we ought to invite new worlds. (Cover 1983, 68)

It is difficult to see how redemption and jurisgenesis can be established through a pre-articulated, pre-inscribed established legal system, even one of a higher degree of generality and abstraction such as a constitution. Reasoning from within the rigid institutional contours of a legal *system* will always have a jurispathic effect, it will always silence reasoning informed by other narratives, different conceptual schemes that are, as I have been arguing, rooted in different *laws*. Claims stemming from such alternative bodies of law can only be treated, at best, as exceptions, at worst as altogether illegal. Either way, they will have to be made to fit into the conceptual fabric of institutionalized law. The problem is exacerbated even further in the case of State law, which not only embodies (and often misreads) very specific normative commitments, but also fixes their meaning and ascribes them an objective status. It then shifts the focus from justification and mutual understanding to action and from agreement to the management of disagreement as the necessary condition of social order. This, after all, has been the remit of State law from its very conception and is reflected in much of the philosophical thought about it. State law aims at responding to the indeterminacy and radical subjectivity of morality, which account for the improbability (if not impossibility) of moral co-ordination. This task is built into the very systemic character and operations of State law and is revealed in various concepts, institutions and practices culminating in the rule of law. The rule of law is little else but a way of establishing the differentiation of State law from the moral and the political, while at the same time reconciling it with them (although largely failing so to do) by recasting systemic rigidity as equality before the law. So not only does State law have narrow boundaries of meaning but it can also only operate by way of establishing and embedding its closure and passing it as its greatest virtue.

This does not prove the complete bankruptcy of the principles of the rule of law. It is, however, a strong indication that alternative legalities, new *nomoi*, cannot flourish within an already established legal system – a closed system grounded on and incorporating specific commitments and forms of life. This being so, alternative legalities and new *nomoi* can only flourish in a political forum, where the possibility of openness and flexibility is genuine. And if we give up on the idea that all law is *necessarily* and *fully* systemically closed, it will be possible to reconcile its two natures of law as a medium of justification *and* action. Of course this will not eradicate disagreement. The point has been made that the law is principally about managing disagreement rather than confirming agreement (Webber 2006; for a response, see Schneiderman 2006). According to the same argument legal pluralism kicks off from a fallacious premise, failing to appreciate something essential about the law, namely its adjudicative character. This line of reasoning clearly echoes the classical understanding of State law, which I spoke about in the previous paragraph. I would suggest that it starts from an ideological adherence to the Hobbesian misconception of human nature as necessarily antagonistic. The point is that we do not need to turn to any argument about human nature in order to address the question of law. All we need to do is closely examine the sense of law in order to see that the focus is on autonomous agreement with disagreement and the use of force being the exception rather than the norm. The argument from disagreement fails to see that there is always a sense of failure in the use of force, irrespective of who is to blame for it. Arguing that law is *primarily* about adjudication, force and advocacy runs counter to some of our most powerful intuitions about avoiding conflict and pursuing understanding. Genuine law is about dealing with this sense of failure in enforcement, not by mystifying it as a fact of human nature and presenting it as normal but by reconciling with the tragedy in it and shifting the focus from disagreement and force to agreement and the potentiality of resolving eventual disagreement *meaningfully*. Thus, not only will the space for action not disappear but it will also be widened, so as to place in the first instance co-operative action in light of mutual understanding rather than forceful action without further ado. Moreover, the sense of fallibility will take centre stage and give us reasons for always leaving open the possibility of revisiting and revising our reasons for action and restoring the harm done. Perhaps it will be felt that makes for too much uncertainty. It does not. It simply reconciles us with the inevitable uncertainty stemming from the finiteness of all our resources without, at the same time, buying into some sort of eschatological teleology, which deprives one from present rightness or, indeed, happiness.

I believe that, despite the conflicting signals that his writings often send out, this is how Cover should be interpreted. Certainly, the doubts he expresses concerning the ability of the courts to be sensitive to or even aware of other *nomoi* (at least in the first instance) provides a basis on which to reject any *institutionalized context* as the site of jurisgenesis. But I would suggest that Cover sees a space for meaningful dialogue between dispersed *nomoi*, a space opened up by the universal values embedded in the universal sense of law. This dialogue is not antagonistic. Rather, it would have the aim of discovering commonalities that would enable participants to co-exist and communicate without the intervention of a State. I interpret Cover's insistence on constitutionalism as a defence of those fundamental norms and values that underpin a constitution but *not* the way they have been determined in any specific jurisdiction. I also read Cover as expressing the hope that judges could in time recognize the need to transcend the boundaries of State legality and become attentive to other instances of jurisgenesis.[8]

And there is also the question of violence that needs to be dealt with. Cover is said not to be interested in 'splitting epistemological hairs' (Sarat and Kearns 1992, 219) in the discussion on violence. Some see this as a virtue, others as his main weakness. The concept of violence is notoriously elusive and often strategically misused.[9] The conceptual boundaries between violence, legitimate use of force, coercion and other related concepts are fuzzy to say the least. Things get even harder and counterintuitive when talking about the law *as* violent. A now classic exchange between Robert Paul Wolff and Jeffrie G. Murphy revolves precisely around the controversy of whether the law is violent or whether, on the contrary, it tempers violence (Wolff 1969; J.G. Murphy 1970). I think the reason why Cover is loath to get tangled in what he considers to be semantic controversies is that he strikes the middle way between Wolff's anarchism and Murphy's faith in the rule of law. It is precisely because he sees law as aiming at tempering violence that he criticizes *State law* as a non-genuine instance of law, which therefore becomes violent. Cover, I believe, sees clearly what I called earlier in this chapter the sense of failure in any kind of force, whether it is backed by reasons or not. Not only is the use of force regrettable (anyone with their heart in the right place would agree on this) but it also always signifies total rejection. This is true even in the case of punishment meted out as a reaction to an unquestionably wrongful act. There is always an asymmetry between the wrongful act and the crushing response. Take the death penalty, incarceration, military intervention, war, even fines. Right as they may seem at first, they are always a rejection of a person or the group as a whole. Cover's aim is to bring this to the fore and rethink the law as rooted in the possibility of understanding rather than the inevitability of strife and domination.

Conclusion

In this chapter I defended a theoretical understanding of legal pluralism as contextualism. I argued with Robert Cover that we can make sense of the plurality of *nomoi* as contextualizations of a universal sense of law in light of participants' real commitments and normative experiences. This already provides a solution to the conundrum of the compatibility between conceptual schemes and the commensurability or not of context-bound concepts, because the focus is shifted from the philosophical analysis of the possibility of plural concepts to the real conditions of contextualization and specification of the law. At the same time, it departs from the internalist–externalist debate, which in a legal context is rather

8 For an account of how legal pluralism can be taken seriously while still reserving for the State the role of 'legal executive' (with emphasis on Islamic law), see S. Jackson 2006.

9 For an analytical account of the meaning of violence in relation to neighbouring concepts, see Geuss 2001, 21–8.

sterile and tends to lead nowhere. It does so by maintaining the possibility of there being a universal sense of law with both ontological and normative aspects, without needing to take a stance as to whether this sense is part of the fabric of nature or purely socially constructed and yet constant through time. Furthermore, Cover's contextualism dissociates the law from the State without giving up on its institutional autonomy and differentiation from other normative orders, thus addressing the shortcomings of other theorizations of legal pluralism. In the same move it reveals both the violence potentially committed by State law (or any *nomos* with the same imperialist tendencies) by substituting and representing people's commitments with a claim to universality. Even more importantly, Cover's contextualism forces us to rethink the law as primarily about mutual understanding rather than force, about the way we make normative sense of our shared experience world rather than the necessary suppression of inevitable irreconcilable disagreement, while reserving a place for a set of universal values, which account both for communication between *nomoi* and serve as the appellate jurisdiction in the case of disagreement. Its critical potential is thus wed with an emancipatory one.

However, it is also the case that Cover's faith in the jurisgenerative potential of State law and courts does not sit comfortably with the rest of his argument. The foreclosure of meaning that State law relies on stands in the way of the repoliticization of the question of law in light of a universal sense of legality. In the next chapter I will argue that, at least in the first instance, such a discussion can be hosted in the realm of legal theory, understood as an interperspectival, open, democratized dialogue, relieved from the constraints of expertise.

Chapter 4
Interperspectival, Critical Legal Theory

Introduction

In the first two chapters I advanced a critique of the most influential legal theories on grounds of their methodological one-dimensionality, which forecloses pluralism. I also provided an exposition and critique of the main theories of legal pluralism available. In Chapter 3, I explored the possibility of legal pluralism by defending a qualified contextualism, which rests on a thin but universal sense of law, which would account both for its factual and normative aspects. This detour into the substantive core of legal pluralism was necessary in preparing the ground for this chapter, in which I shall discuss, in a rather programmatic fashion, how legal theory can make the most of the pluralistic nature of the law by abandoning a purely functionalist or a purely normative agenda and adopting an interperspectival, critical method informed by the possibility of accommodating pluralism within a normatively meaningful universe. First, though, I will revisit some of the arguments in Chapter 1, but this time recasting the mainstream, monistic legal theories, which have been my main target, as expert cultures situated well within the epistemological project of modernity.

A Critique of Legal Theory as an Expert Culture

The emergence of specialized expertise is of course not an exclusively modern or even a particularly recent phenomenon. Any kind and degree of division of labour usually goes hand in hand with the emergence of specialists and experts.[1] Expertise has *some* trans-epochal characteristics. Experts generally hold and *with*hold knowledge over a specific domain, which is usually either altogether inaccessible to those outside the circle of experts or inaccessible without special training and/or some initiation rituals. This monopolization of knowledge gives experts theoretical authority backing claims to true knowledge. At the same time, both pre-modern and modern expert cultures tend to become autonomous and closed and use their object of expertise as the main weapon in jurisdictional turf wars (Abbott 1988).

1 Whether the two are one and the same is debatable. If we understand expertise as axiologically tainted, then there is a difference: experts are exceptionally *good* at what they do, whereas specialists simply do something very specific. If not, there does not seem to be anything distinguishing specialists and experts. In any case, the question is not of particular relevance in this context.

However, modernity saw the transformation of expertise into something rather distinct and historically unique. This transformation is informed and became possible by the epistemological shift experienced in the Enlightenment. Perhaps the most central characteristics of that shift are the separation of the mind from the world and the move from the particular to the universal and from induction to deduction. Since we saw ourselves not as mutually constituted but in separation and *inter*action with the world, a distance was established between knower and known, observer and observed, and everything was seen as being structured around a set of discoverable universal principles. Thus truth started being measured against the correctness of the classification of facts under universal categories. This already demystified knowledge which ceased to be the privilege of the few naturally or otherwise gifted ones and was opened up to anyone who could master the necessary methods of enquiry. From being a by and large locally contained and person-bound phenomenon, the emergence and gradual domination of abstract systems of thought and meaning meant that expertise became de-personified. At the same time, knowledge was separated from experience. The phenomenology of the world and the way that people lived it were reduced at best to mere indications as to what may be the universal principles governing the world and their exceptions.

The obvious emancipatory potential in this demystification of knowledge was, however, soon undermined proportionately to the increase of societal complexity and the transition from *Gemeinschaft* to *Gesellschaft*. The possibility of reifying the world was, perhaps inevitably, divorced from the encyclopaedic ideal and the enquiry into truth was fragmented afresh, albeit still guided by the potential universalization and de-personification of knowledge. Professional classes emerged and the subject matters marking their boundaries became more and more narrow. Ritualistic procedures, such as university education, took centre stage in deciding who had the potential of being an expert in specific fields. This was accompanied by claims to scientific adequacy and accuracy in the training of experts. Indeed it is still the case that various disciplines, which have proliferated since the second half of the twentieth century, defend their status as autonomous disciplines precisely by forging scientific agendas and methodologies. In combination with the separation of true knowledge from experience, this led to the dependence of 'lay people' on experts and professionals. Thus expertise was able to stretch its reach over a global scale, with experts taking on the task of mapping the world, and expertise became the central mechanism for the reduction of complexity and the management of uncertainty, thus making co-ordination and control of expectations possible.

The optimism about certainty did not last very long. From the age of faith in scientific authority, we soon moved into a new age of doubt and disagreement. In Bauman's words, experts were transformed anew from legislators to interpreters (Bauman 1987). Bauman interprets this as an indication of modernity's end and the entry into post-modernity. Giddens takes issue with this reading (Giddens 1990). He maintains that rather than these changing attitudes to truth signifying its end, the democratization of scientific dialogue is very much part, if not the culmination, of modernity. To the extent that this dialogue is guided by the presupposition of commensurability and aims at the constant reformulation of universal principles, it is indeed difficult to see any genuine departure from modern ideals. What is crucial is that this is not simply a matter of historical or theoretical classification. It has important substantive extensions in that what is at stake is modernity's emancipatory agenda. Incommensurability necessarily implies that the only way of reconciling, to allude to de Sousa Santos again, regulation and emancipation is cognitive, normative and physical domination. But this will also be the only alternative in the absence of a non-hegemonic, inclusive method of enquiry. Later on in this chapter I will revisit this point with special reference to legal theory.

Modern expertise should also be seen in conjunction with the transformation of the role and content of authority. The emancipatory aspirations of modernity and the transition from traditional and charismatic authority to the authority of rules and the fixation (in all senses) of normative expectations were combined with the sense that true knowledge and a full rational explanation of the world are possible. This combination soon led to the sense that the scientific outlook enjoys epistemological priority over any other way of understanding the world. In this scheme of things, it becomes easy to make the giant leap from speculative to normative knowledge: once we form sufficient knowledge about something, then the right course of action will pretty much reveal itself to us. As a result, modern expert cultures raise claims to practical, alongside that to theoretical, authority. Experts in modernity are there to be trusted as legislators, as being able to tell non-experts *how* to live their lives and set their practical priorities by virtue of the *truth* of their specialized knowledge.

The predominance and growing authority of modern expertise has generated a very rich debate in social theory and the philosophy both of the natural and the social sciences. The expert mediation between agents and the world and the manipulation of time/space relations on the part of experts becomes suspicious when scientific knowledge and expert opinions are ascribed normative force determining policy and, more worryingly, issues of justice (for a comprehensive overview of the literature, see Reed 1996). As a result of this deferral of questions of justice to expert discourses, democratic dialogue is by-passed and disabled. Foucault famously recorded the danger in this transformation of knowledge into power. Similarly, Habermas locates a problem in the way that expert cultures colonize the lifeworld, that is, the space of ordinary, open communication not fettered by system-maintenance imperatives, in the form of unaccountable policy makers, within the administrative, bureaucratic nexus that cuts through the lifeworld at its expense (Habermas 1987; for a critique of expertise, see also Bereiter and Scardamalia 1993; and for a more militant stance, see Martin 1991). Even moral philosophers have grappled with the question of whether their professional capacity vests them with any moral authority to instruct people how to lead their lives (Singer 1972).

Oddly enough legal theory has immunized itself to the debate in a way that it has become unable self-reflexively to revisit its research programme and methodological directions. To be sure, there are some instances of critique of the role of expertise in the field of law and legal theory. Perhaps the most influential critique of the epistemic isolation of legal theory has been American legal realism. The realist critique was very much a reaction to one of the earliest and most prominent attempts at establishing legal theory broadly conceived as an expert culture with claims to being a science, namely Dean Langdell's case method libraries as laboratories vision (Duxbury 1995). Although it is difficult coherently and consistently to reduce realist arguments to a set of core theses (for such an attempt, see Llewellyn 1931), it is perhaps not unwarranted to argue that their main concern was to recover lawyers' sensitivity to the real context of legal practice and all those factors, external to the letter but very much part of the actual 'life' of the law, determining adjudication as well as legislation.[2] However, this early attempt at setting out an interdisciplinary agenda had a curious effect. As Auerbach notes, instead of making legal practice more attuned to the social environment, it resulted in an even more radical separation of legal discourse into the two branches of theory and practice, and the emergence of academic legal expertise as an autonomous domain (Auerbach 1976). According to Auerbach, far from liberating the study of law from the imperatives of legal practice, in most cases academic legal experts nurtured the elitism of 'high standards', which accentuated and perpetuated class, ethnic, gender and other divides within American law schools. How much American legal realism departed from the critique of expertise becomes all the more obvious if we accept the very plausible argument that it is genealogically related to the law and economics, which is founded on the reduction of questions of law to questions of cost effectiveness as determined by, whom else, experts.

There is also plenty of criticism of the use of expertise *in* the law (the literature in this area is extremely rich. *Cf.* Brewer 1998; Pardo 2005; Ward 2006; for a defence of technocratic expertise in the context of the EU, see Majone 1993; 1994; 1996; 2002; Moravcsik 2002; 2004; and for powerful responses, see Shapiro 2005; Follesdal and Hix 2006). One of the sources of the problem is that two incommensurable genres of discourse are artificially merged and, inevitably, one colonizes the other (I am alluding to terminology introduced by Lyotard 1988). The appeal to expert witnesses to assist with legal decisions is justified by a claim to scientific neutrality, thus concealing that scientific knowledge is already normatively determined. As a result, the justificatory complexity which should characterize any instance of legal decision making is reduced by invoking the scientific claims to objectivity and neutrality. This has a twofold result. First, the contested moral and political agenda silently determining scientific research seeps into legal discourse and establishes itself even more firmly, vesting itself with normative authority through the legal justificatory process.[3] Secondly, by directly translating scientific into moral knowledge, the law is stripped of its sensitivity

2 Interestingly, Jerome Frank defended expert evidence in court as neutral, objectively accurate and not posing any threat to democracy (Frank 1949b).

3 This is even more strikingly evident in popular perceptions of the law. One need look no further than works of popular culture from Agatha Christie novels to the *Crime Scene*

to the particular by reducing people and events to the universal categories of science, which represent them not as agents any longer but as objects of enquiry in the natural environment. There is a plethora of examples here. In the context of criminal law, provocation in cases of homicide committed by battered women tends to be understood as a pathological reaction rather than a moral or political issue; in serious cases of fraud, juries have been replaced by experts on the grounds of their complexity and difficulty for 'lay people', thus enabling the unjustified practices of the market to be normatively galvanized through fact-finding court procedures. Of course, there are also pragmatic problems with fact-finding being prioritized over justification and these problems are revealed most painfully when the single expert (and due to economic imperatives, the number of experts is being steadily reduced) gets things wrong.[4]

But although legal theory seems aware of the problems caused by the interweaving of expertise with the law and theoretical with practical authority, it is striking that it has failed to view *itself* in that light. In fact, as I shall try to show in the following, the two arguably most influential trends in legal theory have, each in its own way, espoused and established the character of legal theory as an expert culture.

Hart's *The Concept of Law* came theoretically to confirm the expert culture of legal theory, which had gradually developed since the modern emergence of legal specialization and the law as a distinct epistemic category. In the opening paragraph of *The Concept of Law*, Hart famously noticed the persistence of the question concerning the law's ontology:

> Few questions concerning human society have been asked with such persistence and answered by serious thinkers in so many diverse, strange, and even paradoxical ways as the question 'What is law?' Even if we confine our attention to the legal theory of the last 150 years and neglect classical and medieval speculation about the 'nature' of law, we shall find a situation not paralleled in any other subject systematically studied as a separate academic discipline. (Hart 1994, 1)

This passage can be read as a programmatic declaration properly inaugurating legal theory as a 'separate academic discipline' by delineating its object of enquiry. Hart displays an anxiety as to what exactly the remit of the legal theorist is and laments the fact that all previous efforts have been unsuccessful. But although he correctly emphasizes that the question has been asked in the wrong way, he fails to consider whether it is asked by and addressed to the right people. The reason is that he appears to be more than convinced about the role of the expert in ascertaining what the law

---

Investigation television series, in which the question of crime becomes one-dimensional and its meaning is exhausted in its empirical dimensions.

4 A recent example from a British context is the expert testimony of a paediatrician, whose expert but wrong advice on cot deaths led to the conviction of a mother for the murder of her two sons. See <http://www.guardian.co.uk/society/2005/jun/29/childrensservices.NHS> (last accessed 5 March 2008).

is. Hart promotes the legal philosopher as the one equipped with the intellectual and cognitive skills to understand folk theories of law and extract from them the universal and a-temporal framework of legal thought. It is revealing how he employs Wittgensteinian ordinary language philosophy, in order to produce a conceptual analysis of the law in the sense of drawing the framework of legal thought. As Nicola Lacey points out, he failed consistently to apply a Wittgensteinian method in that he was not attentive enough to the forms of life giving rise to conceptual schemes and the rules of language games (Lacey 2004). This is even more obvious in his *Causation in the Law* (co-authored with Tony Honoré), which reads more like a linguistic analysis of contemporary legal doctrine as developed through the linguistic conventions of experts (in this case legal officials) rather than as a discussion of law in terms of the social practices and shared understandings underpinning it (Hart and Honoré 1985). In other words, Hart may have been successful in showing that institutional facts come about within an institution, but he failed to discuss the emergence of the institution in the first place, as well as its conditions of possibility. Conceptual analysis of the Wittgensteinian kind requires empirical work, in order for usage to be observed and concepts to be clarified. But Hart bypassed this need for empirical labour by simply recording as an expert from well within the internal point of view a conception of law as mirrored in the way that both academic and practising experts seem to make sense of what the law is.

Thus, Hartian jurisprudence is unmistakeably placed within the project of modernity but also takes it one step further. Although Hart denied any such influence with astonishing vehemence (Lacey 2004, 230), what he did is little more than usurp Weber's sociological observations and misrepresent them as a conceptual paradigm with implicit claims to universality. He treated an instance of social mutation that went hand in hand with the project of rationalization and the reduction of societal complexity as a manifestation of a trans-contextual paradigmatic case.[5] This is manifested both on a methodological and a substantive level. Not only is the legal philosopher the privileged party in answering the question of law, but also legal officials are those whose reflective attitude towards a certain set of rules lends the latter their validity *qua* law. Weber spoke about the rationalization of the legal institution (the identification of which did not require a fine-tuned conceptual analysis of the legal category for his purposes). This rationalization was accompanied by the emergence of the legal caste and the gradual process of specialization and separation of the law from its epistemic and normative environment (Weber 1968; Kronman 1983; Ewing 1987). Hart picks up this lesson and disguises it into a conceptual argument, and, in the lack of any proper and careful indexical qualification,[6] we can assume that he tries to vest with

5 For an account of the modern State in terms of the development of bureaucratic structures, see Geuss 2001.

6 Perhaps it can be inferred that Hart sees the emergence of the concept of law as a modern phenomenon and thus not a transcendental category by the distinction he draws between small-scale, 'primitive' and complex communities. However, he fails to qualify

universal validity what is nothing but the recording of an historical phenomenon.[7] Legal expertise thus ceases to be regarded simply as a contingent occurrence, but is transformed into the very conceptual cornerstone of legality.

If we dig a little deeper, it will also become apparent that Hart's approach is not normatively neutral. As I argued with Stephen Perry in Chapter 1, there is a strong normative undertone in Hart's account of the transition from pre-modern systems of primary rules to the emergence of formalized legal systems enriched with secondary rules. The systematicity and centrality of Hart's 'law' provides a *good* solution to the problems of uncertainty, ineffectiveness and rigidity of pre-modern systems. And, of course, there is always the Hobbesian undertone in Hart, which MacCormick explicitly admits:

> The ultimate basis for adhering to the positivist thesis of the conceptual differentiation of law and morals is itself a moral reason. The point is to make sure that it is always open to the theorist and the ordinary person to retain a critical moral stance in face of the law which is. (MacCormick 1981, 24–5)

In order for any this to be possible, there must be a *definitive* and relatively simple way of conceptualizing the law and fixing its conceptual boundaries. This is precisely the task which Hart entrusts to experts: to establish the core of meaning of the concept of law and thus minimize the penumbra of uncertainty, which is modernity's worst nightmare. In other words, Hart sees the professionalization of legal theory, its development as an expert culture and the subsequent centralization of the control over the concept and institution of law as the desirable way of reducing and controlling conceptual and moral complexity.

One would have expected normativist legal theories to depart from this image of the legal expert as the final arbiter of legality. And yet, this is not the case. Dworkin provides a good example. In the latest instalment of his interpretivist theory of law, he subscribes to, without fully endorsing, Stavropoulos' reworking of law-as-interpretation in the light of the Kripke-Putnam semantics (Kress 1987; Stavropoulos 1996; 2003; Dworkin 2004). I say he does not fully endorse it in that he does not accept that legal concepts have a micro-structure available in nature and pre-existing our cognition of it, but rather introduces the idea of interpretive concepts, which have an objective existence and content needing to be discovered.[8]

---

his claims any further, for example, by speaking of *our* concept of law in specific historical and social circumstances, and we can therefore assume that he sees his concept of law as spatially universal, if not diachronically so.

7 Sean Coyle acknowledges the fact that particular conceptual analysis cannot help being indexical and offers an excellent account of the development of the concept of law in an Anglo-American context (Coyle 2007).

8 Surprisingly, Dworkin does not actually offer a clear account of objectivity. He seems to be using the latter as a regulative ideal or a fiction guiding the process of discovering the meaning of law that is law-as-integrity without accounting for the difference between this

But who is to discover that content? In Putnam's causal theory of reference, referents are fixed as rigid designators by the community of scientific experts and are subsequently divulged to the rest of the linguistic community as a matter of division of labour (Putnam 1973). Dworkin seems not to deny the same need for expertise but this time in law, politics and morality. The expert is ascribed the task of locating the best possible reasons cohering with the pre-existing institutional framework, as well as with established political morality rather than the semantic criteria sufficient for the existence of law, as in Hartian jurisprudence. But what is crucial is that Dworkin's Herculean philosopher-judge, who has full command and grasp of all the relevant principles available in the political community, takes on the impossible task of representing the normative commitment of others in an authoritative manner. Dworkin fails to see that the project of democratization of legal discourse must extend to the very question of the institutional contours of the legal, which ascribes legal experts their status as such in the first place. He also fails to see that the question of the law, whether it be seen as a conceptual or a substantive one, cannot be asked in the absence of those to whose commitment it owes its normative force in the first place. Habermas takes issue with the Dworkinian idealization of the legal expert, who can single-handedly and monologically represent the 'self-understanding of the legal community':

> The paradigmatic preunderstanding of law in general can limit the indeterminacy of theoretically informed decision making and guarantee a sufficient measure of legal certainty only if it is intersubjectively shared by *all* citizens and expresses a self-understanding of the legal community as a whole. This also holds mutatis mutandis for a proceduralist understanding of the law, which reckons from the start with a discursively regulated competition among different paradigms. This is why a cooperative endeavour is required to remove the suspicion of ideology hanging over such a background understanding. This single judge must conceive her constructive interpretation fundamentally as a common undertaking supported by the public communication of citizens. (Habermas 1996, 223–4)

Dworkin's naturalism implies not only that *only one* out of the plethora of competing interpretations of the meaning of law can be true, but also that this right interpretation can only be that of an expert, who has achieved knowledge of all the possible interpretations, practices, principles, values, goals and so forth *together*, thus making this knowledge esoteric and inaccessible. This, in combination with Dworkin's pure normativism, reveals an implicit disregard for people's in-common experience of normativity. Non-experts' experiencing of the law becomes not true or potentially true, but rather potentially, and in fact probably, *false*.

To revert to the debate introduced earlier on in this chapter, Hart sees experts as legislators, who construct and consolidate the conventions constitutive of the law.

---

process and its final outcome. This seems to undermine law-as-integrity, making it very easy for it to slip into a version of hard-core pragmatism.

Dworkin, on the other hand, sees the law as somehow inscribed in nature and experts as those who can provide an authoritative, all-encompassing interpretation. But, despite it leaving room for corrigibility, this is far from what Giddens envisages as the emancipatory potential of expertise in late modernity, let alone what Bauman sees as the transformation of expertise in the era of post-modern reconciliation with uncertainty. Law-as-interpretation not only does not encourage disagreement and dialogue but, instead, it explicitly aims at coercively suppressing it. It is thus even more of an expert theory of law than conventionalist positivism, in that it dismisses people's fragmentary and local experience and self-understanding as irrelevant and unsophisticated by the standards set by the expert culture.

The excessive faith in and reliance on legal expertise goes part and parcel with another distortion of the nature of legal theory, namely the radical separation between the social-theoretical and the philosophical study of the law. In *Between Facts and Norms*, Habermas highlights the inability of purely sociological (especially functionalist) as well as purely normative accounts of the law to be fully attentive to the dual nature of the law as an action system and a normative order (Habermas 1996). He argues that the former disregard the normative self-understanding, the normative commitments of participants in a legal system, by assuming epistemological authority in recording the phenomenology of legal systems. This fallacy can readily be traced in Hart's project. He takes the social-theoretical (albeit not empirical) expert perspective in order to single out the conditions of existence of legal systems, by explicitly arguing that the participants speak about the law and the expert legal philosopher is in position to grasp the real meaning of their self-understanding. At the same time, he places emphasis on normativity and obligation without being able to achieve a committed understanding of the reasons behind legal rule-following. As a result, he is unable to tease out the moral, political and pragmatic parameters of legal obligation and thus assume a critical position *vis-à-vis* the substantive content of law. Thus legal theory as an expert culture becomes little more than a contemporary historiography of power. The rise and establishment of expertise in legal theory marks the de-democratization of the question of law, as the participants in legal linguistic communities are excluded from the project of bringing to the fore their normative commitments, as well as the conditions of institutionalization of their legal code.

Normative accounts, on the other hand, fail to account for the institutional nature of the law and the necessity and conditions of translating moral imperatives into legal code. Dworkinian interpretivism, for example, relies on the moral and political expertise of the legal philosopher, or the philosopher-judge in the case of Dworkin, and their ability single-handedly to make sense of and reduce value pluralism and complexity through legal, institutionalized procedures. As I have already suggested in Chapter 3, moral rightness may be objective on a thin, indeterminate level, but soon this will have to be concretized, contextualized and institutionalized in order for it to be able to determine anything in a real context of legality. The parameters of this institutionalized normative order rests on the commitments of the participants, not in the trivially conventionalist fashion described by Hart, but in direct relation to the way they experience in common the world, as well as the possibility of transforming it normatively.

Legal theory as an expert culture objectivates the conditions constitutive of the law as well as the discursive processes through which those presuppositions are concretized and situated in context, and treats this dynamism of legality as an object of scientific enquiry in laboratory conditions. Thus, the meta-narrative of expert legal theory mistranslates and transforms the genre of legal discourse by radically separating the constative from the performative, which in law form a unity, and placing the emphasis on one or the other depending on which side of the descriptive/normative divide the theorist chooses to stand. Moreover, in dislocating legal discourse from the social, it already performs a quasi-legal task by reallocating jurisdiction and authority to determine the meaning of law.

Stephen Turner provides a useful taxonomy of modern experts in relation to their audiences as well as an account of their suspect relationship with liberal democracies (Turner 2003). The five types Turner singles out are: a) expert groups whose authority is generally recognized, such as doctors; b) those who carve out a cognitive space for themselves and create their own audience, such as the authors of self-help books; c) experts who address specific groups, such as theologians; d) experts 'whose audience is the public but who derive their support from subsidies from parties interested in the acceptance of their opinions as authoritative' (Turner 2003, 40); e) lastly, those who address and whose opinions are taken as authoritative by public administrators. Expert legal theories, both the meta-theories that I have been discussing and legal theories more narrowly conceived as theorizations of the specificities of State law, do not fit very neatly in any one of these types. However, they can fruitfully be understood in terms of a crossover. Expert legal meta-theories create their cognitive space in tertiary education institutions so as to vest themselves with the authority of the first of Turner's categories. Equipped with this status, they go on to provide the necessary cognitive legitimation both to substantive legal theorists and officials, enabling them to claim the authority of Turner's type (d) experts and help determine the content and meaning of the law. Hart does this explicitly and Dworkin implicitly by centralizing as a matter of necessity the enquiry into the legal and simultaneously accepting the current institutional structures of State law as suitable for the pursuit of 'legal truth'. And this seems to have permeated legal theory generally to such an extent that even legal pluralistic theories have resorted to an appeal to experts in non-State legal orders authoritatively to represent the latter, inform State law and enable it to become attentive and fair to such legalities (Shah 2005). But this simply reproduces and perpetuates both the image of State law as able objectively to accommodate and adjudicate between other legalities, as well as the reification of legality.

The argument has been made in the context of science, and indeed some social sciences, that there is nothing wrong or undemocratic about experts. It only makes sense, the argument goes, to rely on the extensive, specialized knowledge of experts, as long as procedures of accountability are in place both in respect to how the research programme is set and carried out. And even if we accept that some degree of co-operation between stakeholders and experts is necessary in order to ensure, or at least facilitate, accountability, this by no means makes expertise redundant or *necessarily* undemocratic. Even Turner, generally a harsh critic of expertise, admits that the first two categories above do not pose a great political threat to democracy (Turner 2003).

I have strong doubts that this argument holds even in the natural, let alone the social, sciences, especially in light of the economic and regulatory framework in which they develop, but here I would like to focus specifically on law. As I argued with Cover in Chapter 3, precisely because they are the very source of legality, the participants in a legal order cannot be substituted by experts or be treated simply as co-operating agents. The two necessarily linked questions of the law, namely the ones concerning its institutional boundaries and its substantive content, can only be asked and answered by those on whose shared experience depend the possibility of making sense of the world and changing it as a matter of normative rather than causal necessity. The speculative knowledge built into the law does not have a normative content in itself before being vested with the participants' commitment. This already weakens the normative power entrusted to scientific and other experts, although it must be conceded that in order for this disempowerment to be complete and their input not to taint legal discourse, there must be a structural transformation at a stage prior to that, that is at the stage of formation of scientific knowledge. In any case, to the extent that the law can only be thematized intersubjectively, it is done injustice to, when not tackled in a participatory, democratic way. This can only be done with empirical work in the sense that participants in various legal orders must be brought into the frame as observers and observed in a self-reflexive, dialogic process. In the next part of this chapter I make some suggestions as to how this can be possible and what the advantages of such a methodology are.

Interperspectival, Critical Legal Theory

So far I have identified a number of challenges that legal theory must rise up to, if it is to become sensitive to the pluralism of experienced normative commitments dispersed in the normative universe and, at the same time, not abandon the possibility of self-reflexive critique: it must attune itself to the detranscendentalized, situated character of the normative commitments constitutive of law; it must become aware of the inevitability of its own context-bound character; at the same time, it must recognize that legality necessarily rests on a set of conditions making possible the convergence of normativity and facticity as well as the transcontextual communication and observation of various normative self-understandings; it must seek to spell out these presuppositions; it must re-democratize *itself* by abandoning the expert perspective and opening up the discourse about the law (for an argument for the democratization of knowledge generally, see Derber, Schwartz and Magrass 1990).

I would suggest that this will become possible, if the epistemological field of legal theory is expanded so as to rid itself from the pretence of descriptive, neutral objectivity as well as escape from the institution of State law, in which most kinds of normativism try to confine it. In order for this to be achieved, legal theory must become interperspectival and inclusive of all those whose participation and commitment gives rise to instances of legality.

In the words of James Bohman:

> [The] second-person perspective has a special and self-reflexive status in criticism. It is within this perspective that the social relationship of critic and audience is established in acts of interpretation and criticism. Such dialogical relations employ practical knowledge in the normative attitude, that is, knowledge about norms and the normative dimensions of actions and conditions of success. It is knowledge of the normative from within the normative attitude. As the attitude of the second-person interpreter, such practical knowledge is manifested in interaction and in dialogue and proves itself in terms of the success of dialogue and communication: in the ability of the interpreter to offer interpretations of the normative attitudes of others that they could in principle accept. (Bohman 2001, 106)

This multi-perspectival social enquiry is inspired by Habermas' discourse theory and the pragmatist slant given to it by Thomas McCarthy. What the latter has in common with those versions of pragmatism in the tradition of William James through to Richard Rorty is that it situates social enquiry in particular contexts, taking seriously the claims raised by participants as potentially true, thus treating these participants as rational, knowledgeable and accountable agents prepared to justify their actions with recourse to reasons. The content of such context-bound discourses is infinitely diverse and encompasses a wide range of arguments and experiences from morality to aesthetics or narratives. The critical enquirer cannot distance herself from those discourses, not least because she herself is firmly situated in context. To that extent, McCarthy's pragmatism departs from the tradition of idealism which informed much of recent critical theory. At the same time though, it distances itself from trans-perspectival critique, such as the Marxian critique of ideology, as well as the kind of pragmatism, which is not prepared to make any concessions to any notions of a-contextual truth or rightness, in that it acknowledges the need for the possibility of adjudication between those infinite, diverse self-understandings. It is for this purpose that McCarthy turns to Habermasian communicative reason. Like all discourse, the interperspectival dialogue between self-understandings and worldviews is subject to universal pragmatics and the conditions of free discourse.

The advantage of Habermasian discourse theory in this context is that it is able to detranscendentalize and situate reason in context while, at the same time, retaining the possibility of objectivity. This time, however, objectivity does not transcend the discourse but is rather built into the conditions of intersubjective understanding. Claims raised by participants in discourse are always subject to problematization. In such instances, the participant raising a claim in discourse must be able to defend its truth or rightness with reasons. This justifiability is always inescapably incorporated into all utterances as a condition of the rationality of communication. The inescapability of justification and accountability goes back to the very initial moment of engaging in communication in a serious and efficacious manner. The very act of entering into rational, non-strategic discourse entails that the participants aim at persuading not only their actual but also an idealized, universal audience as to the truth and rightness of their claims in the light of four fundamental presuppositions built into the very nature of rational argumentation: inclusiveness, absence of coercion, truthfulness, equality in participation.[9] These presuppositions guarantee both a 'universal egalitarianism' (Habermas 2001) but also the possibility of participants self-reflectively to assess their own positions and possibly deal with their own errors of judgment or self-deception.

However, the universalism insinuating itself into discourse through formal pragmatics is not all pervasive. Therefore, it is not necessary that *all* claims must be universally endorsed at all times. There is no doubt that agents always already enter discourse from within their own experienced context. Some of these claims will be inextricably tied up to the particular, local, experiential and normative circumstances. It suffices that, given the orientation of discourse towards truth and rightness under the inevitable idealizations of universality, those particular instantiations be acceptable on a thin, universal level. In this light, diversity is recast not as incommensurability or intercontextual unintelligibility any longer, but rather as acceptability on a certain level of universality.

The relevance of this interperspectival pragmatism in the context of the question of the law is, I believe, immediately obvious. To be sure, the conceptual and normative clarification of the law is not an instance of problem-solving akin to the issues facing other social sciences. However, as I have already argued and will explain further in the next chapter, the law question is marked by the same organic link between experience and normative commitment, the blending of constative and performative. Therefore, the aim of legal theory is both to describe the experiential basis accounting for the institutional existence of the law as well as its normative substratum. Crucially, it must be able to engage in practical criticism so as to bring about change. Interperspectival, pluralistic, critical legal theory is the only one that can do justice to this dual nature of the law and strike the balance between description and normative critique, which purely sociological or purely normative legal theories fail to acknowledge. It can do so by avoiding the fundamental shortcoming of idealism, namely the illusion that there can be a grand, all-encompassing social theory, which can adequately, sufficiently and uniformly

9 These presuppositions have remained unchanged since the very early stages of Habermasian discourse theory. In a very interesting article, Habermas draws the genealogical continuity between discourse theory and Kant's account of theoretical and practical reason (Habermas 2001).

explain all social phenomena. At the same time, it does not have to concede to pragmatism an inability to reach inter-contextual understanding, which, as I argued in Chapter 3 against Tamanaha, in view of the plethora of possible interpretations would bring the social scientist in an impossible epistemological position. Interperspectival, critical legal theory relieves the tension between understanding and critique by employing intersubjective enquiry as the means of testing beliefs and normative commitments in the light of the conditions of discourse. The first and third person perspectives are still useful but only as *prima facie* indications of what those practices consist in or what, indeed, they may mean.

Interperspectival, critical legal theory requires the legal theorist to enter into discourse with the participants in the practices which she observes, in order to start a process of self-reflection and justification under conditions of equal participation. This social theory of law rids itself of the delusion of superiority, the Archimedianism that Dworkin argues against, while at the same time remaining committed to the possibility of theory. Interperspectival social enquiry makes the legal theorist part of the legal universe rather than a mere observer, whether it be an external one or a participating one with pretences of objectivity. All beliefs and practices, including those of the legal theorist, are put to a constant test and they are always open to substantive intersubjective criticism and revision. The aim of socio-legal enquiry is thus not to find practices which fit predetermined concepts, or to judge the effectiveness of means and worth of ends from the external point of view, but rather to kick-start a process of self-reflection, which will result in the refinement of everyone's conceptions of their practices, a better mutual understanding and the co-ordination of the pluralistic universe by letting surface the loose connections between beliefs and conceptions.

Interperspectival, critical legal theory can also bridge the gap between the sociological and the philosophical study of the law. As Tamanaha too argues, the divide between legal theory and socio-legal theory is false. Interperspectival legal theory is necessarily sociological to the extent that it focuses on the examination of all instances of legality. At the same time, it is philosophical, to the degree that it formulates general hypotheses about and constantly revises the thin and a-contextual sense of law. This already addresses the fundamental problem of late modernity which I identified earlier, namely the discrepancy between the universal and the particular, regulation and emancipation, the global and the local. The point of discourse is to see how the thin and universal is transformed into the particular in experienced contexts. And all offers as to how this happens are *prima facie* valid until they have been put to the test of self-reflexive and mutually critical discourse.

The difference of this kind of legal theory to what seems to be the norm in Western legal discourses is striking. One can single out at least three distinct focal points in Western legal theory broadly conceived as any kind academic discourse about the law. There is, of course, the doctrinal study of the law, black-letter law as it is often referred to in a pejorative way. The rapid development of legal academia, its increasing integration into general academic culture and the shift of emphasis from effectiveness in vocational teaching to innovation and originality, has meant that this kind of scholarship is slowly withering. In the European context this seems to be the case not only in the UK, where academia developed its own market logic very rapidly, but also in the rest of Europe, where academia is more resistant to sudden transformations. Legal theory in the narrow sense, that is legal philosophy or jurisprudence, has still not managed to break free from the natural law/positivism debate or its variations (internalism/externalism, inclusiveness/exclusiveness and so forth). Most legal philosophers, although by no means all, are too busy locking their horns over the law and morality question. The debate is philosophical in nature and borrows heavily from metaphysics, philosophy of language and moral theory. Thus it often becomes almost oblivious to the law's necessary social texture, which it treats as another concept in the process of analysis rather than a reality, which should somehow be observed and be taken seriously. In the margins of that debate, critical legal theory, including post-modern and feminist legal philosophy, focuses on the criticism of the presuppositions of mainstream legal theory and seeks to highlight the irresolvable tensions in the law as manifestations of its political genealogy, and embarrass the law and mainstream legal theory by disclosing the fallacy of their claims to universality. However, very rarely does critical legal theory become aware and try to rid itself of its self-undermining aspiration of integration. While it highlights and criticizes the imperialism of State law and its tendency to violently exclude the Other, when critical theory moves beyond criticism, its aim seems to be the recognition and acceptance of the Other's point of view *by* State law. Alternatively, as I argued in Chapter 1, it all too easily resorts to a nefarious mysticism, which reveals a yearning for a messianic moment. On the methodological level, critical theory has not managed to wed the sociological and the philosophical either. Legal sociological projects either take for granted a State-centred concept of law or they stretch the concept so as to include all forms of social control (for a typical such example, see Leith and Morison 2005). At the same time, much of socio-legal theory refuses to engage with philosophical arguments about the law.

Interperspectival social legal theory is well equipped to avoid these potholes. It combines the philosophical and the sociological in a substantive and organic way. Its focus is on the sociological exploration of how various communities employ legal language and it also engages in discourse with them in order to assess the rightness of their linguistic and normative practices. *Prima facie* indications of the legal nature of such discourses are provided by the concepts, terms and practices that participants show a commitment to. This obviously entails active, empirical sociological research. At the same time, the starting point and the outcome of enquiry and discourse are both practical and philosophical, to the extent that they are based on a loose and thin understanding of the law, which is shared trans-contextually, and, indeed, necessary for discourse to be possible at all, and they result in the refinement and qualification of that conceptualization of the law.

Concepts, terms, practices and beliefs should not be bought into wholesale simply by virtue of them being employed by a community, as Tamanaha suggests (see Chapter 2). They should form the point of departure for a practical discourse concerning participants' beliefs and the justification of their actions. Thus it will be possible for them to reflect on their practices as well as for the legal theorist to review her beliefs concerning the law. But this does not mean that there is one right answer to everything or that, if all-encompassing convergence and consensus are not achieved, only one of the competing beliefs will be true or right. The point of socio-legal enquiry is not to expand and establish 'law's empire', to colonize other legal discourses with one context-specific interpretation under the pretension that it is possible to integrate the plurality of *nomoi*. On the contrary, the aim is to bring to the surface that plurality and maintain and nurture it without, at the same time, painting a picture of the world as disjointed and therefore meaningless as a whole. And this should be the task of all legal theory and not only philosophy of law narrowly conceived. *Every* instance of theorizing about the law should take an interperspectival, critical turn and test a general theory of law, as well as concepts within the law, discursively against the beliefs and communicative inputs of participants in other linguistic-legal communities. Thus, those concepts will be clarified through the identification of their context-determined limits.

The point has been made forcefully by critical theorists that systemically integral, institutionalized law cannot accommodate pluralism. Institutionalized legal systems code its functions and fix the meaning of concepts and the content of norms in a way that excludes alternative interpretations, worldviews and normative universes. Institutionalized law cannot be attentive to the other without assimilating the latter or sacrificing some of its own integrity because of its historical and political baggage. This realization often leads critical theory to despair, thus exhausting itself in critique, which understandably makes its critics rejoice and accuse it of nihilism. Interperspectival, critical legal theory offers a solution. The metaphysical and normative relative closure of the concept of law is one of its fundamental premises but it does not allow that closure to disable it or limit its scope as a practical, critical venture. On the contrary, interperspectival legal theory *becomes* the forum of politicized, practical discourse about the legal and its content. Dworkin is correct in not accepting any difference between conceptual and normative analysis in the context of law. Every utterance about the law is a substantive one concerning its content and everyone speaking about the law engages in legal theory in one way or another. However, Dworkin is wrong in reserving for State law the special role that he does as the forum of principle, in which the right answer on *all* questions will shine, because institutionalized law is necessarily univocal. The judge *is* a legal theorist but not one who can assume the third or second person perspectives, so as to understand the communicative inputs of all of the participants in institutionalized legal discourse. But the legal theorist outwith the institutional confines of State law has that ability to realize that hers is only one offer in the discourse concerning the law.

Thus, the distinction between legal pluralism and legal monism collapses. *All* legal theory ought to be pluralistic. Otherwise, it simply *is not* legal theory but rather a first-person account of intrasystemic coherence. Interperspectival, critical socio-legal enquiry cancels out the distinction between legal pluralism and legal monism, which various theorists have been focusing on for so long. Legal pluralism ceases to be just another socio-theoretical strand or school and legal centralism ceases to be legal theory at all. Every methodologically sound theorization about the law is conscious of the plurality of its object of study, which is symmetrical to the plethora of ways of theorizing the legal. The point of legal theory is the critical, discursive testing of tentative concepts of law, the self-reflection of every legal theorist and legal community on their practices and preconceptions and the establishment or re-affirmation of a thin and indeterminate common metaphysical and normative point of reference.

To return to the critique of expertise which introduced this chapter, once (what counts today as) legal theory takes an interperspectival, critical turn, it will become aware that it is not in a privileged epistemological position. The expert culture of legal theory, confined so far in academia and State courts, will acknowledge its limitations. Discourse about the law will be transposed into a political space, and thus be liberated and opened up to all participants in all possible *nomoi*. Thus the question of the law will be re-politicized both on the descriptive and the normative level. This, however, does not mean that the law will lose its action-guiding potential. On the contrary, not only will the discursive forum of interperspectival, critical legal theory not normatively debilitate the various *nomoi* constituting it but, to the extent that it facilitates the understanding and co-operation between all these *nomoi*, it will create the necessary conditions for them to function unhindered. At the same time, though, it will operate as a contemporaneous appellate tribunal, albeit one based on co-operation rather than heteronomy, in which self-understandings, beliefs and normative commitments will come to the fore and be put to discursive tests, and thus remain always falsifiable and in need of defence.

Conclusion

In this chapter I questioned the expert culture of legal theory and advocated a change of direction from undemocratic, colonizing expertise to an interperspectivism facilitating both self-reflection and critique. This, I argued, will make possible the mutual understanding and co-operation between dispersed *nomoi* both conceptually and normatively. Thus, legal theory will be dissociated from the external (and thus potentially unjust) point of view, but will also stop simply regurgitating normative arguments from well within the internal point of view and then trying to export them, lending them a false pretence of universality. Legal discourse will be repoliticized and opened up so as to do justice to the diversity of normative experiences and commitments in the world as well as its own inescapable internal pluralism.

But, as I have already implied, one cannot help starting from the most familiar of places, home. The first communicative offer to the discourse concerning the institutional existence and normative content of the law is always uttered in the first person. This is what I will try to do in the next two chapters. I will shift the focus from the methodology of legal theory to a closer analysis of the substance of the legal phenomenon and try to articulate a *prima facie* conceptualization of law, hoping that it can be used as a universal basis for the enquiry into the legal. In the last two chapters, I will return to a critique of State law, demonstrating that it fails to see through its claim to universal application precisely because it is institutionalized on a very foundational level by encoding itself around specific experienced presuppositions which cannot be meaningfully exported to other *nomoi*, at least not in their entirety.

Chapter 5

The Contours of Institutionalized Legal Discourse

Introduction

This is how my argument has unfolded so far: mainstream legal theories, especially Hartian conventionalism and Dworkinian normativism, are unable to make sense of and do justice to the pluralist potential of the law and legal theory, because they developed as expert theorizations and rationalizations of the contingent modern phenomenon of nation-States and territorial law. At the same time, theories of legal pluralism tend to commit similar errors. Some fail carefully to account for the dual nature of the law as an institution and an action-guiding order. Others paint a counterintuitive and undesirable picture of legal pluralism as an aggregate of hermetically closed legal systems, which cannot meaningfully, let alone critically, communicate with each other. At the same time, they do not account for how it is possible to even recognize such legal orders as such in the first place. All these problems stem both from methodological errors as well as, relatedly, from a misconceptualization of the law from the outset. In Chapter 3 I used Robert Cover's work to defend a contextualist image of the law on the basis of a thin, and always open to thematization, sense of law. In Chapter 4 I returned to the methodological question and argued that legal theory must cease to be an expert culture and, instead, it ought to be recast as the discursive space, in which all *prima facie* legal orders can communicate and undergo a constant process of self-reflection and critique.

Throughout the first four chapters of this book, I have repeatedly implied that any suggestion as to what the sense of the law, which will form the basis for interperspectival enquiry and discourse, may entail is inevitably bound to the experienced normative context of the speaker. Still, it is possible to at least *try* to transcend one's context and raise claims to universality, as long as one is always aware of the corrigibility of these claims. I also consider such substantive suggestions as to the sense of the law inevitable in any interperspectival, critical legal discourse. In this and the following chapters, I try to articulate some suggestions as to where to look for the law, at least in the first instance. My starting point is the pragmatics of State-bound legal discourse, while I try to transcend the context to the extent possible. Once I have explained what accounts for the institutional autonomization and, somewhat paradoxically, the possibility of openness and communication between various legal orders, I will turn to State law and provide a critique of the latter on the grounds of its inability to acknowledge its closure and its simultaneous insistence on monopolizing the normative universe.

Legal theories advocating the connection of the law with other normative orders generally either explicitly revolve around or implicitly accept the thesis that legal discourse is open to all information and to all potential participants. It is only under such conditions of openness and inclusiveness that a claim to rightness can be raised and it can be purported that just decisions have been made. I will build my argument by arguing against what I consider to be the most powerful such account of the necessary connection between law and morality grounded on the openness of communication, namely Robert Alexy's Special Case Thesis (*Sonderfallthese*), a discourse theory of law which rests on Habermas' theory of general practical discourse. Although I agree with Alexy's connection thesis, the problem is that he does not provide a convincing account of the differentiation of legal discourse from other practical discourses. In other words, the *Sonderfallthese* does not offer a convincing explanation of the institutionalization of legal discourse. I will show that legal discourse necessarily rests on the commitment of the participants to their shared way of normatively making sense of the world. That is revealed as a set of fundamental assumptions embedded in all legal utterances, which provide the necessary bedrock that makes communication possible. These assumptions are the basis of the institution of legal discourse, to the effect that their problematization signifies a departure from the latter.

The chapter is structured as follows: first, I give a brief exposition of the groundwork of Habermasian discourse theory and Alexy's Special Case Thesis (*Sonderfallthese*). I conclude that the *Sonderfallthese* begs the question, to the extent that it does not properly account for the distinctness of legal discourse. The reason for this seems to be that it rests on the same fallacious presupposition as Hartian positivism and Dworkinian interpretivism, namely the necessary association of the concept of law with the contingent phenomenon of modern Western States. I then use speech act theory in order to trace what underpins legal discourse making legal utterances and communication within the law meaningful. In the course of this enquiry I identify a set of assumptions tacit in legal discourse, which I deem to be expressions of the shared normative experiences, in which the constative and the performative are merged, giving rise to legal discourse. Finally, I explore this idea further by highlighting how the existence of these presuppositions concerning, to use Cover's terminology, the translation of word into deed, and vice versa, is revealed in State law and discourses about State law, as well as how the latter prioritizes systemic coherence and cannot, therefore, be attentive to those normative experiences.

A Discourse Theory of Law

There is no need to give a full exposition of Habermas' universal pragmatics here so the following is only by way of introduction or reminder. For Habermas the truth of utterances should be tested on the pragmatic rather than on the semantic level. In other words the truth of what is being said should be judged according to the soundness of an utterance rather than vice versa. In that way it would be possible to ascribe truth value to normative sentences as well as to non-normative ones. On the illocutionary level, everything is translatable and comprehensible by all, as long as it is properly uttered. Each speaker aiming at reaching an understanding through discourse incorporates four validity claims in her utterances: a claim to intelligibility, a claim to validity, a claim to rightness and a claim to truthfulness (Habermas 1995, 159). These claims correspond to the universal pragmatic functions of language which a speaker must have mastered in order to partake in a discourse. Thus, we can form formal criteria in order to distinguish between sound assertions, valid arguments and sound transitions from statement of fact to normative statements. To put it simply, even normative utterances can have a truth value, as opposed to a correctness value, for they are judged on the level of universal pragmatics.

Habermas also draws a distinction between actions and discourses. 'Actions' are language games in which the claim to validity implicated in speech acts is tacitly recognized. By contrast, in 'discourses' claims to validity that have become problematic are made the subject-matter and are scrutinized as to their soundness. In the process of discourse new experiences cannot be acquired. Although experiences do enter in the realm of discourse, it is exclusively problematic validity claims that are being dealt with by means of argumentation (Habermas 1995, 130–31).

Robert Alexy grounds his theory of law in Habermas' theory of general practical discourse but also qualifies the latter in substantive respects. The crux of Alexy's legal theory is the Special Case Thesis (*Sonderfallthese*), which addresses the problems of adapting a theory of general practical discourse in a 'real' discourse such as law (Alexy 1989a).

The *Sonderfallthese* can be summed up in three basic points:

1. *Legal discourse is practical discourse, that is, it deals with practical questions*. Communication in the law is an instance of discourse, that is an instance of exchange of utterances raising validity claims. To the extent that legal discourse deals with and provides reasons for action, it is practical discourse. Alexy is happy to accept that empirical arguments are permissible in the course of legal discourse. According to one of the numerous rules of legal discourse that he identifies, namely one of the *transition rules*, empirical statements can be discussed at any stage of the discourse: 'It is possible for any speaker at any time to make a transition into a theoretical (empirical) discourse' (Alexy 1989a, 206). He goes on to say that 'Speakers often agree about normative premises but are in dispute about the facts. It is frequently the case that the necessary empirical knowledge cannot be attained with desirable certainty. In this situation there is a need for rules of reasonable presumption' (Alexy 1989a, 206).

   Apart from empirical ones, *discourse-theoretical* arguments, that is, arguments concerning the way discourse is being carried out as well as *linguistic-analytical* arguments, that is, arguments concerning the use of language, can be discussed at all times during legal discourse. In short, in legal discourse everything can in principle be problematized at all times.

2. *Legal discourse, like all practical discourse, raises a claim to rightness.* This is a highly contested point, as it concerns the necessary connection of law with morality (for the debate on the claim to correctness, see Alexy 1989b; 1992/2002; 1997; 2000a; 2007; Raz 2007; Bulygin 1993; 2000; Heidemann 2005). I will return to it in the following chapter, when I discuss the possibility of normative communication between various legal orders. For now it is necessary to clarify one point that often gives rise to misunderstandings. The claim to rightness does not mean that the law is *necessarily* morally right or that it so happens that it *is* always morally right. Legal propositions raise a claim to rightness in the sense that, if they did not or if they even raised a claim to wrongness, a performative contradiction would be committed (Alexy 1989a, 215).
3. *Because of the institutional constraints, legal discourse is a special instance of practical discourse* (Alexy 1989a, 212–13). It is this third point that will be the point of departure of my critique in this chapter, although it will be related back to the previous two aspects of the *Sonderfallthese*. Alexy tells us that legal disputes are not 'to be viewed as discourse in the sense of non-coercive unfettered communication, but only that, in legal disputes, discussion proceeds under a claim to correctness and accordingly by reference to ideal conditions' (Alexy 1989a, 219–20).

Although in other contexts, such as in academic legal debates, legal discourse can be free and unimpeded, in institutionalized instances, such as in legal proceedings, there are some obvious hindrances to the realization of ideal conditions.[1] So, it seems that what Alexy has in mind when he refers to constraints to legal discourse in those contexts are constraints relating not to the immanent but rather the incidental conditions of institutionalized legal dialogue: the involuntary participation of the defendant, the inevitable temporal limits of the trial, the strict regulation of the procedure, the interest of the parties in profiting as much or losing as little as possible. In short, the parties' interest in discovering the truth as well as arriving at a decision is filtered through their self-interest but also the empirical limitations in legal proceedings, thus potentially tainting the end result.[2]

1 The difference between these instances of legal discourse seems to be that, before a court action, discourse is always oriented towards action. In Chapter 6 I shall show that, if we focus at the conditions of discourse rather than its apparent aims, the distinction between these instances is cancelled out.

2 Alexy 1989a, 212. At an early stage, Habermas argued that the trial is an instance of *strategic action* rather than *discourse* (Habermas and Luhmann 1971). If this were true, then the *Sonderfallthese* would stand indefensible, which is why Alexy attempts to address the problem.

This account focuses on the external circumstances of legal discourse. As such, Alexy argues, they do not pose any real problem to the *Sonderfallthese*. He claims that, although it is of course the case on certain, if not most, occasions that the parties are concerned with their own interests, in arguments exchanged in court a claim to correctness *is* raised irrespective of the intention of the parties. All legal communicative interactions are rational exchanges of arguments with reference to ideal conditions (for the influence on Habermas on this, see Perelman 1980), to the extent that the parties purport to convince any rational audience of the correctness of their argumentation. According to a later thesis by Habermas, the strategic conduct of the parties during the course of a trial is neutralized by the procedural rules that exclude external hindrances from the outset and 'define the bounds within which parties can deal with the law strategically' (Habermas 1996, 237). Apart from that, and along the same lines as Alexy, he argues that it is crucial that the arguments brought forward by the parties are addressed to the judge, who is the guarantor of the application of the procedural rules and it is from her point of view that a decision will be reached.

It seems that Alexy chooses to play down the institutional character of legal discourse by reducing it to a sociological phenomenon that can be shrugged off by way of idealization or abstraction. It is undoubtedly trivially true to say that the law must be interpreted by a person or that a trial cannot last forever, but a decision must be made sooner or later. In fact, it can be argued that the purposes of justice are best served when a decision is made and action is taken as promptly as possible or that constraints to discourse are facilitative or, indeed, necessary for action. Thus conceived, the institutionalization of legal discourse only gives rise to incidental constraints to communication. They are incidental, because they are contingent, they do not have to do with nor do they affect the conditions of communication in legal discourse or with the essence of legal discourse as practical discourse that can yield just results.

However, a closer look will reveal that Alexy's denial of the importance of those constraints to legal discourse conceals a fundamental shortcoming of the *Sonderfallthese*, namely that it does not include a convincing account of what differentiates legal from general practical discourse in the first place. Alexy argues that:

> legal reasoning is characterised by its relationship with valid law, however this is to be determined.
>
> This highlights one of the most important differences between legal reasoning and general practical reasoning. In the context of legal discussion not all questions are open to debate. Such discussion takes place under certain constraints. (Alexy 1989a, 212)

So, Alexy already presupposes the existence of legal discourse as a distinct and autonomous instance of practical discourse. In fact, very frequently he makes references to *institutionalized* legal discourse, indicating that he already understands legal discourse as organized in an institution that differentiates itself from moral discourse or other practical discourses. It is precisely this presupposition that allows him to form the argument regarding the constraints present in legal discourse. However, he fails to ask the logically prior question as to what this institution exactly consists in and what its relation is to the development of communication in legal discourse.[3]

The importance of that question cannot be overemphasized. On the intuitive level of everyday language, we speak of 'the law' and we find it possible to communicate on a common understanding of that concept. We disagree about what the law is in each case, or what is prescribed by law according to a different reading, having tacitly established a basis upon which our agreement or disagreement lies. The same happens in legal proceedings. Disagreement there revolves around the particularities of the law and practical questions facing the court or other legal officials, but communication about these disagreements is still possible. By the same token, there come times that disagreement becomes so radical that it seems to cancel the possibility of communication. There are instances of insular societies or militant political groups coming in contact with the law of the State but communication collapsing from the outset, despite the fact that their communicative offers are intelligible and truthful. So it seems that legal discourse takes place in a pre-set communicative framework which is not contingent and incidental, is unique and specific, and also remains beyond problematization, at least in certain contexts. Participants in legal discourse seem already to have a common bond upon which they base their communication. In what follows I shall try to trace what lies at the basis of communication, in what I have tentatively and intuitively called institutionalized legal discourse.

Speech Acts and the Conditions for their Felicity

In the following two sections, I shall analyse legal utterances in the light of speech act theory, which informs Habermas' and Alexy's thought. The objective is to find what lies at the basis of meaningful communication in institutionalized legal discourse and track down what it is that participants in legal discourse share before entering legal discourse and in order for them to be able to do so.

As I have already indicated above, Habermas' theory of communicative action, as well as Alexy's *Sonderfallthese*, rely heavily on speech act theory. Their aim is to show that by using language correctly and by conforming to the formal rules of rational, meaningful communication, it will be possible for the best argument to prevail, that is convince any possible rational audience of its correctness without this precluding the possibility of it being questioned and perhaps quashed in the

3 Habermas and Günther have taken issue with Alexy's failure sufficiently to differentiate between legal and other normative discourses. I shall have more to say about their objection in Chapter 6.

future. In turn, communicative correctness also guarantees the correctness of the justification of practical arguments.

It is not possible to offer a full exposition of speech act theory in this context but it is nonetheless useful to give a short introduction in order to make the following analysis more accessible. Speech act theory was introduced by John Langshaw Austin and further developed by John Searle. The basic premise of the theory is that in speaking, we do not only make a statement about the truth or falsity of a state of affairs but also perform a certain act. Within a speech act three acts can be distinguished: i) the *locutionary* act (which can be subdivided into the phonetic, the phatic and the rhetic acts) is the expression of a sentence with a specific meaning; ii) the *illocutionary* act is the act performed *in* saying something, as opposed to the act performed by saying something; iii) the *perlocutionary* act is the one performed *by* saying something, the effects of the utterance, which do not necessarily coincide with the illocutionary act. For instance, the utterance 'Watch it!' could be perceived either as a warning or as a threat.

According to Searle, this analysis of the structure of speech acts makes the distinction between performative and constative utterances redundant. Whether it be accompanied by a performative propositional indicator such as 'I promise', 'I convict', 'I now pronounce you husband and wife' and so on, or not, every utterance on the illocutionary level is a performance of an act. Therefore, assertions too can be conceptualized as speech acts. However, since this disagreement between Austin and Searle does not have a bearing on the arguments in this chapter, but also for the sake of simplicity, I shall continue to refer to explicit performative utterances as performatives and to assertions as constatives or statements of fact.

Like all games, language is permeated by rules. Therefore, in order for speech acts to be successfully performed, some conditions must be met. Austin sums up these necessary conditions in three twofold rules. Firstly, there must exist a conventional procedure with a certain conventional effect (A.1) and the participants and circumstances must be the appropriate ones (A.2). Secondly, the procedure must be observed by participants correctly (B.1) and completely (B.2). Thirdly, where the procedure is designed for use by persons having certain thoughts or feelings, or for the inauguration of certain consequential conduct on the part of any participant, then those persons must in fact have those thoughts or feelings, and the participants must intend so to conduct themselves (Γ.1), and further must actually so conduct themselves subsequently (Γ.2).[4]

Searle introduces a slightly different categorization of the conditions necessary for the successful performance of speech acts. He analyses promises as an exemplary case of a performative and singles out nine conditions necessary for the non-defective and sincere performance of a promise. These conditions are then abstracted and systematized in five rules: the *propositional content* rule, according to which the illocutionary force indicating device can be uttered only in the context of a sentence, which performs the respective act; two *preparatory*

4 Please note that I follow Austin's original Greek letter numbering.

rules, which roughly refer to the mutual expectations of the communicating parties regarding the instance of communication; the *sincerity* rule, which in the case of promising refer to the intention of the promisor to keep her promise; the *essential* rule, which is a *constitutive*[5] rule and prescribes that the utterance of an illocutionary force indicating device (such as certain verbs in the first person singular indicative, for example, I am promising, I am warning, and so on) counts as a certain performative act. Stated in this way, these rules apply specifically to the case of promises. However, with some necessary, albeit not substantive, amendments they can be extended to cover all illocutionary acts. A necessary and very important implication of this is that even assertions are not judged according to their correspondence to an extra-linguistic reality. Their truth value is assessed according to their abidance by the corresponding constitutive rules. To return briefly to the context of legal discourse, it is this point that allows Habermas to formulate his thesis that utterances imply validity claims and Alexy to formulate his thesis concerning the connection between general practical and legal discourses.

Whether one opts for Austin's or Searle's version of the conditions necessary for the felicity[6] of performatives, one cannot deny that these conditions are embodied in the illocutionary act in an expressible way.[7] To return to Austinian speech act theory, there are at least three ways, in which those utterances are connected. A proposition might *entail* another proposition. For instance '*the cat is on the mat*' entails '*the mat is under the cat*'; a proposition can be implied in another proposition. For example, '*the cat is on the mat*' implies that the speaker believes things to be so. A proposition can be presupposed by another proposition. For instance, '*All Jack's children are bald*' presupposes that Jack actually does have children.[8]

To take the same point one step further, to the extent that they are entailed, implied or presupposed, utterances can *infect* other utterances. The kind of infection depends on the missing conditions. When Austinian conditions A and B are not in place, the performative act is cancelled altogether. For example, my attempt to rename the LSE Old Theatre into the 'Ryan Giggs lecture theatre' would clearly have no effect without the proper authorization by a proper body of LSE staff with the proper jurisdiction and so forth. The lack of conditions Γ1 and 2 simply makes the act problematic but not invalidated. So, for instance, a promise is defective albeit still a promise, if the promisor does not intend to keep it.

---

5 *Constitutive* rules 'create or define new forms of behaviour' whereas *regulative* rules regulate 'antecedently or independently existing forms of behaviour' (Searle 1969, 33).

6 The term felicity in the context of speech acts is coined by Austin. Searle does not espouse it but does not reject it either. In fact he acknowledges that it is a term very close to his defective and non-defective speech acts (J.L. Austin 1962, 54).

7 According to Searle's principle of expressibility, whatever can be meant, can be said (Searle 1969, 19–21).

8 J.L. Austin 1962, 47–52.

This surely rings somewhat counterintuitive. How can one claim to have made a valid promise, if one does not feel obligated to keep it? Similarly, how can one perform a warning, when one does not believe that there is a present danger? To explain this schematically, let us look at an example used by Austin. In trying to explain and justify the sharp distinction between statements and performative utterances, Austin uses the example of the utterance '*I warn you that the bull is about to charge*'. What depends on the truth of the statement '*The bull is about to charge*', that is what depends on whether the bull *is* about to charge or *not*, is not the happiness of the warning but its falsity or mistakenness. The utterance will still be a warning but it will be a superfluous one. In any case, and for the time being, it cannot be denied that the felicity of the performative utterance depends not on the knowledge but on the *belief* of the speaker as to whether the bull is about to charge or not (J.L. Austin 1962, 47–52).

The problem can be remedied with reference to Searle's version of the theory. Searle argues that linguistic philosophy of the classical period consistently but also fallaciously equated *meaning* with *use*. Because some words seemed to be strongly associated with certain acts, it was assumed that the performance of that specific act coincided with or was part of the meaning of the word.[9] The alternative explanation Searle offers is that the 'quasi-necessary'[10] truth that certain words refer to certain speech acts has to do with their embeddedness in the specific institution rather than with the inherent meaning of the word. It is this qualification that enables Searle to set the *sincerity* and the *essential* rules. It is also precisely this analytical platform that enables Alexy to ground a performative contradiction each time a legal proposition is uttered but its rightness denied.

Be that as it may, we can now safely say that performatives are not all they appear to be; they are underpinned by other utterances, which set the conditions for the felicity of these performatives. This is of paramount importance, not only for the felicity of illocutionary acts themselves but also, perhaps more crucially, for the success of communication.[11] Those implicit utterances express the

9 It is this misunderstanding that also gives rise to three fundamental fallacies: the *naturalistic fallacy fallacy*, according to which descriptive claims cannot entail evaluative ones; the *speech act fallacy*, which confuses the meaning of a word with the fact that it is characteristically used for the performance of a certain act (for example, 'good' and the act of commending); the *assertion fallacy*, which collapses the conditions for the performance of the speech act with the analysis of the meaning of certain words that appear in certain assertions (Searle 1969, 131ff).

10 It is true that Searle is a little ambivalent as to whether this is a quasi-necessary or a necessary truth (see Dascal 1994).

11 Advocates of Gricean pragmatics (see Grice 1992) explicitly question the connection between successful comprehension and communication on one hand and the felicity of speech acts on the other. They argue that in order for comprehension and communication to be achieved, it is not necessary for the speaker to know that she is performing a speech act at all (see Sperber and Wilson 1995, 244). This dispute between schools does not concern

assumptions[12] necessary for the discourse to take place in a way that will be meaningful to all the parties. In turn, these assumptions form the pragmatic context of communication and it is against this background that newly acquired information is tested and then added as a new set of assumptions. The content and, subsequently, the degree of generality of those assumptions may vary depending on the instance of communication as well as the content of the exchanged utterances. The relevant but extremely general assumptions are stored as encyclopaedic knowledge that needs not be retrieved explicitly.[13] The more specific assumptions must be processed in the light of the context, in order for communication to proceed meaningfully. So, when a lecturer tells a student: '*You are awarded the LSE Law Department Lecturers' Prize in Jurisprudence*', in order for that communicative offer to be comprehended correctly by the student so that the discourse can take place without serious misunderstandings, the student must assume (but not necessarily know) a number of things of various degrees of generality: what the prize is, how it can be won, that the lecturer was either on the competition panel or has been informed by someone who was, that her Jurisprudence essay got the highest mark amongst her fellow students' essays and so on.

These underlying assertions, the correctness of which is *assumed*, can be distinguished in two categories, the importance of which will become apparent, when we return to the context of institutionalized legal discourse. On the one hand, they are assertions about institutional facts. Institutional facts are juxtaposed to brute facts and are those brought about by constitutive rules. For instance, the fact that the 'LSE Law Department Lecturers' Prize in Jurisprudence' exists is not part of the make-up of nature but, at the same time, it is also a cognizable fact. The truth of it does not depend on its correspondence to some external state of affairs but to whether and to what extent the rules that prescribe the ways in which such a prize can be established have been observed. On the other hand, the assumptions implicit in utterances also refer to brute facts. These brute facts can be connected to institutional facts as the operative facts of constitutive rules, or they can be self-standing.

---

me in this context to the extent that, for my purposes, I examine the felicity of a speech act and the success of communication separately.

12 In this instance it is not necessary to establish whether the pragmatic context of communication must be based on the mutual *knowledge* of the parties or whether it suffices that they have some shared assumptions. It is also not important precisely how these assumptions are employed and how they facilitate communication. For a discussion of those issues, see Sperber and Wilson 1995.

13 Sperber and Wilson (1995, 120–21) doubt the very relevance of such self-evident assumptions. It seems to me that telling the reader that she is reading a book might be trivial and unnecessary but this does not make it irrelevant.

Happy Legal Utterances

Let us now take the discussion back to a legal context and see how the above applies. Alexy understands legal discourse as consisting mainly in performatives, which usually give rise to institutional facts. A judge pronounces a sentence; two parties form a contract, in which they promise the fulfilment of certain obligations; an MP votes for a motion in Parliament by shouting 'Yes', when her name is called. There is no question, and this has been shown very convincingly in the literature, that what takes place in all these instances is not only the utterance of the relevant proposition but also a separate act, in our examples an act of sentencing, promising and voting respectively. To that extent legal propositions are indeed performative.

However, as I have already shown, this is not all there is to performatives, especially in an instance of discourse and argumentation: performatives are always underpinned by constatives. Such is the case in legal discourse as well. In order to show this, I shall use as an example a proposition drawn from sentencing. Sentencing provides an ideal context in which the material aspect of legal discourse is revealed clearly and forcefully, for it is one of the moments of culmination of legal discourse, in which the boundaries between the distance between the abstraction of rules and their material consequences is minimized radically.

I borrow an example used by Alexy: a judge decides that '*Mr N is hereby sentenced to ten years' imprisonment*'. There is no doubt that this is a performative utterance. The judge does not describe a state of affairs; she performs a distinct act by sentencing Mr N to imprisonment. To be precise in Austinian terminology, it is an *exercitive* act: 'It is a decision that something is to be so, as distinct from a judgement that it is so' (J.L. Austin 1962, 155) And elsewhere: 'the exercitive is an assertion of influence or exercising of power' (J.L. Austin 1962, 153). The felicity of exercitives such as 'I award', 'I absolve', 'I sentence' and the like is based on *verdicts*. So, in our example, the judge's sentencing utterance is based on the previous verdict delivered either by the judge or, more likely, a jury. In other words, one cannot sentence without a previous judgment on guilt. I should note here that, for the time being, I leave aside the question of whether the act of sentencing can be understood independently of its justification. Later on in this book it will become clear that I do not believe this to be possible. But for now, I will just provide an analysis on the basis of pragmatics.

Verdictives are another Austinian category of illocutionary acts that involve the exercise of judgment. Austin goes on to say that verdictives have an obvious connection with truth and falsity. In other words, there must be some statements of fact implied by this performative utterance that make it meaningful and guarantee its felicity as a performative utterance in the first place. Seen from the point of view of the possibility of comprehension, the implicit utterances account for the success of communication. Let us, then, look behind the above sentencing proposition, in order to discover the utterances which set the conditions, making it happy autonomously as well as meaningful in the communication between the judge and the accused. The diagnosis of the relevant propositions can be systematized around Austin's and Searle's five rules for the felicity of illocutionary acts.

What must be established first is whether the propositional content rule is abided by, that is, whether there is correspondence between the grammar and the syntactical structure of the utterance with the act purported to be performed. Then it must be examined whether Austinian conditions A and B, which correspond to Searle's preparatory conditions, obtain. Is the judge really a judge or is she an impostor? Have all the procedural rules been followed? More importantly, has a guilty verdict been passed? Were all the facts proven, before and in order for the verdict to be reached? To rephrase, were all the constitutive rules followed and were the statements describing their operative facts true? At the same time, and now we are moving to Searle's sincerity rule or Austin's Γ1 and 2 conditions, did the jury sincerely believe that Mr N was guilty? Moreover, there is the assumption that it will be possible for the sentence to be carried out: there is such a practice as imprisonment; there are buildings designated as prisons, in which Mr N will be taken and which he will not be able to leave, and he will also not be able to carry out certain activities that he otherwise would. It is clear that trying to give an exhaustive list of all the relevant conditions would be a tedious and fruitless task.

However, there is a different kind of implicit utterances at play deserving closer attention. Legal discourse is predominantly discourse about extra-discursive facts, which have either taken place in the past or their occurrence is predicted and projected in the future. Therefore the implied or presupposed information is not immediately testable with the senses of the participants. The most obvious example is that the jury and the judge have no way of knowing that all the facts have indeed taken place. In some cases, it is not the facts themselves but the way facts are connected which is being assumed. For example, if no one saw Mr N committing the crime but he was found at the crime scene shortly after the crime was committed with a smoking gun, one could legitimately assume that he was the perpetrator.[14] The specific assumptions concerning the specific case can now be called *first-order assumptions*.

Soon it becomes clear, though, that in order for the first-order assumptions to be true, a further set of assumptions is needed, which will concern the general method in which facts are being reconstructed, the correctness of that method and, crucially, the linkage between factual and normative content. What participants in legal discourse must assume is the felicity of general statements about the world and their normative significance. This is where the constantive and the performative are merged and give rise to law. These assumptions do not concern the particular topics of discussion but rather *legal discourse* itself. They define the way in which the venture of legal discourse is understood by the participants; they incorporate their shared perceptions of what exactly it is they are doing in entering legal discourse.

14 MacCormick offers such a coherence theory of historical truth in MacCormick 1991.

Legal discourse is indeed practical discourse to the extent that it provides reasons for action. Not only this, but the interruption of discourse and the transition to action is built into the very character of the law. So, if legal discourse can be said to be able to raise a claim, then this would be that *it can mediate between the real and the ideal by, firstly, evaluating and, secondly, authorizing action.* But in order for that claim to be raised at all, the possibility of that mediation, of *normatively linking material facts*, must be presupposed. To revert to Cover's terminology, this is the way in which law bridges *alternity*, the gap between reality and vision. I suggest that this assumption refers to the shared normative experience of participants in a legal discourse, which, as I have been arguing throughout this book, lies at the basis of every instance of law.

I propose that these underlying assumptions should be understood as part of the *experiential make-up of the participants*. They are connected to the way the participants normatively relate to the world in common, the way they normatively understand themselves in their environment and interact with others. In other words, they refer to the way they experience in common the possibility of binding themselves normatively and also transforming the material world. Now we can move from the *prima facie* intuition that legal discourse is organized with a certain degree of closure in an institution and conclude that the contours of this institution are defined by the shared normative experiences of the participants. Institutionalization does not refer only to the emergence of institutional facts or the empirical reality of courtrooms, prisons and so on. More importantly it refers to the demarcation of the limits of communicative meaning. Thus, institutionalized legal discourse contains those communicative offers that can be traced back to those fundamental presuppositions.

Arguing with Robert Cover and elaborating further on a theme in his work, I would also suggest that, if the pragmatics of legal discourse are followed down to an elementary level, it will be seen that these shared normative experiences refer to the possibility of transforming word into deed and vice versa in a real spatial and temporal context. Legal reason and reasons is the constant intertwining of theoretical reason and revisable practical reason(s). In our running example, what is implied in the sentencing utterance is not only that the norm *can* be translated into action (in this case, imprisonment) but also that there can be an accurate way of converting the norm into action or, to revert to Habermasian terminology, to make the transition from discourse to action. In order for legal discourse to lead to action, there must be a way of translating communication into action, of bringing about the consequences prescribed in legal rules. This should not be misunderstood as a claim about sanctions and the dependence of legal validity upon them. Whether it prescribes sanctions in the strict sense or not, legal discourse as a whole is about decisions and reasons for action, that is about the translation of language into acts. The currency of this conversion is immanent in legal discourse as a fundamental assumption about the world.

Seen from the opposite perspective, the law presupposes the possibility of transforming deed into word. For legal discourse to operate in an institutionalized manner, it must implicitly rely on the translatability of action into norm. If we turn to our running example again, it is implied firstly that there is a connection between the facts and the norms, on which Mr N was convicted, but also that there is a way of reconstructing historical truth independently of the relevant norms and then classifying the facts of the case under the latter. There is always an elusive element there lending coherence to these connections, an element that must be assumed and, in fact, must remain so.

Drawing a rough parallel to Kant's account of pure intuitions, I would argue that this quasi-causal function of the law is complemented and, indeed, framed by the assumed connection between normativity, space and time. One of the dimensions of existence of the law is the possibility of *correlating normative force with space*. In narrow legal terms, this could be understood as jurisdiction but in reality it is much broader than what this would suggest. Jurisdiction is only one manifestation of the topology of legal discourse. In institutionalized legal discourse, it is assumed that the normative force of utterances has boundaries usually coinciding with the country's physical boundaries. Physically crossing the boundary automatically amounts to being included in or excluded from legal discourse or determines how one is to participate in legal discourse. Because legal discourse sets its own topology, it becomes ubiquitous in the sense that nothing can possibly exist outwith it; it is always with reference to those boundaries that communicative offers can make sense.

The law's normative topology is complemented by its chronology. In order for it to exist as an institution as well as to lead to action, a conception of time is built into legal discourse. In order for it to be able to operate as institutionalized practical discourse, legal discourse must assume its synchronization with the world. The only way of achieving this is by developing a uniform perception of time and thus creating a temporal framework within which its operations take place. In Mr N's case, this is revealed quite forcefully. Ten years' imprisonment constitutes appropriate and just punishment, because of the assumed calculability of those ten years in a standard, assumed way, which is also the same way in which the convicted experiences time. It is this calculability of time that transforms it into an exchange value. To the extent that one of the points of departure of legal discourse is the possibility of such exchanges, the calculability of time must be assumed.

The intuition that there is something always elusive and unspeakable in the law has been expressed in a variety of ways. In his 'Force of Law', Jacques Derrida speaks of the *épokhè of the rule* as one of the *aporias* of the law. A just decision must be a free decision, one that is not constrained by a pre-existing rule, one that reaffirms the rule, creates rather than applies with a 'reinstituting act of interpretation, as if nothing previously existed of the law, as if the judge invented the law in every case' (Derrida 1992, 23).

This prerequisite of freedom for the justice of a decision leads to the paradox of the impossibility of a just decision in the present. A decision can claim to be legitimate, legal but *not just*. This connects to Derrida's third *aporia* of the law, namely 'the urgency that obstructs the horizon of knowledge' (Derrida 1992, 26). Justice belongs to the future as *avenir*, it is always yet to come. This is not possible in the law. Legal decisions are urgent, they are a violent interruption of the process of deciding, rather than its natural conclusion. Therefore, for Derrida, in law justice becomes a calculation of the incalculable.

As I argued in Chapter 1, this view of the law (not just the law of the State but all law) is at times frustratingly eschatological and almost yearns for a messianic mediation between the addressors and addressees of the law with a view to annulling this hegemonic relationship. At the same time, it is rather counterintuitive, as it necessarily dismisses *every* instance of legality as ideological. But this already compromises both its explanatory and, very importantly, its emancipatory potential. What I am trying to argue in this book is that there is indeed something that remains silent in legal discourse, but this something is at the same time constitutive of the law. The reconceptualization of the law in terms of shared normative experiences reconciles with the corrigibility of our beliefs on rightness, while at the same time providing us with some certainty in the law which is bound to the materiality of the here and now.

However, Derrida's *aporias* can still be seen as characteristic of *State law*, because the latter developed as a bureaucratic system of fixing of expectations rather than being attentive to what makes such normative expectations possible and sustainable. In what follows I will explore further the idea that the law is bound to shared normative experiences and the merging of the constative with the performative, at the same time as highlighting that State law necessarily obstructs this 'horizon of knowledge'. The most obvious context in which word is transformed into deed, or in other words norm is transformed into action, is that of the criminal law. Thus I will use sentencing as a paradigmatic case. On a substantive level, I will show how shared normative experiences are revealed as the tacit, undiscussed missing element in the justification of sanctions. At the same time, I will show that all the arguments for the justification of punishment are found wanting to the extent that they do not account for the apparent arbitrariness in their claim to calculability, especially when it comes to selecting a specific punishment for specific offences.

From Word to Deed

The justification of punishment could be analytically broken down to various levels of generality. On a first level, what needs to established is the wrongfulness of an act. I shall not say more on this now but will return to it in the next section. In any case, this is not all there is to it. Much work needs to be done in the next step, that is, in the transition from the wrongfulness of an act to the need to respond to it in any way and, especially, to respond by way of punishment. There is no shortage of theories here. In their effort to make sense of the morality of punishment, various theoretical strands range from extreme utilitarianism to almost metaphysical forms of rule-fetishism. The two basic strands emerging are utilitarianism and retributivism. The distinction is not watertight, as sometimes the differences between various expressions of each strand are such that classification calls for re-evaluation of the original categories, but it is sufficiently serviceable for the purposes of exposition (for some accounts of theories of punishment, see Ashworth 1992; Honderich 1969; Walker and Padfield 1983; Lacey 1988).

Consistent with its philosophical roots, utilitarianism views punishment as a means to an end rather than an end in itself. What has often been promoted within the project of maximizing utility as the general objective of punishing is the reduction of crime rates. This is meant to be achieved by preventing known offenders from committing more crimes or by punishing them in a paradigmatic way so that others are deterred. The general category of utilitarianism can accommodate various sub-strands. The aim of *reform* or *rehabilitation*,[15] which has rather fallen from grace over the last couple of decades, is about making the offender realize the immorality of her actions and teaching her to abide by the law on moral rather than utilitarian grounds. Seen from a different perspective, it is about the internalization of the law as a normative order. Punishment is not only an imposition of a certain harm, it is all about forming morally better citizens. *Deterrence* of others is another scope and justification of punishment. The punishment of offenders is to prevent others from committing the same crime by symbolically emphasizing that the price to pay is greater than the goods gained by the crime.

Retributivism can be said to be looking backwards; it is concerned with the past, with the crime committed, unlike utilitarianism which focuses on the future and the outcome of punishment. Most retributivist theories revolve around Kant's thesis that the duty to punish is a categorical imperative: we ought to punish offenders, because otherwise the shame of the breach of the moral law will burden the community. However, punishment is not to be treated as a means but rather as an end in itself. Retributivism is usually articulated in the language of 'just deserts'. Andrew von Hirsch argues that penalties should comport with the seriousness of the crime so that the punishment reflects the culpability of the wrong-doer's conduct (von Hirsch 1976).

Despite their seeming incompatibility, a retributivist theory of punishment with traces of utilitarianism was put forward by H.L.A. Hart (1970). He suggests that the justification of punishment should cover both its general aims as an institution as well as issues of distribution. To the latter belong the calculation of punishment for specific offences and the rightness of punishment in particular cases, including the proviso that it is only the guilty who should be punished. The utilitarian side of his thesis is that the general justification of punishment should be a forward-looking one.

So, theories of punishment purport to be offering answers to the two interconnected but analytically separate questions of 'why wrongful acts ought to be punished' and 'how wrongful acts ought to be punished'. The former refers to the justification of punishment in general, whereas the latter concerns the concrete

15 The distinction is to a large degree historical rather than substantive (Hudson 1996).

implementation of the answer to the first question, that is, it refers to the justification of specific sanctions, of sentencing. That wrong-doing provides good reasons for *some* response is considered generally uncontroversial. Disagreement by and large revolves around the character and source of such reasons. Utilitarianism all but collapses the two questions into each other by attributing punishment an instrumental character. Thus the crucial question is that of calculability, the general possibility of which is taken for granted. Retributivism, on the other hand, grounds punishment as a moral *a priori* discarding any pragmatic calculations at this stage. To this extent, retributivism has much more of a potential of approximating justice in punishment. However, it still seems incomplete. All instances of punishment, or indeed any *material* response to wrong-doing, entails the commensurability of one act with another through the mediation of norms, even before the appropriateness of a specific material response is considered. This becomes all the more obvious when it comes to the justification of specific sanctions for specific offences, as there is no logical, conceptual or *a priori* moral connection between the two. The imposition of specific sanctions constitutes a real intervention in the material conditions of the existence of a person. At the same time, the intervention in people's materiality means that new moral milieus are being pervaded. To phrase it slightly differently: the justification of punishment concerns the question of whether some harm ought to be inflicted upon the wrong-doer, whereas the justification of sanctions concerns the question of what kind of harm ought to be inflicted upon the wrong-doer.

The question concerning the rightness of specific sanctions is in the first instance answered only with *negative arguments of value*. Moral arguments would be restricted to the examination of whether, and to what extent, a sanction unacceptably or disproportionately violates the autonomy of the person and whether it clashes with other norms, principles or values. If the justificatory process were left here, the Derridean *aporia* of the law would already be proven inescapable. One would never be able to say that a sanction is just in any sense. The only claim that could be raised is that it is not evidently wrong. However, this is clearly not a sufficient guarantee of rightness. Justice must be positively established, it must be based on certitude, it cannot be exposed to contingency and uncertainty.

Such a certainty is pursued usually by recourse to *effectiveness*. The considerations that enter the equation are the safety and welfare of the general public, the reform of the perpetrator, the available punitive technologies, the political and economic implications of forms of punishment and so forth, depending on the overall aim of punishment that has been selected. In other words, the questions asked are: 'will this punishment reform the perpetrator?', 'will the public be and feel safer if we punish the wrong-doer in such or such a way?', 'will social peace be safeguarded and guaranteed?', 'do we have the necessary financial and technological reserves to implement that punishment?' and so on, always in view of the crime and the assumed moral status of the perpetrator. In short, the positive side of the justification of a penalty as a response to a wrongful act is, first of all, a *purpose-rational activity* attempting to connect the (proven or provable to be right) objective of punishment with the chosen practice. In any case, it still cannot be said that 'S is just'. The *aporia* has still not been done away with. The sanction is a calculation, a connection of the desired outcome and the available means. It is an aspiration and aspirations as projections of desires in the future cannot be right or wrong. And this is something that even an unqualified retributivism, which tries to justify sanctions by and large in terms of *a priori* universality, cannot shake off. Retributive sanctions are also grounded in a calculation that is incapable of meeting the criteria of justice set by retributivism itself. In fact, this time the calculation is completely arbitrary, as it is incommensurable entities that are being weighed up. How can it be shown that inflicting pain or depriving someone of her freedom compensates for a wrong done by that person? If left there, retribution reduces punishment to an exchange, which cannot possibly have any rules except for ones externally and authoritatively imposed.

Kant himself concedes this shortcoming of the *jus talionis*. He acknowledges that the 'eye for an eye' equation cannot always be just. Even it were possible to justify depriving a thief of as many goods as she stole, how can one justly calculate the punishment for rape or murder? Norrie summarizes this tension between ideal and actual:

> The strength of the retributive doctrine of equality of punishment is that it flows from the metaphysical justification of punishment, and sets an ideal limit on what may be done to a criminal. But that is also its weakness, for the *jus talionis* is an attempt to cash in the practical world the ideal cheque of metaphysical justice. Between the two currencies – the ideal and the concrete – there is no adequate point of contact, no workable exchange rate. The ideal principle of equality is incommensurable with a world of infinite practical variation. (Norrie 1991, 61)

Von Hirsch argues that the principle of proportionality can provide a secure and certain way of making this exchange (von Hirsch and Ashworth 1992). But this hardly solves the problem. On the contrary, it highlights it. Discourses of proportionality are paradigmatic cases of the attempt to bridge the ideal and the actual, the law's alternity, to return to Cover's terminology.[16] Seeking proportionality in punishment is nothing but the attempt to establish some symmetry between the action and the reaction. Nicola Lacey objects to this:

> The practical issue is that of determining just what type and measure of punishment is in (moral) fact proportionate to the offence committed by the offender. The difficulty of principle underlying this problem is that the two elements are actually incommensurable; there are no acceptable common units of measurement in terms of which we can assess the relationship of equivalence. In deciding just what punishment a murderer or robber deserves, we seem to be thrown back on the unacceptable lex talionis, or on some conventionally

16 See Chapter 2.

> established scale of penalties, or forced to admit that this is a matter for the untrammelled discretion of the legislator or sentencer, perhaps for her determination on consequentialist lines. (Lacey 1988, 21)

The *aporia* is still not overcome, if we view punishment as the fair redistribution of benefits and burdens (Morris 1968). Such a view still leaves open the question of what makes for benefits and burdens and how exactly their equilibrium can be and has been disturbed and how it can be restored. In order for us fully to grasp the practice of punishment and, in doing so, in order to grasp the foundations of law, we must look into the constitutive conditions of those benefits and burdens. In other words, we must look closely at the interplay between constative and performative, between normativity and our experience of the world.

Retributivism comes close to capturing this when resorting to arguments from social contract. The negative moral argument, as I have already mentioned above, provides some sort of a guarantee that the response of the criminal law and the criminal justice system will not violate the boundaries of the humanity and dignity of the defendant. The social contractarian argument rests on the assumption that all members of a community have tacitly or explicitly consented to the imposition of some kind of constraints to their liberty and self-determination, and some intervention to the materiality of their lives, to the extent that this will promote or protect the interests of the community. And to the extent that the wrong-doer owes a debt to others, punishment in cases of the violation of criminal law rules is one of these instances of an acceptable constraint to one's autonomy.

Alexy takes a slightly different tack:

> [...] if one conceives justice as comprising all questions of distribution and retribution, then problems like that of the welfare state and that of punishment have to be treated as questions of justice. The answers to these questions depend on many reasons. Among them arguments about how one should understand oneself and the community in which one lives play an essential role. By this the just depends on the good. Changing one's self-understanding or one's interpretation of the tradition in which one has been bred up can change one's conception of justice. (Alexy 1999, 379)

Alexy's aim in the passage is to show the unity between the various aspects of practical reasoning. His argument is that practical reason is not simply a blending of its three aspects but rather the unity of their internal interconnections. Effectively, he claims that questions such as the justification of punishment are inevitably decided on the ethical level but, at the same time, that discourse cannot violate the universalizable moral point of view. Habermas argues along similar lines. Pragmatic arguments are acceptable in law-making discourses as long as they are underpinned by existing values of the community and they do not violate universalizable moral norms (Habermas 1993).

The perception of punishment put forth by Alexy and Habermas is, to a large extent, based on Habermas' distinction between pragmatic, moral and ethical employments of practical reason and the conditions under which these are acceptably interconnected and combined. Habermas draws on the Kantian tradition and seeks creatively to combine it with Aristotelian ethics and utilitarianism through the spectrum of discourse theory. He proposes, therefore, a distinction between the different employments of practical reason. Namely, he distinguishes between the *pragmatic*, the *ethical* and the *moral*.

Pragmatic reason refers, in short, to purposive rationality. It provides answers to questions concerning action or reasons for action on grounds of resources and expected outcome. Ethical rationality is different to purposive, in that moral imperatives enter the reasoning. Nevertheless, they are not pure moral considerations. Ethical rationality is contextual. Individual life histories or the real conditions of existence of a specific community enter the discussion as catalysts. Pure moral rationality is employed in moral discourses. The contingencies of the real conditions of existence are irrelevant. Moral imperatives are beyond subjects or communities. The rather vague difference between the moral and the ethical employment of practical reason means that ethical reason refers to what is *good* for a particular society, whereas moral reason is about what is *just* (Habermas 1993).

Let me approach the same issues from the point of view of the unity of practical reason which Alexy advocates and at which MacCormick hints (MacCormick and Weinberger 1986). Indeed, we cannot distinguish clearly between different kinds of argument in practical reasoning in the sense that all are inevitably intermeshed. Practical decisions are based on pragmatic and moral considerations. Although these do not stand in a strict hierarchical order, a decision which raises a claim to moral rightness must not lose sight of universalizable imperatives. MacCormick's argument is not exhausted there. In his discussion of the requirements of practical reason, he argues that value rationality must be at least second order rationality (MacCormick and Weinberger 1986). When we provide reasons for choosing one reason for action over another, that second order reason ought to be a value or principle sustained consistently over time and universalizable over persons and cases. Second order reasons have to be *good* reasons rather than merely strategies or means–ends calculations.

Let us accept the distinction between the ethical and the moral. Let us also assume that the justification of punishment is an ethical question permeated by some conception of justice. Let us finally accept the unity of practical reason and the important role of pragmatic rationality in the formation of strategies and the weighing up of means and ends in a community. It is far from clear that we will be able to tell the full story, even with this trinitarian yet uniform essence of reason and the interplay between the moral, the ethical and the pragmatic under our belt.

On the contrary, the breakdown of reason in its three constituent parts highlights even more clearly that there is still something missing.[17, 18]

It is indeed necessary to make the transition from the general to the specific before the law can claim to be able meaningfully to regulate social co-existence. But recognizing the need to bridge the space between the common and the specific, the moral and the ethical, does not explain everything in and by itself. What still remains to be accounted for is what precisely makes the transition possible. To return to our current example, even appreciating that the proposition that wrongful acts are punishable is of a different order to the proposition that a specific sanction is the right punishment for a specific offence, does not do away with the sense of contingency accompanying the choice of a specific sanction over another. For instance, how can the law determine that the sanction for theft ought

17 Resorting to the ethical in order to make sense of the justification of sanctions implies that the universal needs to be localized and stranded to the context. The same concern has been expressed in many ways. Aristotle famously distinguishes between *common* and *specific* law:

> Just and unjust actions have been defined in reference to two kinds of law and in reference to persons spoken of in two senses. I call law on the one hand *specific*, on the other *common*, the latter being unwritten, the former written, specific being what has been defined by each people in reference to themselves, and common that which is based on nature. (*Rhetoric*: I. 1373b)

Similarly, Thomas Aquinas distinguishes between the *lex naturalis* and the *lex humana*. One of the reasons motivating such arguments is the fact that on the moral level (or the level of natural law) very little is determined. The general principles of morality not only lack the necessary thickness for them to be able to guide action but they also need to be ascribed an ethical, contextual relevance in order for them to become responsive to the specific needs of the community by becoming able somehow to interact with the physical world. So, the law comes as the *determinatio* of the natural law, as its implementation and contextualization, which is expected to solve problems of appropriateness in light of the material circumstances of the community.

18 Klaus Günther's theory of appropriateness, which is also a discourse theoretical approach to law, cannot be of much help either. His theory of application discourses is an attempt to temper Kantian rigidity in norm application through recourse to the fluidity of Aristotelian *phronesis* and systems theory. Application discourses are based on a 'weak universalization principle', according to which a norm is right, when its consequences will be accepted by everyone *under unchanging circumstances*. Discourses of application consist of taking into account all the relevant facts and valid norms. In the case of the law, that means that a judge has the ability to evaluate both the situation as past and the decision as future. But this does not solve the problem. Even if a particularly right judgment can be passed, the judge has very few options concerning the pronouncement of a penalty. The choice is limited to the details of the sanction, namely its duration, the mode of its implementation and so on. To allow the judge to freely choose a sanction would obviously have severe repercussions for the rule of law (Günther 1993a; 1993b).

to be imprisonment for up to seven years?[19] We could, of course, turn to external explanations. From a distance one could argue, for instance, that the decisive factor is the contingent material development of a community. So, the choice of specific sanctions over others is determined by the technologies in existence, the state of material culture and so forth. But from this hermeneutic point of view, it is impossible to see the link between normativity and materiality, which allows the concretization of general normative propositions into propositions that legitimate specific action. Any such external vantage point will have to rely on the observer's sense of that connection and it will not be able to grasp how it is that a ethical, legal order can raise a claim to correctness or even appropriateness raised by sanction-imposing legal rules.

So this is where the idea of shared normative experiences kicks in. In order for the arguments from proportionality or appropriateness in the light of the distinction between the moral, the ethical and the pragmatic to get off the ground in the first place, what needs to be in place is a basic presupposition in the ability to bridge the gap between factuality and normativity, as well as the way in which this bridging may happen in the real context of a community. I argue that the law becomes specific to a community of people, who have come to experience the world and their ability to transform it through their normative commitments in a shared manner. There is nothing in the categorical content of the legal norm that determines its application or individuation, despite the normative aspect of that individuation. At the same time, there is nothing that the natural sciences can teach us about the connection of the punishment to the offence or, indeed, to effectiveness, which is already normatively textured. So both seem necessary but neither will suffice separately.

The Other Side of the Coin: From Deeds to Words

The embeddedness of the law in shared normative commitments is revealed not only in the transition from word to deed but also from deed to word. It is what allows us to ascribe normative significance to facts so as to translate them again into action. This is revealed most clearly in the ascertainment of facts in legal processes. In what follows I shall refer to three classic critiques and one defence of legal fact-finding, and revisit them in the light of the idea of shared normative experiences as constitutive of law.

Amongst the American legal realists, fact sceptics drew attention to the fact that, as well as an instance of rule following, the trial purports also to be a process of discovering, ascertaining and establishing facts. The distribution of substantive justice depends on the correct application both of the appropriate or right rule and the correct and accurate diagnosis of the facts. Prominent amongst fact sceptics, Jerome Frank bases his critique of legal fact-finding on a general critique of formalistic legal culture. In his *Law and the Modern Mind*, he challenges the 'demand for

---

19 This is the case in England and Wales (Theft Act 1968).

an impossible legal stability, resulting from an infantile longing to find a father-substitute in the law' (Frank 1949a, 178). He criticizes the 'basic myth' that the law provides certainty and justice under all circumstances. Frank ridicules this childish longing for a fatherly presence, which is manifested in institutions guaranteeing generalization, impartiality and predictability, such as the big legal codifications, the jury and so on. According to Frank, the law far from offers such stability.

Aside from the common American legal realist thesis that judicial decisions are rationalizations shrouded in the ideology that there are definitive rules for every case, Frank also highlights that the fundamental myth of the possibility of the harmonious combination of certainty and predictability with justice is also maintained on a different level, namely that of fact-finding. In his *Courts on Trial*, Frank criticizes legal finding on various grounds, which have one common denominator: the 'discovery' of truth in the course of a trial is subjective and biased. Frank sees the process of adjudication as not having yet advanced from magic to rationality. In primitive societies, the truth was established by way of ordeal, be it of a material, corporal character or a spiritual one such as the oath (Frank 1949c, 37ff). Such were the guarantees that witnesses and parties in disputes were telling the truth. The 'rationalization' of law, Frank argues, has not signified the end of the era of magic but merely the transition to a different kind of magic, one indeed much less square than the primitive one (Frank 1949c, 47). Processes of fact-finding will always be haunted by subjectivity, either because not enough information is available or because the judge or the jury are fallible and thus unable to ascertain the truth. Therefore, the final judgment always relies on a leap of faith, a magical moment of assuming that the judge or the jury are insightful enough correctly to evaluate the produced facts. This 'modern legal magic' is based on the faith that the rules have the power to filter the facts and lead the fact-finding procedure. Behind the faith that subjectivity does not substantively affect the decision-making process, Frank finds the 'magical notion that uniformity in the use of precise legal rules must yield approximate uniformity in the decisions of specific cases, if only the judges conduct themselves properly' (Frank 1949c, 61).

Frank has much to say about the manipulability of judges, witnesses and juries by lawyers, the unequal distribution of resources between parties compromising the quality of legal representation and so forth. However, it is another, perhaps not as central, argument of his that is particularly interesting, in that it does not focus on the distortion of verbal communication or the inadequacy of the input of information in the courtroom but on the very form of communication. This is an argument from *Gestalt* theory (Frank 1949c, 165ff). Roughly, according to *Gestalt* theory, perception is not always exhausted in language. There are ideas and thoughts that are too complex to be expressed propositionally in the linear and orderly way in which language operates. Frank refers extensively to Susanne Langer's work. In her words:

> this restriction of discourse sets bounds to the complexity of speakable ideas. An idea that contains too many minute yet closely related parts, too many relations

> within relations, cannot be 'projected' into discursive form; it is too subtle for speech. (quoted by Frank 1949c, 172)

In those cases in which the object of perception is too complicated to be propositionalized, perception can only take place in wholes. Langer illustrates *Gestalt* with melody as an example: we do not perceive of the melody as each separate note and pause. We register it as a continuum, as a whole.

Frank applies *Gestalt* theory to the legal fact-finding process. The judge or the jury, he tells us, do not and indeed cannot verbalize all the information they are exposed to. Their reaction to evidence is a combination of rational assessment of data, emotions and intuitions. Precisely because the perception of facts as presented before the courts is to a large extent extra-linguistic, it cannot be compared to and described by rules. The containment of that *Gestalt* experience in rules can only be a selection of certain propositional elements of that experience. Therefore, the application of the rule is selective and it cannot do justice to the situation or the parties.

Frank's use of *Gestalt* is insightful and promising, if rather incomplete. Bernard Jackson points out that Frank does not quite drive the argument from *Gestalt* home (B. Jackson 1988, 14). According to Jackson, Frank's claims are exhausted in the claim that communication is also possible with means other than language and that external stimuli can cause decisions. This, Jackson argues, does not challenge the belief that external reality can be fully represented and communicated. Frank adheres to a referential understanding of the relationship between facts and statements, thus disregarding the intensionality of processes of representation. Therefore his critique of legal fact-finding is critically undermined. Indeed, this is the most crucial shortcoming of Frank's critique. He seems to assume the existence of an objective truth, even if its discovery is impaired by the ways in which courts go about looking for it. This background belief becomes evident by the fact that Frank proposes some practical solutions to the fact-finding problem, such as improvement of legal education, the psychological screening of judges and jurors, and so on. Thus he overlooks a logically prior question, namely whether the law can accommodate such an objective truth, even if such a thing exists. Nevertheless, Frank's critique is insightful in that it implicitly grasps the complex relations at play in legal discourse. Moreover, his critique of modern legal fact-finding as a different kind of magic alludes tacitly to the fact that, just like magic, the law operates with a distinct rationality of its own, an internal coherence, which cannot be accessed from outside.

Bankowski raises a similar objection to Frank's fact scepticism and puts the latter into a new perspective (Bankowski 1981). What is sought in the trial process, Bankowski argues, is the construction of coherent stories which plausibly accommodate the pieces of concrete evidence. As for the accusatorial, adversarial form of the process, not only does it not impede the discovery of the truth but it actually facilitates the testing of the stories presented before the court. Bankowski puts forth an argument which still revolves around the reconstruction of events in the courtroom and the role of the jury in deciding on the truth of the facts. However, it goes beyond the pragmatic aspect of the trial and draws attention to an immanent feature of legal fact-finding. Bankowski sees a flaw and a potential great danger in the epistemological claim that the truth of the matter can be discovered in a merely representational way, that is, without any method and theory underpinning the process of discovery. In other words the truth of the matter cannot be seen disjointedly from justification. If the search for the truth is separated from any kind of normative basis, there will be no constraints in the collection of evidence. The reasons justifying the method vary between various instances of the discovery of truth. For instance, the police are not constrained by the same rules when acknowledging the probability of someone having breached the law by arresting her as the jury when actually convicting the defendant. According to Bankowski, the problem is that, since justification is inevitable in the discovery of truth, the jury have a clearly substantive role in the trial process. The danger lies not in their perception of the facts but in the extent to which the jurors have exceeded the (justificatory) powers allocated to them by procedural rules.

In *Images of Law*, Bankowski and Mungham advance a more far-reaching critique of legal fact-finding (Bankowski and Mungham 1976, 117ff). They criticize the dominant view that facts are a-historical and a-temporal, so they can be reported as they really took place. They subscribe to an epistemological paradigm, according to which the truth (or at least historical truth) is inevitably the product of the dialectic relationship between consciousness and the world. Facts are not radically separated from perception. In that respect Frank is wrong, Bankowski and Mungham argue (Bankowski and Mungham 1976, 118). He seems to be relying on science as the only vehicle of rationality. State law and its institutions base their operations on precisely the same premise. Science guarantees objectivity and this, in turn, guarantees justice. However, Bankowski and Mungham tell us, the reductionism in the first part of that equation is already a fallacy. The outcome of scientific research is not infallible statements about the world as it really exists and waiting to be described. These results are already social, they exist in the world and they are connected to a decision which is to a large extent extra-scientific. So mainstream, axiologically and socially laden, science is utilized and perpetuated by courts, thus precluding alternative understandings of the world and their political, social and moral substrata.

To be sure, there are some problems with Bankowski and Mungham's critique of fact-finding on grounds of the latter's necessary axiological character. Although they are right to reject the reductionist understanding of the world as a correspondence between statements and actual events, the alternative they offer is not sufficiently powerful to the extent that they seem to rely on robust epistemological and ontological arguments without seeing them through. Nevertheless, their critique is valuable in that it concerns the structural inability of State law to make sense of other understandings of the world. To this extent it is in line with the argument in this book: that State law is unable to be attentive to shared normative experiences, because it fixes the epistemological of meaning in view of systemic imperatives and its historical baggage.

Jackson gives the same point a semiotic slant and draws a stronger connection between rules and facts and, subsequently, narrative and justification. He looks at Biblical and older law examples and concludes that the distinction between norms and facts is only a by-product of the codification of laws and the professionalization of legal practice (B. Jackson 1988, 97). The emergence of law as a separate profession and discipline led to an increasing abstraction of rules and their categorial separation from facts:

> The difference between the modern, abstract legal rule, and the ancient narrative model has a sociological as well as a formal dimension. The abstract model requires specialisation and training; one has to know how and what to abstract, before one can deduce. (B. Jackson 1988, 98)

However, Jackson argues, this separation is neither universal nor necessary (B. Jackson 1988, 90). Apart from facts, norms too are narratives. Therefore, adjudication is not a question of inference from a major and a minor premise, as the positivist school of deductive justification want it. This is in fact impossible according to Jackson, because abstract and diachronic rules can only relate abstract and diachronic conditions to universal consequences. But they cannot refer to real cases, there can be no inference from the combination of a rule/major premise and a set of facts/minor premise (B. Jackson 1988, 37ff). Decision-making is rather a process of structural comparison of two separate narratives: that of the norm and that of the facts. In other words, the justification of decision-making is a case of narrative pattern-matching. The frequent difficulties in this matching of narratives explain the existence of 'easy' and 'hard' cases in legal reasoning.

In defence of the rationality and coherence of fact-finding, Neil MacCormick extends his thesis on coherence as a prerequisite of legal reasoning (MacCormick 1978). He claims that we can safely draw conclusions about the truth of historical facts based on a theory of coherence, which is 'being presented not as a theory about the meaning of "truth", but as a theory about procedures for proof of all such statements as cannot be directly checked for their present correspondence with present facts' (MacCormick 1980, 47).

However, coherence comes into play only when there is no direct evidence concerning the facts. Sceptical of relativistic scepticism that rejects the law as having nothing to do with the truth (MacCormick 1995, 116), MacCormick maintains that objectivity is possible and that there is a reality accessible by our senses (MacCormick 1991). Although narratives are important and indeed inevitable, the truth is not exhausted in them. As far as facts produced in court are concerned, it is of course true that our only access to them is by way of interpreting narratives. And assessing those narratives is already an evaluative affair. Moreover, most of the truisms about the fallibility of perception, memory and so forth are true. Nevertheless there are mechanisms capable of successfully testing stories, coherence being the most prominent and important amongst them.

As far as the possibility of the normative coherence is concerned, MacCormick insists that application/instantiation and classification are indeed possible. Although there is indeed a problem with the inference of conclusions from major and minor premises, that problem is not one of reference (MacCormick 1991), it is one of universal instantiation. Reasoning is a combination of interpretation and classification. And he concludes that:

> [T]he problem of matching major and minor premises in a normative syllogism is the problem of securing sameness of sense of the predicates deployed in both. Narrative modes of argumentation can have real value here, but not to the exclusion of other modes. That it is only in minor premises that predicates are used referentially, with reference to particular features of particular concrete cases, while their use in major premises is non-referential, poses no difficulty for this theory. (MacCormick 1991, 174)

So for MacCormick, narrative coherence can guarantee the success of the ascertainment of facts and, in combination with normative coherence, it can guarantee the justice and fairness of the outcome. And, by implication, he argues that there is nothing in State law impeding the process of establishing such coherence other than, perhaps, the same incidental constraints singled out by Alexy as well.

But how convincingly does this argument rebut the critiques of legal fact-finding? MacCormick's argument seems to rest on a straightforward separation between law and facts. The assumption is that there is a way of coherently describing and individuating events. The law then comes to ascribe legal meaning to those events. But such a strict separation of the realms of fact and law fails to account for how State law reduces complexity by picking certain facts as normatively or rather *legally* relevant. As Csaba Varga puts it:

> In law [...] all kinds of operation with facts have to start from the search after and with the identification of what is relevant. But in contrast to non-legal fields, relevancy is pre-codified here: [...] formally defined in a normative way, it is given to each and every kind of, and situation in, legal processes. Accordingly, legal relevancy canalizes any business directed to gaining [...] facts in a given path from the very start; at the same time, it closes any other path [...] (Varga 1995, 68)

The image of the world and the law as two coherent wholes, portions of which correspond to each other on a one-to-one basis, fails to capture what Jackson, Bankowski and Mungham, and Varga hint at in different ways. Namely, that in law the constative and the performative are merged and become inseparable, that legal norms are always already hinged on facts, they incorporate a specific understanding of the law. The problems of legal fact-finding are only an indication of this inseparability of law and fact. If we go one step back, we will discover the productive aspects of that connection and see that the law does not develop separately from the way people normatively experience the world, but is rather constituted by those experiences.

MacCormick, however, gives a very good description of State law, which operates on the assumption of the separability of the two self-contained and coherent realms of facts and norms. This allows it to introduce universal categories, which are supposed to guarantee certainty and predictability, in that they cover all, or at least most, possible factual situations. So, instead of being attentive to the way normativity develops and is being experienced in concrete, lived contexts, State law rests on the artificial radical distinction between fact and norm and the pretension that legal normative meaning is adaptable to any combination of facts. Thus it silences the fact that selection and individuation of events is already guided by a merging of the constative and the performative, which in State law is pre-coded and remains tacit.

Conclusion

This conversion of word into deed and deed into word, of the performative into constative and vice versa, can only be presupposed and experienced by the participants in a *nomos*, and it is only against this background that one can even begin to ask what counts as a crime or which punishment fits the crime, let alone the specific technicalities of the sanction and its appropriateness for particular defendants. However, modern Western State law, as well as the legal theories that have accompanied it since its emergence, are oblivious to the fact that there is something contingent and context-bound built in the very heart of the legal and which, crucially, needs to be acknowledged as one of the building blocks of the very sense of law. Social contractarian arguments (explicitly employed by some retributivists and implicitly present in MacCormick's defence of legal fact-finding) are strongly indicative not only of an anxiety somehow to fill this gap but also of the character of State law, which such theories reflect. State law is concerned with the maintenance of its systematicity and the fixing of normative expectations. Even the social contract imagined by the tradition of big civic revolutions seeks to guarantee that the contracting parties will give up part of their practical autonomy and authorize others to determine the law, so that moral and political complexity is reduced.

According to State law and legal theoretical orthodoxy, issues of appropriateness, sanctions being again a prominent example here, may not be met with universal consent (for example, I may disagree that imprisonment is the right punishment for theft and consider fines a more suitable sanction for offences against property), but at least there is nothing immanent in legal discourse that does not allow such discussion to get off the ground. But what makes this assumption possible is that it is rooted in the State law internal perspective. This means that the horizon of possibility has already been set and limited in light of the State's remit as the guarantor of stability through authoritative representation, a remit which is typically expressed as the requirements of the rule of law. This is something that theories of law generally, and of punishment in particular, are blind to, not because they all place the rule of law and certainty centre-stage (Dworkin, for instance, does not) but to the extent that they conceptualize the law as inseparable from the State.

Nevertheless, all this does not amount to saying that we need to despair, as many critical theorists tend to do. If anything, the fact that State law is incapable of doing justice to spontaneous and diverse alternities urges us to consider those as constitutive of the law, rather than giving up altogether on the possibility of reconciling regulation and emancipation.

Chapter 6
Shared Normative Experiences and the Space for Legal Pluralism

Introduction

In the previous chapter, I made the first step towards formulating a thin sense of law, which can be used as a *prima facie* (and therefore defeasible and temporary) guide for pluralistic, interperspectival socio-legal theory, the forum of discourse on the law. I argued against Robert Alexy's discourse theory, which I consider to be the best representative of theories advocating the normative openness of the law, that the institutionalization of legal discourse entails more than most legal theories assume. Marshalled by an analysis of State legal language in terms of speech acts, I arrived at the conclusion that at the bedrock of legality lie certain presuppositions on the part of participants concerning their ability in common to transform the world through their normative commitments. These presuppositions I termed shared normative experiences in order to capture the nature of the law as 'alternity', in Cover's terms as what bridges word and deed. In this chapter I will try to clarify the idea of shared normative experiences and how thinking of the law in such terms may serve the project of legal pluralism.

True Presuppositions or Presupposed Beliefs?

Talk of assumptions and presuppositions will already have raised the suspicion that my argument is quite close to Hans Kelsen's neo-Kantianism. There are indeed some affinities between the two projects although there are important differences as well. In what follows I will use Kelsen's legal philosophy as a springboard helping me to clarify my conceptualization of the law.

As is well known, Kelsen wanted to avoid the pitfall of empiricist legal positivism, which committed the naturalistic fallacy by accepting that normativity can emanate from a fact such as the social practice of acceptance of the normative force of a set of rules. His aim was seriously to account both for the separability of law and morality and the separation of law and fact, and thus formulate a theory of law which would be pure in two intertwined senses: first, in proving the autonomy of the law in relation to its normative environment and, secondly, in establishing the epistemological autonomy of legal theory. In the many versions of his *Reine Rechtslehre* (*RR*) he sought to explain the law's autonomy in terms of the category of imputation, the quasi-causal connection between material facts in and through reconstructed legal norms, and the transcendental presupposition, which he terms as the *Grundnorm*. The individuated norm (for instance, the judge passing a sentence) is based on another norm and so forth until we hit the historically first constitution. This historical, constitutional origin is not preceded by anything but the transcendental presupposition that is the *Grundnorm* lending the whole of the legal system its validity and unity. It is only because of this cognitive presupposition that people are able to ascribe legal meaning to physical facts.

Kelsen revisited the nature and content of the *Grundnorm* several times over his very long writing career (see Heidemann 1999; Paulson 1998; 1999). In the concept's last phase, it ceased to be a transcendental presupposition and became rather a fiction (Duxbury 2008). As my aim is not to provide an exegesis of Kelsenian text or a biographical account of Kelsen's theoretical oscillations, I shall refer to the *Grundnorm* in its neo-Kantian sense as an epistemic presupposition, as this seems to me to be its most interesting interpretation (Kelsen 1992). Stanley Paulson reconstructs Kelsen's Kant-inspired transcendental argument and points out an essential problem about it. According to Paulson, the transcendental argument knows a progressive and a regressive version, which, though inseparable in Kantian thought, neo-Kantians had to split, in order for them to apply the argument in specific epistemological contexts and establish the autonomy of various disciplines. The initial premise of the progressive version of the transcendental argument consists in data of consciousness. In order for those data to be available, a category must be presupposed. As a further conclusion, we can then infer statements about our cognition. For example, we observe that knocking over a thing will cause it to fall over but in order for us to make sense of this relationship, we must presuppose causality as a category. Therefore the category of causality *is* presupposed and we can then go on and formulate natural laws about and around causality as further conclusions.

It is this further conclusion concerning statements about our cognition that neo-Kantians use as their starting premise in the regressive version of the argument, in order to establish the autonomy of various separate domains of knowledge. And this was Kelsen's aim in the context of the law: to establish the autonomy of knowledge of law and the fact that such knowledge is *constitutive of the law itself*. It is therefore clear that Kelsen could not have used the progressive version of the argument, because then he would effectively concede that imputation is identifiable as a material fact, thus undermining the very foundations of the *RR*. Therefore Kelsen argues along the following lines: we have cognition of the law and speak about it meaningfully. In order for this to be possible, the category of imputation (and at the end of it, the *Grundnorm*) must be presupposed. Therefore, imputation and the *Grundnorm* are true.

Paulson raises a challenge to this regressive form of the transcendental argument. He argues that, if the aim of the transcendental argument is to disarm sceptics (and, I would add, conventionalists), it fails, as the latter would not have to accept the initial premise concerning legal cognition at all. This, after all, is what they would object to in the first place. But even if that were not the case, the premise that legal cognition is possible only on the presupposition of imputation and the *Grundnorm* is even more problematic, as these are two of many (in fact, an infinite number of) possible candidates accounting for the possibility of legal cognition. As Paulson shows, two options would then be available to Kelsen. The first would be to deal with each alternative explanation of legal cognition separately, which would of course debilitate his project by leaving it perpetually open and unproved. Alternatively, he would have to demonstrate that imputation *is* the case, which would clearly amount to returning to the progressive version of the transcendental argument and conceding too much to legal naturalism.

Paulson's argument is a variation on a theme set by Stroud with his famous argument that transcendentalism must sooner or later collapse into verificationism (Stroud 1968; Brand-Ballard 1996). This is how Stroud's objection unfolds: transcendental arguments are supposed to prove that certain propositions must hold transcendentally *true*, in order for all other propositions to be *meaningful* at all. However, a sceptic can always claim that the set of propositions that transcendentalists hold as transcendentally true are merely people's *beliefs* about the state of affairs. In that case, one would be able to talk about them in a perfectly meaningful manner, while, at the same time, being utterly wrong and deluded about everything. In order for a Kantian transcendentalist to counter this argument, she will have to show that there is a way of telling apart meaningfulness from truth. But that would already amount to conceding that, in order for transcendental conclusions to hold, they must be verifiable. Therefore, transcendentalism already regresses into verificationism, which is fatal both because the latter rests on the refutation of the possibility of the transcendental validity of any proposition and because it has already been discredited as a theory of truth in its own right.

The ghost of verificationism haunts the *RR* from the outset. Two related objections can be raised in different stages of Kelsen's transcendental argument. What is stated in the first step argument is simply the fact of our cognition of legal norms. As I said previously, given that the existence of legal norms is not sensibly identifiable, a sceptic could already raise an objection by arguing that there is nothing that she *recognizes as law*. Indeed, some would argue that not everyone has a use for the concept of law in the sense that there is no generally accepted convention allowing some communities formally to recognize the law and differentiate it from any other way of normatively ordering their lives with any consistency. Plenty such examples are available in legal anthropological literature. In his study of the Nuer, Evans-Pritchard reports that:

> In the strict sense of the word, the Nuer have no law. There is no one with legislative or juridical functions. There are conventional payments considered due to a man who has suffered certain injuries – adultery with his wife, fornication with his daughter, theft, broken limbs, &c. – but these do not make a legal system, for there is no constituted and impartial authority who decides on the rights and wrongs of a dispute and there is no external power to enforce such a decision were it given. If a man has right on his side, and, in virtue of

> that, obtains the support of his kinsmen and they are prepared to use force, he has a good chance of obtaining what is due to him, if the parties live near to one another. (Evans-Pritchard 1940, 293–4)

Faced with cases such as the Nuer of Southern Sudan, Kelsen would have had to concede that there is nothing universal about the category of the legal ought and that its existence is just a matter of historical contingency. He therefore deals with the objection by avoiding it. He tells us explicitly that it is not the sceptic whom he is trying to persuade and that imputation and the *Grundnorm* are true only for those who already inhabit a legal system and have cognition of the law (Kelsen 1992, §16, 34).

I believe that Kelsen concedes too much too soon. The objection that there may be some communities who do not have law at all can only be sustained if what we are looking for are instances of the word law or a synonym or, indeed, law as a system of rules with some formal characteristics, or what Evans-Pritchard calls law 'in the strict sense of the word'. My argument in this book is that we must go beyond such a formal and rigid understanding of the law. I suggest that our *prima facie* sense of the law should reflect its context-bound nature as the shared belief of participants in a *nomos* in transforming the world normatively and in common. Whether there is semantic coincidence between the ways that various languages choose to refer to law thus conceived or whether some institutional arrangements recur across contexts become irrelevancies. Therefore, one who raises the objection that some communities do not have cognition of law will have to show a great deal more than simply that these communities do not have a use for the word 'law' or that there is no uniform source of legality. Their task becomes much more difficult in that they must prove that these communities do not share a way of ordering the world in common and which is associated with their conditions of existence. It will then be up to the sceptic to prove that cognition of the law in that sense is not universal, that there are communities without normative practices differing to some extent from their normative environment.

Arguing this does not amount simply to by-passing the problem. The intuition that legality is inescapable, and the *prima facie* historical evidence supporting it, are so strong as to reverse the onus of proof. If committed to the universality *and* absolute determinacy of morality, one who raises such an objection would have to show that the social arrangements in her community are in no way specific to that community alone and that they can freely be transposed to any other possible context, as they all belong in the universal moral order. If, on the other hand, the claim rests on moral relativism and consists in that all, even the most trivial and technical, normative arrangements in that imaginary community are both purely moral and context-specific, the counterintuitive nature of such a claim would mean that she will have the burden of proving that morality is fully determinative of as well as somehow accounting for the formation of the moral context in a way that is significantly different to the universal, presupposed concept of legality. But until such an argument is made convincingly, in other words while the intuitive distinction between law and other normative orders persists, then we can assume that the fact of cognition of legal norms holds universally.

The second objection to Kelsen can be raised in the third step of the argument, which concludes that the transcendental category of legality is *true* because it is presupposed, thus making legal cognition possible and legal communication meaningful. However, going back to Stroud's objection to transcendentalism, even if one accepts that the first two steps of the argument hold true, the same is not the case in the third step. It is true that this objection seems insurmountable for Kelsen and something will have to give. This is where the fundamental difference between Kelsenian transcendentalism and my suggestion concerning the experiential basis of legality lies. Firstly, I do not believe it is necessary (or indeed possible) to prove the truth of the presuppositions underpinning legality as an *a priori*. What I term 'normative experiences' of participants in a *nomos* do not have a transcendental dimension. They are shared, embedded *beliefs* of the participants concerning their ability normatively and in unison to transform their environment.

The fact that I downgrade, so to speak, the interrelated, shared normative experiences to beliefs rather than *a priori* truths does not mean that the scheme collapses into Hartian conventionalism. Hart's main concern was to establish the autonomy of the legal system by grounding it on a non-contingent basis. If that basis were normative then one would either be led to infinite regress or would have to concede the necessary connection of law with other normative orders, most importantly morality, at that foundational stage. So, instead, Hart opted for an empirical, sociological basis for the legal system, namely the social practices of the participants. At the same time, and precisely because he projects the existence of a legal system onto pre-existing truths about humanity, he concedes that there is a 'minimum content of natural law' in every legal system.

The underlying Humean idea of contingently emerging institutions of justice that facilitate the peaceful co-existence of essentially benevolent human beings is served by the conception of legality as a matter of conventions (see Postema 1986). Marmor extends Lewis' account of social conventions (Lewis 1969) so as to include not only conventions, which resolve pre-existing co-ordination problems, but also conventions, which constitute the very point of the practice which they govern (Marmor 1996; 2001; 2007). Structured games such as chess provide the typical example here. There is clearly no pre-existing co-ordination problem which chess provides a solution to (it would be rather strange if there were!) but, even if we did view practices such as chess as solutions to co-ordination problems, we would hardly understand the rules of chess and the point of the practice itself properly. Rather, Marmor argues, the whole character of the game is determined by its very conventions, which he views as constitutive of the practice. Of course, like all social conventions, these conventions are *arbitrary*, according to Marmor, in the sense that they could freely be otherwise. Nevertheless, they are *not indifferent* to the extent that they are the product of historical experience and the embedding of certain principles espoused by the respective legal community. This relative arbitrariness of the conventions purportedly constituting the autonomous practice of the law is problematic in its own merit but I will return to it, however briefly, in the next section. For now I will focus on the idea that the autonomous existence of the law is tied up to the emergence of certain conventions, which are historically contingent.

A conventionalist account of the law would perhaps successfully explain the emergence, autonomization and differentiation between various actual legal systems. Marmor himself resorts to the divergences between common and civil law systems as an example of the autonomy and relative neutrality of legal conventions. This, however, would again amount to little more than giving a quasi-Weberian sociological analysis the veneer of conceptual analysis. But the unqualified conceptual analysis raises a claim to universality, and in a rather univocal way, as I argued in Chapters 1 and 4. So the question is whether conventionalism can see this task through. The only argument available to conventionalist positivism would be that conventions for the recognition of the law are the only necessary and sufficient condition for the emergence of the legal as an autonomous practice. Every time we have a convention in relation to the legal, there will be law, and every time there is law, there will be such a convention. This is unconvincing on two grounds. Firstly, it is counterfactual. It flies in the face of the fact that legal language, that is, somehow and to a certain extent differentiated normative language, has developed despite the absence of such explicit conventions. Examples to that effect abound both in historical and contemporary contexts. Therefore, conventionalism will have to concede that it has already parted ways with careful, attentive linguistic analysis. Alternatively, and this is even more of a contradiction on conventionalism's part, it will have to admit that it describes either modern legal systems, which developed in specific historical environments, or *good* legal systems, which are able to co-ordinate action in an objective, thus fair, way.[1]

A second, interconnected problem is that explaining the law in terms of conventions stops short of what may really lie at the basis of the emergence of the legal. In other words, Hartian conventionalism never asks what exactly it is that allows the shared practices and institutions to arise in the first place. Even if we concede that conventions are indications of the existence of a legal system, the prior question that needs to be asked concerns the conditions of possibility of emergence of these conventions. This, in turn, leads to the conditions of possibility of the differentiation of the legal and its institutionalization as an autonomous practice. In other words, law must have a deeper structure than just being attributed to a contingent, albeit historically embedded, decision. And this deeper structure cannot be purely normative. If it were, that is, if, say, common law systems were grounded in the moral commitment to the authority of the wise judge and civil law countries to the public identifiability of the law in comprehensive codes, then the boundaries between law and morality would collapse. This would not simply be an internal contradiction of conventionalist positivism but also, and more importantly,

1 Stephen Perry makes this point (Perry 2001). Note that this is only one step away from Fuller's 'inner morality of law' (Fuller 1964).

it would run counter to the intuition that the law is somehow contextually situated and that the law arises from the close interplay between empirical reality and normativity. And, although conventionalist positivism seems to be informed by this insight, it fails to go to the very roots of it.

The problem is addressed, I suggest, if we accept that what underlies the practice of law are the tacit shared normative experiences which constitute the dimensions of the legal. The undiscussed, tacit commitment to their common normative experiences can explain the co-ordination of action as well as the construction of institutionalized legal discourse on that basis. This commitment is not guided by a pre-existing rule and it does not give rise to any other rule. However, it is a commitment in the sense that it is part of how the participants understand themselves as individuals, as well as in their collectivity in the world. It is also a commitment to their ability to transform and stabilize the real, situated world normatively. And recognizing that this empirical reality simply qualifies and predicates normativity and thus makes it specifically legal without treating them as synonymous, means that the pitfall of reductionism is avoided.

To explain this a little further: the assumption of shared normative experiences is not empirical, in the sense that it does not consist simply in observations of facts in the world. The participants in legal discourse do not form an external knowledge of those experiences. If this were not the case, a number of problems would arise. Firstly, it would still be possible to look for further sets of assumptions that underpin those. In other words, they would be cognitively falsifiable or ascertainable and thus reducible to other statements about facts. Secondly, if the claim were that they are empirical, the argument would be reductive. How can the norms at play in legal discourse be reduced to facts? This would surely amount to committing the fallacy of collapsing the descriptive and the normative. At the same time, they are not *purely* normative either. Although, as I have already argued, they conform with and are answerable to a universal normative order, they themselves are the product of the combination of normativity with experienced reality.

In exactly the same way that my suggestion does not raise a claim to transcendental validity, it also does not raise a strong claim to truth. As I made clear in the previous chapters, my intention is to provide a hypothesis as to what may be what underpins the legal phenomenon, which will inform, or perhaps even kickstart, a self-reflexive interperspectival discourse on the ontological and normative contours of normativity. To be sure, this hypothesis is grounded in the intuition that the legal, in the sense of contextualized normativity on the basis of shared experiences of a community of people, is indeed marked by universality and diachronicity. Whether this is indeed the case or whether the content of those presuppositions is what I suggest they are or not, is a matter that can only be discussed (and perhaps never settled) in legal theoretical discourse, as I described in Chapter 4. Indeed, legal theory is the *only* forum for such a discussion, as these beliefs, which are foundational of legality, cannot be problematized from within the law itself, because they set the latter's institutional contours, which in turn set the boundaries of meaningful communication. In other words, thematizing them from within a legal framework would amount paradoxically to questioning the very existence or parameters of a language game from within that language game itself. This may be possible in cases of legal commitments marked by procedural flexibility and self-reflexivity, where it is easier for small revolutionary moments to transform the character of the game without any systemic resistance by the latter. However, it can certainly not be the case in closed systems of legality such as State law, which organize their operations around coherence and systematicity.

A Detour: Normativity, Law, Morality

I will now make a brief detour and turn to a point on which, as I have announced from the beginning, I will not say much, because it goes beyond the scope of this book. Although I hint at the connection between law and its normative environment, I cannot delve into exactly how this connection is possible. The primary aim of the book is to take a new tack on explaining how legal thought becomes possible in a way that will go beyond the necessary connection between the law and the State and the disjunction between the philosophical and the socio-theoretical study of the law. At the same time, though, it is informed by the underlying idea that law and morality cannot but be interconnected to an extent, which is also what makes critical, normative communication between various *nomoi* meaningful. In the following I shall briefly explain what I envisage the point of connection to be.

The dual aim of positivism is to account for legal normativity while at the same time maintaining the epistemic or ontological separation of law and morality. There is something counterintuitive about this claim, though, and this becomes obvious in instances of stress, when there seems to be a genuine conflict between law and other normative orders. Cases of principled disobedience to the law are such paradigmatic instances. In such cases, positivism would have to concede that the law can be judged to be morally unsound but this does not take anything away from its legality. But what is already built in legality is the sense of obligation. So, the very concept of normativity is radically fragmented, leaving the agent helpless as to what she should do. The onus of proof regarding this radical fragmentation of normativity and obligation lies firmly with those who raise the argument.

In order to substantiate this intuition I would argue with Alexy and his correctness thesis, which purports to prove the impossibility of breaking down normativity in that manner. The crux of the correctness thesis is this: every law raises a claim to correctness and this provides the link between law and morality. Alexy uses two examples to substantiate the claim. First, the imaginary example of a constitution, which declares that 'X is a sovereign, federal and unjust republic'. From the outset, there is a striking absurdity in both these utterances, argues Alexy. This absurdity is not simply a moral defect, in the same way that one would be prepared to deem a constitution morally unsound, if it explicitly excluded people of a certain race from the law. Such a constitution would have been substantively unjust but, at the same time, it would still be classifiable as a constitution. Neither is it simply a conventional defect, in the sense that the constitution does not abide by some general conventions. The absurdity at play here can only be conceptual and it can be explained with reference to speech acts. A condition of the felicity of the constitutional clause is that it is directed towards achieving justice in whatever way justice may be conceived. Therefore, in refuting its character as such, a performative contradiction is being committed. In the second example, a judge decrees that 'the accused is sentenced to life imprisonment, which is wrong' in the sense that the decision is grounded in incorrect interpretation of current law. Again, the claim implicitly raised by the judge as a participant in the legal system is that her decisions result from a correct interpretation of the law, a claim which is explicitly contradicted by her in the decision.

To use a real example: in 2002 the House of Lords dismissed Diane Pretty's request to commit suicide assisted by her husband.[2] In response to her initial request to the Director of Public Prosecutions, the latter said: 'Whilst I believe that I have no choice but to refuse your request, I deeply regret any further suffering that this refusal may cause.'[3] Lords Steyn and Hope seemed to be adopting this kind of rhetoric by saying explicitly in their opinions this was a very sad and unfortunate case and that Diane Pretty's suffering was enormous. However, after discussing at length issues concerning the Suicide Act 1961, the Human Rights Act 1998 and the European Convention of Human Rights, as well as employing consequentialist arguments from public order, they dismissed her appeal. The central question here is whether and how it is possible to reconcile the rhetoric of empathy with the unfavourable decision. One way would be to divorce questions of emotion from practical questions. But this does not seem to have happened in Pretty's case and, even if it did, their Lordships would have had to try very hard in order to convince us that feelings of regret had nothing to do with the rightness or wrongness of their decision. What seems to me to be surfacing in their speeches is an intuition that what they are deciding is ultimately morally wrong, albeit legally correct. But by implicitly waving the '*dura lex, sed lex*' flag, they already commit a performative contradiction by fragmenting the notion of rightness and giving it two contradictory and mutually exclusive contents. To the extent that the law and morality both concern practical questions, they can only exist in an uninterrupted continuum as far as the rightness of decisions is concerned.

But so far, there is nothing that a positivist could not happily accept. Indeed, Raz argues against Alexy that the claim to correctness is nothing but a requirement of any kind of purposeful, intentional action (Raz 2007). All such action, and not just legal action, is subject to certain standards of correctness. Viewing the claim to correctness as a necessary requirement of intentional action, though, and not something specific to the law, recasts it as formal and, therefore, neutral. In other words, the fact that a claim to correctness is raised cannot in itself specify the

2 <http://news.bbc.co.uk/1/hi/health/1682321.stm> (last accessed 17 July 2008).

3 The Queen on the Application of Mrs Diane Pretty v. Director of Public Prosecutions and Secretary of State for the Home Department [2001] UKHL 61.

standards to be applied in order for that claim to be satisfied. Even a group of bandits can establish its own criteria of correctness for assessing their actions. Case, then, not proven.

Alexy rebuts this objection by resorting to three arguments. First, he argues that the claim to correctness raised in the law is not akin to that raised by a gang of bandits in that *it is accompanied by a claim to objectivity*. The imaginary constitution or judge in the examples mentioned above do not claim that their utterances are correct just for themselves, because these claims are true to their own personal preferences for a good life or some such subjective reason. Those claims are objective in that they must be addressed and be acceptable by all. But this argument would again not perturb positivists, who would argue that the cohort of addressees of the claim comprises those who have the participant's perspective in a particular legal system. In response, Alexy employs two further arguments (Alexy 2002b). The law, he tells us, is about issues of distribution and balance. Such questions are necessarily questions of justice. Therefore, justice becomes the yardstick, which the claim to correctness is assessed against. All this is corroborated by a further two arguments: the argument from injustice and the argument from principles. Very briefly, and I shall explain in due course why I do not devote more time to these arguments, the argument from injustice is based on the formula which Radbruch developed as a response to the paradox of calling law such a profoundly morally unsound legal system as the Nazi one: where there is grave injustice, there is no law. According to the argument from principles, which is not all that different from Dworkin's distinction between rules and principles, principles are 'optimization requirements' and, as such, they form the point of entry, so to speak, of morality into the law.

I said I do not insist on Alexy's further two arguments, because I do not consider them necessary in order for the success of the correctness argument to be established. In order to show that there is no necessary connection between law and morality, one will have to show that correctness is somehow fragmented in different, incommensurable kinds, so as to make external critique of standards of correctness fruitless precisely *because* it is external and can never be anything more than that. Thus, the gang of bandits can only be criticized as wrong from the external perspective without it being possible to show that there is something inherently problematic with the very practice of judging in their specific manner. This runs counter to the fundamental intuition that standards of rightness are universal and uniform at least on a certain level, an intuition which informs the universal claims we raise at least some of the time. Furthermore, it presupposes an understanding of humanity as an aggregate of self-interested individuals who, far from avoiding and regretting separation and conflict, invite and thrive on it. This, however, is both an inaccurate and undesirable picture of humanity.

A convincing attempt to ground the uniformity of prescriptive language and the subsequent necessary connection between law and morality is made by George Pavlakos. The argument's basic philosophical premise is that, in the attempt to reconcile objectivity with normativity, a third way is available between mentalism or representationalism and referential realism. In the context of legal theory, the former would refer to conventionalism and the latter to essentialism of all varieties. The problem with representationalism is that it cannot account for a large range of linguistic symbols, from unicorns to abstract concepts, and the latter sooner or later slips into indeterminacy. Pavlakos argues for a *Practice Theory of Law*, according to which 'legal facts can be known objectively, if we conceive of legal practices as a normative activity of making assertions (judging)' (Pavlakos 2007a, 2). At the basis of the practice theory of law lies what Pavlakos terms the philosophy of 'pragmatic rationalism'. Pragmatic rationalism provides an alternative to representationalism and referential realism in that it departs from the approach to objectivity as the distance between mind and world and substitutes this with intelligibility as the link between thought and environment. In order to establish the conditions of intelligibility, Pavlakos turns to *grammar*, as the rule-governed structure of language, which makes possible not only communication but in fact *any* attempt of capturing the world. Grammar is seen as consisting not only in static rules of semantics and logic but also as a practice sensitive to particular domains and facts therein, which function as reasons against which the truth of sentences is assessed. This requires that pragmatic rules connected to the specific purposes pursued in a domain be included in the practice of grammar. Thus the latter becomes flexible enough as to be sensitive to the context and, at the same time, guaranteeing objectivity *qua* intelligibility. Very importantly, viewing grammar as a practice of rule-following directed towards knowledge paints an image of agents as capable of rational judgment, capable of handling and applying reasons.

In this last point Pavlakos echoes Christine Korsgaard whose argument kicks off from the premise that the reflective structure of our consciousness accounts for the fact that we require reasons for acting (as opposed to acting spasmodically, simply responding to impulses or desires) and we form and need conceptions of the right (Korsgaard 1996). This practical conception of ourselves is what makes possible all normativity. Our endorsement of any practical identity, from which obligations will stem, is directly linked to the endorsement of our identity as reflecting subjects. This is not merely a formalistic empty shell. Our identity as members of humanity, of the Kingdom of Ends to employ Kantian terminology, itself gives rise to certain obligations, as do all practical identities. This time, though, it is not only an inescapable identity, because it is a prerequisite for all others, but it also sets the outer limits of all other obligations. In other words, some obligations stem from our humanity and it is precisely by virtue of this that such obligations cannot be side-stepped because of our membership of other communities. Which ones or how many of these obligations there may be is a different, open question. But even if, as I maintained in Chapter 3, this universal morality is only very thin and limited, it can still provide the common vocabulary of ethical possibility and thus serve as a common point of reference of critical, self-reflexive interperspectival dialogue.

Even with this rough sketch of Korsgaard's and Pavlakos' arguments, it becomes, I hope, obvious that the positivist assumption that various normative orders are of a different kind and that they do not communicate in any way and on any level is wrong. Not only are all instances of normativity and practical identities formally traceable back to our reflective consciousness, but they are also subject to a set of moral standards stemming from our membership of humanity. The positivist project was, in this respect, misguided from the outset and, unfortunately, it misled the whole of legal theory and, as I argued in Chapter 1, it self-defeatingly disarmed itself as a critical theory of law by excluding the very possibility of meaningful critique from the remit of legal theory.

Klaus Günther arrives at a similar conclusion, albeit following a different route (Günther 2001). His point of departure is that legal pluralism is a fact that must be taken seriously. To support this claim, he focuses on recently emerged transnational bodies such as the WTO, the IMF and various NGOs. On Günther's analysis, these bodies have become *de facto* legislators and, in some cases, they even emulate State-centred legal systems by setting up adjudicative and enforcement agencies. He then proceeds in a constructivist fashion and observes that all these essentially legal orders do communicate with each other on a certain common ground. Moreover, this common ground can be discerned from the way Western, but not only Western, legal systems have evolved. Günther terms this common ground *the universal code of legality* and concludes that it may be possible to divorce the concept of law from the State, but it is not possible to disengage it from this universal code which would include democratic self-determination and a basic list of human rights at the very least.

My conclusion is similar to Günther's, although there are two points of disagreement that I ought to stress. First, much as the convergence of various legal orders to some basic values or norms is indicative of common moral ground, the latter ought to be discovered and established in an *a priori* manner, which would exclude the contingent particularities of specific legal orders – particularities which do not necessarily belong to the universal description of the legal. Secondly, the way that Günther fleshes out the universal code of legality seems too thick and determinative. As I have already argued, in order to reconcile emancipation and regulation, diversity and order, the commonalities between non State-bound legal orders must be discerned in the light of practical reason's conditions of possibility *and* through interperspectival, self-reflective, critical dialogue.

The Specificity of the Legal: Determinacy and Autonomy

So, to return to the central theme of this chapter, I consider the biggest challenge for legal theory to be explaining and dealing with the specificity of legality rather than accounting (or not) for the connection between the law and morality. This concerns, first, the determinacy of norms in singular situations and, secondly, the institutionalization and autonomization of the legal. And I believe that understanding the law in terms of shared normative experiences helps us tackle both aspects of the question.

The problem of determinacy was picked up by Klaus Günther, who argued, against Alexy, that the *Sonderfallthese* insufficiently accounts for how legal norms determine singular situations (Günther 1993a, 1993b). Günther correctly points out that general moral norms can conflict with each other, thus making impossible their concretization in specific situations in a way that will do justice to the particular circumstances. Both the rigid application of a norm (for example, do not lie, even if this will result in an innocent person losing his life) or the selective one (for example, applying one norm without considering other relevant but conflicting ones, thus hiding behind their rigidity and indeterminacy) cannot do justice to particular situations. Günther thus counter-proposes that the law be seen as an application discourse rather than a justification one concerning the validity of the relevant norms. Application discourses start from the concrete situations with a thorough examination of the facts of the situation in hand with regard to all the relevant norms. In the next step, a singular normative proposition is formed and justified, thus deciding the given case. The institutional constraints present in the application discourse minimize the space of the discursively possible in the sense that they limit the horizon of reasons that can be used in determining the outcome of the process. Habermas has endorsed Günther's idea of application discourses while, at the same time, insisting that justification discourse take place in the realm of democratic deliberative politics. For Habermas it is only the latter that can guarantee that the rules of discourse will be observed and that the norms available in institutionalized law will enjoy legitimacy (Habermas 1996). This also introduces procedural and substantive constraints to the creative, discretionary input of the judge, who will then act as the universal audience, which transforms the strategic action of the parties in a dispute into an instance of rational discourse.

As a constructivist account of current institutional frameworks and conceptions of the law, this may be a useful one, not least because, in removing from the judges the task of justification, it partly departs from the approach to the law (and legal theory) as an expert culture. At the same time its critical potential is severely tempered by its over-reliance on the assumption that procedural constraints to the subjectivity of actors in legal institutions enjoy democratic legitimation and that the existence of these constraints alone guarantees the democratic application of legal norms. But, more crucially for my purposes in this book, the main shortcoming of viewing the law as an application discourse is that it still presupposes the radical separation of legal normativity from reality, thus not explicating convincingly what makes the application of norms to real contexts possible at all. In other words, what is that elusive element allowing the complete description of a singular situation *in the light of legal norms*, thus allowing the transition from the norm to a positive act in a determinate manner raising claims to appropriateness, if not rightness?

The second, interconnected, aspect of the question of the specificity of the legal has to do with the autonomization of the latter as a normative order. To return to Kelsen, although he insightfully perceived the need for something non-conventional, non-empirical lending the category of legality its autonomy, he failed to specify what exactly this may be in its specificity. Take, for example, how

Kelsen deals with cases of transformation of the content of the *Grundnorm* in the first version of the *RR:*

> A band of revolutionaries stages a violent coup d'etat in a monarchy, attempting to oust the legitimate rulers and to replace the monarchy with a republican form of government. If the revolutionaries succeed, the old system ceases to be effective, and the new system becomes effective, because the actual behaviour of the human beings for whom the system claims to be valid corresponds no longer to the old system but, by and large, to the new system. [...] One presupposes a new basic norm, no longer the basic norm delegating lawmaking authority to the monarch, but a basic norm delegating authority to the revolutionary government. (Kelsen 1992, §30, 59)

Although he pays lip service to the distinction between the *Grundnorm* and its content, Kelsen does not consistently adhere to it. In the above excerpt, for instance, he clearly suggests that the new, post-revolution regime establishes a *new* basic norm. This, however, is tantamount to accepting that there is nothing transcendental about the *Grundnorm* on any level and that it can only exist and be determined in specific contexts. Thus Kelsen implicitly and in a rather roundabout way accepts the charge of verificationism, as his analysis implies this: 'Look at cases of people starting from scratch. They form a new legal system and through it runs the same thread: imputation and the *Grundnorm*. Clearly, coherent, valid law is happening. Therefore it is *possible* for it to happen.' But this is a trivial point and, in any case, there is nothing transcendental about it. As Heidemann puts it, it is merely a 'contestable metatheoretical presuppositional analysis of existing legal dogmatics' (Heidemann 2004, 376). Otherwise, he would have to defend the absurd argument that some people have the gift of cognizing the law in a transcendental way and others do not.

At the same time, Kelsen seems to be forced to admit that what the *Grundnorm* really refers to is the legitimacy of the political government and that its content ultimately depends on the acceptance of the people in the community. But this effectively amounts to conceding that the law's normativity essentially depends on a fact, namely the social fact of the general acceptance that law is what can be referred back to a particular source. Kelsen himself was not content with this conclusion and he was fully conscious of the fact that it conceded too much to empiricist legal positivism. Grappling with it, he tried to address it by referring to international law as the ultimate stage, on which the *Grundnorm* is determined. Even when there is a radical change in a municipal legal system, public international law is there in order to guarantee a higher level *Grundnorm*, which will lend municipal legal systems their validity.

Having vehemently rejected empiricism, the only possible interpretation of Kelsen's anxiety to reserve such a role for international law is that the category of legality is universal and transcendental but also needs to be concretized in specific contexts. As Paulson puts it:

> Just as Kant's categories require, for their application, a schematization by means of space and time, so likewise the category of imputation requires, for its application, a schematization. In the legal context, too, the schematization calls for spatial (or jurisdictional) and temporal determinants. It is brought about, I suggest, by means of the presupposition associated with the basic norm. The basic norm specifies, as Kelsen states again and again, a *particular* legal system – one that exists at some particular time in some particular place. (Paulson 2001, 58)

It is not entirely clear that this is a very faithful reading of Kelsen but this matters very little. What does matter is this: imputation cannot be akin to the *a priori* categories that frame all experience; legal imputation must differ in *some* way to moral imputation; the law *is* indeed contextualized in the sense that the contingent differences between various legal systems do not seem to affect our general understanding of the law. For all these reasons, there must be something built in the very presupposition of imputation that determines its possible content to a certain degree. To put it differently, if imputation is the quasi-causal connection between material facts in norms, then there must be something incorporated in it which will pre-determine what will make possible this transition in a differentiated manner depending on the context.

I argue that understanding the law in terms of shared normative experiences of the participants in a community provides a solution both to the determinacy and the autonomy problem, although not in the language of transcendentalism any longer but rather in that of conceptual analysis. Starting with the former, the deeply embedded beliefs of participants concerning the possibility of translating norm into act and placing it in space and time make singular normative propositions determinate in that they are based on these shared normative experiences which are fixed and enjoy the status of quasi-truth due to the commitment of participants to them. To be sure, this truth is indexical to the institutionalized legal order and the determinacy is provisional. Its contextual nature means that it can be thematized even from within the institutionalized *nomos*, but only if the possibility of being responsive to stimuli from outside it has remained open. In other words, all *nomoi* must remain open to the interperspectival universal dialogue that is legal theory, so that the participants' normative experiences are constantly subject to the test of discursive universalization. Nevertheless, shared normative experiences explain how participants in a *nomos* feel able to take collective action on the basis of norms.

Regarding the problem of the autonomy of the legal, my suggestion concerning shared normative experiences bears a relation to the Kelsenian notion of imputation. However, there are two differences. First, as I showed earlier, imputation is not transcendental any longer, neither does it have to be shown that it is *necessarily true*. Secondly, imputation now acquires a content that is richer so as not only to differentiate itself from other kinds of possible imputation but also in that it already includes the conditions of its application and contextualization. However, it cannot be overemphasized that this content is specified in its details only once it enters a context and is fleshed out with the shared normative experiential input of participants. There is nothing *in* the idea that shared normative experiences underpin the law that can determine *how exactly* they will be applied in a specific context. All they refer to are the general conditions of applicability of norms and subsequently the boundaries of the legal. Thus, the problem of legal transition is solved because the focus is shifted from the question of why a source of law is accepted as such to the conditions that make law recognizable *qua* law in the first place. What matters is the shared background of normative experiences, against which legality develops.

Ubiquitous Law: The Space for Legal Pluralism

In this and the previous chapter I used examples from State law, and even more particularly the jurisdiction of England and Wales, in order to pursue the intuition that legality rests on shared normative experiences. This, it may be thought, directly contradicts the pluralistic rhetoric in the book. This is not the case at all. I hinted in Chapter 1, agreeing with Joseph Raz, that any conceptual analysis inevitably begins from home. There is no other way of accessing the world of normativity but from one's own experience of it. Nonetheless, this means neither that it is impossible to abstract and depart from that starting point in order to arrive at conclusions transcending the context nor that State legal discourse is actually a genuine instance of law. As I have already stated, what I am trying to do in this book is provide a *prima facie* sense of the law, which may serve as one of the starting points in an interperspectival dialogue concerning the concept of the legal. There is no claim to finality attached, as concepts are formed and reformed in social contexts alone through their experienced application. But the possibility of a universal sense of law, even a thin and indeterminate one, is possible, not least because of the possibility of engaging into such a universal discourse about the concept of law.

Furthermore, my use of State law examples does not mean that State law necessarily does justice to people's shared normative experience and is therefore a genuine instance of legality. On the contrary, as I shall try to show in the next chapter, State law is characteristically blind to that necessary bedrock of legality. Legal language is, however, unique and uniform and, therefore, inescapable, when a claim to legality is raised, as is the case in State law. This is why it served as an example which will enable us to discern the formal requirements of legality. Whether State law really is law in the sense that it supervenes on some shared normative experiences or whether it is an empty ideological construct is not a question that can be answered on this level. As I argued in Chapter 4, such an enquiry requires interperspectival, empirical work. It may well turn out that *some* State legal systems or some *portions* of them are indeed genuine laws whereas others are not. What is crucial is that they are not legal *because* of their association with the State or any other formally identified source. At the same time, the distinction between the formal and the substantive meanings of law is cancelled out, not by dismissing the need for conceptual analysis (in the manner of interpretivism) but rather because the concept of law and conceptual analysis become substantive, dynamic and contingent on the conditions of existence of a community. Discovering how normative experiences come to be formed, developed, shared and applied, and, consequently, what the content of specific instances of legality is, is a matter of empirical, interperspectival, sociological, anthropological, historical analysis, the success of which depends on how well it engages with legal communities and their self-understanding, as well as on how seriously it takes self-reflection and self-critique.

There is one more thing that needs to be clarified. Throughout this book I have been speaking of linguistic and legal *communities*. This, however, does not amount to raising a strong claim concerning the ontological and normative role of communities. The concept of the community is typically understood as all-encompassing and determining both the social make-up of the members of the community as well as the normative criteria of inclusion and exclusion. Such a robust ontological and normative approach to the community can only take us back to the irresolvable tension between individualist liberalism and communitarian theories of politics and law. The understanding of the law in terms of shared normative commitments avoids this pitfall because neither does it presuppose the systematicity and coherence of law, nor does it view the law as necessarily co-extant with a uniform community enjoying priority over its members. People's shared normative commitments may very well be piecemeal and refer not to all but only some of their experiences. Thus the law does not fully subsume the individual, and it therefore does not have to be seen as providing the ultimate authority, substituting agents in the exercise of their practical reason, as law and legal obligation depends not on *ex post fact acceptance* any longer but on common experience and authorship.

At the same time, the conception of the law in terms of shared normative experiences reflects the fragmentation of our identities and memberships. As part of the global condition, to use a neologism, not least through the proliferation of means and forms of communication all but cancelling the necessity of geographical proximity for communities to form, we belong to an ever-increasing number of communities, which do not necessarily demand exclusivity nor require us to forsake other commitments or memberships. Thus, national, religious, lifestyle and other 'identities' are reconciled with each other without putting any strain on the individual. Far from this being a triumph of insular individualism, it points to a healthy combination of the fact that we can only make sense of the world as reflecting, reasoning individuals but, at the same time, that we can only flourish through socialization and co-operation. Similarly, we should be prepared to view the law not as a coherent whole, as a 'seamless web', but rather as existing both in a micro and a macro level, albeit in relative conceptual clarity. To put it schematically, we should be prepared to see law both in the relation between bouncers and clubbers as well as the insular communities such as the Amish and the Mennonites described by Cover.

The argument has now come full circle. This book began with an exposition and assessment of various mainstream legal theories and theories of legal pluralism. In relation to the former, I argued that they err in being implicitly or explicitly, methodologically or substantively, tied up to the State as a necessary presupposition of legality. On the other hand, legal pluralistic theories have not been able to distinguish between legal and value pluralism, because they place too much or too little emphasis on empirical or conceptual analysis. As a result they are either helpful but not ambitious enough or inspirational but not sufficiently clear. My argument rests on the inescapable need to theorize the law, thus placing *some* emphasis on conceptual analysis. Empiricist-positivist theories of legal pluralism were therefore correct to try to identify legal orders by applying some criteria. At the same time, though, our conception of the law must be flexible enough to accommodate the diversity and fluidity which post-conventionalist theories of legal pluralism have correctly identified. Capturing this need, Boaventura de Sousa Santos urges us to turn to the *baroque*, the *South* and the *frontier*. We can do this by conceptualizing the law as distinct within its ontological environment while at the same time in a way that leaves the concretization of the concept up to those whose normative commitments constitute the law in the first place. This, I think, satisfies Desmond Manderson's 'legal chaotics', Margaret Davies' 'pluralistic ethos' and de Sousa Santos' 'legal subjectivities' without committing the same error of conceptual and normative vagueness.

True enough, under my argument the concept of law is significantly expanded. Legality can now be discovered everywhere. The law is then ubiquitous in two senses. First, no source can claim exclusivity over the law. Law can emerge just as suddenly and contingently as the people come to form shared normative experiences. The State is revealed not to be necessary for legality, although this does not, at the same time, necessarily mean that it is not useful for any other purpose. Secondly, the law becomes ubiquitous in that it engulfs our social presence. This may scare some. After all, the whole point of liberal and critical legal theory of the past few decades, if not longer, has been to shrink the law and liberate people from it rather than making it co-extant with all social action. Such fears would be unjustified. The ubiquity of the law is now counterbalanced by the fact that it no longer corresponds to the separation of addressor and addressee of duties, by and large a relationship of power. The law is now acknowledged to incorporate the lived commitments of its participants in a self-reflexive, critical way. This conception of legality in turn acknowledges that rule-following is not incidental but central in the human condition. Normativity *itself* is ubiquitous and human actions are never mere responses to physical stimuli or desires. They are always structured as critical judgments. The same is true of social action. Theorizing the law in terms of shared normative experiences is thus emancipatory because it can both reconcile us with the rule-following character of our co-existence and at the same time establish our dominion over it rather than the other way around. At the same time, the possibility of critique is maintained not only by drawing some conceptual boundaries for the law but, crucially, by building into the concept a universal, albeit thin, normative minimum stemming from the fact of the uniformity of normativity, which will serve as the axiological basis for self-reflection and discussion. Where this discussion can take place, though, is a different question. In this I agree with Günther Teubner that such discourse cannot happen from within State law as a system of action (see Chapter 2).

Conclusion

In this chapter I propose that the presuppositions underpinning the law be understood not as transcendentally true but rather as deeply embedded beliefs, in which norms are merged with fact. Thus our sense of the law will become sensitive both to the necessary continuity between morality and contextualized, institutionalized law as well as the conditions of possibility of existence of the law as an institutionalized normative order. Such a conceptualization of the law revolves around what I have termed *shared normative experiences*, that is the way normativity and beliefs about the world are merged in the common self-understanding of various communities.

Chapter 7
On the Chronology (and Topology) of the Legal

Introduction: A Methodological *Aporia*

The philosophical study of time must face up to a methodological *aporia* from the outset, the very *aporia* that made St Augustine famously concede his inability to define time explicitly, although he *felt* he knew what it was (St Augustine 1912). Equally famously, Wittgenstein explained Augustine's failure to grasp the meaning of time in terms of the use of a wrong language game. Augustine, Wittgenstein tells us, was mistakenly looking for an object the dimensions of which he was trying to define (Wittgenstein 1967). Similarly, Waismann felt that reference to time as a noun can be rather misleading:

> It is true, we can make a person understand the word 'time' by producing examples of its use: but what we cannot do is to present a fixed formula comprising as in a magic crystal the whole often so infinitely complicated and elusive meaning of the word. (Waismann 1968, 58)

But the task I set myself in this chapter is simpler and, in many ways, much more modest than trying to grasp the essence of time. I mentioned in passing in Chapter 5 that a rough parallel is to be drawn between the dimensions of shared normative experiences constitutive of the law and Kant's forms of intuitions of space and time. In other words, I would suggest that central to the sense of law is the temporalization and spatialization of shared normative commitments. In this chapter I will try to pursue this intuition and make a case for the careful enquiry into the normative significance of time and space as a way of gaining a better understanding of the legal itself.

Major legal philosophies generally avoid discussing the law's temporality explicitly, although they inevitably raise claims concerning the law's historicity. The common attitude is to treat the law as ontologically autonomous and belonging exclusively in the realm of practical reason, thus making questions of speculative reasoning, such as that of time, external and largely irrelevant in the discussion of the essence of the legal. At the same time, the few specific theories of law and its connection with time come closer to grasping the law's temporality rather than merely its historicity. I shall argue that, valuable as these latter approaches may be, they remain incomplete to the extent that they do not provide an account of what it is that lends coherence to these manifestations of time in the law and therefore they miss the integral link between conceptions of time with the law. Bringing this link to the fore will also enable us to discern the ways in which State law, with the corroboration of monist, centralist legal philosophy, silences and does violence to those other legal orders, partly by extending its *imperium* over alternative ways of perceiving normativity in time.

Finally, I will make an excursus on the law's topology, that is the inseparability of the law from normative conceptions of space. This time I shall make the case not by way of argument and counterargument, but rather by recounting a few stories which point to space as one of the dimensions of shared normative experiences which constitute the law.

The Need for a Richer Understanding of the Law–Time Relationship

The law is fraught with temporally significant norms. Examples can be drawn from various areas of law and, indeed, various legal systems: imminence in criminal law; the statute of limitations; usurpation over time; sentencing in time units. The question then is what to make of the legal significance of time.

Perhaps under the influence of the Humean disjunction of the *is* and the *ought*, the major and most influential contemporary legal philosophies tend to draw a sharp divide between the concept of law and conceptions of time. They locate the former firmly in the realm of practical reasoning and they reserve a place for the latter in theoretical, speculative reasoning. In other words, as a system of *ought* statements, the law gives statements of fact their normative meaning but does not depend on them for its existence. When legal norms regulate time, as in the examples I mentioned above, they merely ascribe normative texture to reality, as it is authoritatively described by theoretical, scientific discourses. So, according to those theories the concept of law can be grasped independently of the epistemological assumptions existing in parallel with the normative ones incorporated in the law.

To be sure, all these theories have something to say about the historicity of the law and how the law exists in time, depending on which historical moment they promote as the relevant one for the emergence of the law. For positivists situated in the Hartian tradition, that instant would be the moment at which the social practice embodied in the Rule of Recognition was consolidated, and for legal rules specifically, the moment of their formal enactment. In Kelsen's epistemic positivism the validity, that is, the mode of existence, of legal norms has a historical aspect in the sense that it has a specific duration, which is determined intrasystemically. Natural law theories as well as other legal philosophies that see the law in a continuum with morality do not offer a clear way in which ontologically to distinguish the law from its normative environment. Their concern is to emphasize the necessary connection of law with morality but, by doing so, they do not enlighten us as to why it is specific sets of norms and institutions that we call 'law' instead of others. While they draw some distinction, albeit a loose one, between 'human' or 'positive' law on the one hand and 'natural' or 'divine' law or morality on the other, we are none the wiser as to what the former may be. Thus it is more difficult to infer how exactly they place the law in history. The least that can be said is that legal normativity is not temporally co-extant with the convention, which a society may call positive 'law', whatever that may be.[1]

Despite the fact that it is peripheral to their overall project, a useful conclusion can be drawn from this treatment of the law's historicity by major legal philosophies. It appears that both positivistic and substantive legal theories adopt a very specific conception of time. They understand it as an entity observable in an objective way, as an object the ontology of which can be grasped definitively (for a similar argument, see Czarnota 2001). As far as *the form and structure* of time are concerned, it seems to be understood in terms of the distinction between past, present and future. History is the *flow* of events and facts through these three points in time (Schlessinger 1982; Levison 1986). This flow is linear and forward-facing (Newton-Smith 1986; 1980). The movement is from the past to the future in the way of the movement of an arrow. What was the future becomes the present and is finally stored in the infinite database of the past. They are experienced respectively as a bundle of aspirations, plans or hopes, current experience through our senses and, finally, as memories.[2] It is against this background that the law develops as a historical event.

Crucially, this conception of time is objectified and incorporated as an assumption in the law. Returning to my previous point, the law emerges as

1 Perhaps due to the influence of Dworkin's critique of Hartian jurisprudence, the debate soon turned to one concerning adjudication. Seen from the point of view of time, the question is whether legal reasons are to be found in the past or the present/future. In other words, whether judges *declare* or *create* law. The former option presupposes the use of principles as the foundation of legal reasoning and the latter is resigned to the fact of judicial discretion. For a discussion of that problem see Tur 2002. On the question of coherence and its temporal dimension, see MacCormick 1995; Postema 2004.

2 The analytical philosophical problems of this perception of time are endless. In large part the philosophy of time is concerned with the shortcomings of such a simplified and commonsensical epistemology of time. Most prominent amongst them is MacTaggart's claim that time is unreal (MacTaggart 1908). MacTaggart distinguished between two sequences with which we seem to be making sense of time. That of past-present and future (*A series*) and that of earlier and later relations between points in time (*B series*). On a first level he came to the analytical conclusion that time cannot exist without the presence of the A sequence. The predicates past-present-future are clearly incompatible, for nothing can be past-present and future at the same time. Nevertheless, MacTaggart points out, they are obviously attributed to the same event at a given time. Something (say an election) can be future, it becomes present and finally past. The alternative, which MacTaggart and other proponents of the thesis that time does not exist, have to offer is a different perception of temporal sequences. Namely, what is habitually referred to as the B sequence (as opposed to the A past-present-future sequence), according to which events are earlier or later in relation to each other. The opponents of MacTaggart's thesis that time does not actually exist, that is, the advocates of the A series, sought to find a way out of the paradox that he introduced. But by claiming that time actually exists they created, and therefore had to give solutions to, other problems about time, such as its directionality, its dimensionality, the question of causation and so on. See also Rankin 1981; Schlessinger 1983; Prior 1968; Mellor 1981.

a normative order which comes from above to regulate the objective world as described by the natural sciences. Thus, the *concept* of law can be described independently of any epistemological statements. Even when it is grasped with reference to a social practice, as is the case in Hartian jurisprudence, this social practice refers to what the relevant community of people perceive as obligatory and this alone. Thus we get no account of the conditions that give rise to that practice (to that I return later on in this chapter).

But this still leaves unexplained the numerous instances in which time is incorporated in legal language. There seems to be a coherent and consistent mode of making sense of time normatively or, seen from a different perspective, a way in which a commonly accepted perception of time determines the content of the law in a *necessary* manner.[3] If that were not the case, why and how the law is connected to conceptions of time would remain unexplained and wholly contingent. So, a suspicion persists that there is a special connection between *legal normativity* and time, and not simply the boundaries of existence of legal norms or the time interval that the pool of reasons admissible in legal reasoning occupies.[4]

Accounts of Law's Temporality

Time and Law Intertwined but Fragmented

Although the philosophy of time is rich and varied and time has also been theorized in relation to other concepts and phenomena both in the humanities and social sciences (see Sherover 1975; Gale 1968; Le Poidevin and MacBeath 1993; Teichmann 1995), there is not much in the legal philosophical literature by way of theorizing the connection between law and time. A reason for that is possibly the very fact that, as I argued above, the most prominent legal theories discuss the time–law relationship incidentally but nevertheless in a way that seems authoritative and conclusive. In any case, the result is a theorization of the specific connection between law and time, which is rather limited in volume.

---

3 An interesting study of the way the law structures time is Rakoff 2002. What I suggest, however, is different, namely not see how State law determines time but rather how perceptions of time help determine the law.

4 Kevät Nousiainen makes the same point: 'Problems of time are met everywhere in legal dogmatics. [...] A legal act, a crime and an act of judging all seem to presuppose a concept of time that involves the experience of the acting person.' He then goes on to discuss the distinction between objective and subjective time, the former being the linear conception of time, which, as I point out in this chapter, seems to be what the law bases its operations on, and the latter being time as experienced by legal actors. His thesis is that the law shows a tendency to take experienced time more seriously. He illustrates the argument with the example of battered women and the relevance of time-frames for the substantiation of self-defence (Nousiainen 1995).

One such theory was offered in 1955 by Gerhart Husserl. His *Recht und Zeit* is an attempt to systematize and organize the possible connections between time around three questions: How is the law placed in historical time? What is the intrinsic time-structure of legal objects? What are the time perspectives of the legislature, the executive and the judicature (G. Husserl 1955)?

The answer to the first question is a positivistic thesis about the possibility of the law having a concrete history. Not very unlike Kelsen, Husserl understands time as the past-present-future sequence, of which legal systems occupy a well-defined portion. Therefore, past, present and future in the law are understood in an intra-systemic way and do not refer to universal time in exactly the same way that the law does not depend on some extra-legal normativity. However, and this is the answer to the second question, legal concepts do not belong in the same historical time. They are part of an abstract, objective time and, therefore, are not synchronic with the actual behaviours to which they ascribe legal meaning (G. Husserl 1955, 31–2). Thirdly, Husserl distinguishes between past-orientated, future-orientated and present-orientated times, which are used respectively by the judge, the legislator and the executive.

More recently, Ost and van de Kerchove gave a systems-theoretical[5] account of the connection of law and time as part of their account of the systemic autonomy of the law (van de Kerchove and Ost 1993). Depending on the jurisgenerative sources of each legal system, the authors distinguish between respective temporalities (van de Kerchove and Ost 1993, 163). These times are:

1. The constitutional time of foundation. This refers back to the time of origin of the legal system, the one event that marked its emergence: a divine mandate, a revolution, a social contract.
2. The a-temporal time of doctrine:

> While [legal dogmatics] does not appeal explicitly to a fable or origin, it is none the less deployed in the form of an 'omnitemporal' presence designed to suggest the constant self-evidence of the principles appealed to and to shelter them from any historical context that could relativize their significance. (van de Kerchove and Ost 1993, 164).

3. The customary time of the *longue durée*, which refers to the historical development and determination of meaning of the law.
4. The Promethean time of legislation, the conscious voluntary time or law-following.
5. The time of case law or the 'cyclical time of alternation between advance and lag' (van de Kerchove and Ost 1993, 165).

5 In Luhmann's version of systems theory, time is understood not as a past-present-future sequence but rather as intra-systemic earlier-later relationships (see Luhmann 1995a).

Ost and the 'Contrat Temporel'

In 1999 Ost gave a more detailed and specific account of law and time in his *Le Temps du Droit*. There he speaks of the law as measure (*mesure*). A measure in the sense of it 'taking measures', determining public policy, but also a measure in that it sets evaluative standards, drawing the limits of correct action, of right and wrong. At the same time, it is a measure in the sense of the equilibrium, proportionality and prudence. Finally, the law is measure as temperance (*tempérament*):

> Dans son travail d'ajustement permanent, la mesure juridique est rythme – le rythme qui convient, l'harmonie de durées diversifiées, le choix du moment opportune, le tempo accordé á la marche du social. (Ost 1999, 334)

So the law sets the rhythm, the pace at which we organize the governance of our social actions, our existence in common. And this rhythm is set by the four temporalities of the law in their amalgamation: memory, pardon, promise and revision or reproblematization (*la remise en question*). Memory and pardon complement each other with the latter being the possibility of undoing the past (*delier le passé*) and being released from its burden and the former being what facilitates pardon in the first place, the sense of origin and institution, which gives rise to the sense of continuity. Reproblematization (*la remise en question*) expresses radical critique, which puts the act of promising, that is the act of normatively anticipating the future, in the right perspective by releasing it from the asphyxiating embrace of tradition. These four temporalities, Ost continues to argue, are merged in the present, the most elusive and enigmatic aspect of time. Echoing Ricoeur, Nietzsche, Benjamin, but also in a sense Derrida, Ost tells us that the present presents itself as force, an integrating and paradoxical force, in which everything is in the realm of the possible and the not-yet.

And then Ost makes a remarkable point, expressing an intuition or the beginning of a new project, which is yet to begin, and which I shall use as one of the points of departure for the rest of my analysis in this chapter. In discussing responsibility as the third movement of the interlude, as he calls the closing chapter of the book, he writes:

> Plutôt cependant que de mobiliser la catégorie éthico-juridique de responsabilité, n'aurait-on pu, demandera-t-on peut-être, utiliser celle du contrat, et envisager les rapports du droit et du temps sous les modalités de la convention? *Le contrat temporel*, tel aurait pu être le titre de cet ouvrage. Apres le *contrat social*, qui scelle les rapports politiques entre les hommes, après le *Contrat naturel* de M. Serres qui établit les rapports écologiques entre les sociétés et la nature, pourquoi pas le contrat temporel pour dire les rapports juridiques entre les hommes et le temps? (Ost 1999, 339)

Ost quickly goes on to explain why he did not entitle his work *The Temporal Contract*. The contract, it seemed to him, is bound to the instant, it is too momentary to capture the diachronicity of ethical responsibility. And it is this cross-temporality of ethics based on the cross-temporality of humanity, as opposed to the finitude of the individual, and the subsequent intergenerational character of responsibility and justice that Ost thinks is important to recover and take seriously.

I find the idea of the temporal contract fascinating and promising, albeit in need of qualification. But allow me to suspend the discussion of why this extract is of particular importance until after I have made some critical remarks on Husserl's and Ost's accounts of the link between law and time.

The Need for a Unifying Theme

The value in the way Husserl and Ost approach the connection between law and time lies in that they come closer to explaining the intuition that the law's normativity is determined necessarily by a specific perception of time. However, two shortcomings need to be addressed.

First, in both accounts the concept of time as well as that of the law seem to be fragmented in a way that potentially strips them of their exegetic and operative value. Husserl, Ost and van de Kerchove try to combine all the possible *prima facie* temporal perspectives of the law, thus losing sight of the fact that doing so necessarily results in our inability to say anything meaningful and coherent about either the concept of law or the conception of time that legal normativity reveals. If the law comprises all these temporal vantage points, there must be something lending them coherence. It is this elusive element of cohesion that will explain how synchronization in law is possible despite all those different temporal orientations. By themselves each of these viewpoints can be useful as tools for the sociological or even psychological study of legal actors and a specific, context-bound State legal system. It is, indeed, useful to wonder how legislators or judges perceive of time or what perceptions of history and historical information are incorporated in the law. However, this does not reveal anything about the law itself and how it is connected to time.

Ost seems to acknowledge this need for integration, which is why he persistently argues that the four temporalities of the law are merged (*melangées*) and it is through their interconnections and the forceful integrative mediation of the present that the law emerges and forms the horizon of possibility. But it is only in the interlude of his *Le Temps du Droit* that he expresses the intuition of the *contrat temporel*, which could explain how memory, pardon, promise and revision can be merged and how they can form the *melange*, which constitutes the legal. Ost seems to abandon the notion of the *contrat temporel* and prefers to merge law and ethics by implying that intergenerational justice may be achieved through the law. And this is unfortunate because the notion of the contract comes close to capturing the law as the instantiation of normative commitments in view of people's experiences. Therefore an idea such as a contract potentially explains the differentiation of the law from other normative orders. Because there is nothing else that can make these four temporalities specifically legal, nothing that can show that memory, pardon, promise and revision are not part of the temporality of *any* ethical order apart from their connection to the specific form of socialization that marks the differentiation of the law from other normative orders and at the same time its connection to the general, thinner ethical order. This is precisely what the *contrat temporel* hints at: that there is a bedrock, some sort of common ethical and epistemological understanding underlying the legal, of which the *contrat temporel* is one aspect, complemented by other similar *contrats* referring to various aspects of the possibility of being bound by law in common. It is the aggregate of those *contrats* (and it should again be noted that I am using Ost's term provisionally, because as I shall show in the next part of this chapter that they cannot be contracts in the strict sense of an exchange of promises based on the freedom of will) that lies at the heart of the concept of the law.

Secondly, and this point is related to the previous one, those specific theories of law and time seem to be just as bound to State law as the major legal theories that I discussed earlier. The temporalities of memory, pardon, promise and revision, as well as the links between law and time that Husserl singles out, can then be interpreted as just another aspect of orthodox accounts of Western State legal systems as we know them. But if left there, if the argument is simply a retrospective or constructivist reading of State law, then not only is there very little differentiating it from a conventionalist or a social contractarian account of the law, but it can also very easily be hijacked in order to serve State law's false claims to legitimacy. Simply by virtue of it existing in some way, State law can then claim genuinely to incorporate not only some sort of imaginary collective concerning the normative constitution of the community but also all the convictions and commitments of its participants and synthesize them in a coherent and objectively correct whole. Thus State law will be allowed to expand its *imperium* and spread its violence even further.

So the intuition of the *contrat temporel* needs to be refined so that it be placed at the very heart of the legal as one of its constitutive elements and gain priority in the enquiry into the legal over the fact of inscription, which fixes meaning and distances it from participants' self-understanding. In other words, it needs to be recognized that conceptions of temporality and their normative significance are prior to the law, rather than being post-phenomena which can be observed, interpreted and determined in the light of a legal meaning purportedly developing in isolation in the world of pure practical reason. Then we will be able to form a much richer and more critical understanding of the law.

On the Chronology of the Legal

So far I have shown that the major legal philosophies as well as those few specific theories of law and time largely fail to give an account of the necessary connection of the concept of law with time. I then went on to give an account of the way in which I propose we should theorize the legal, namely in terms of shared normative experience of participants in a legal discourse, that is, their shared but tacit way of understanding the world and the possibility of transforming it normatively. In this part, I would like to pursue further the idea that the normative experience of time is one of those elements that form the boundaries of a specific legal order and account for its differentiation from its normative environment.

In one way or another, and however we decide to theorize it, we exist in time. At the very least, this means that we draw connections between events, which we access with our senses, and those that we cannot experience in that way yet or any longer. Our language is by and large tensed even if only in the very weak sense of including certain indices that draw the distinction between the intuitive categories of past, present and future.[6] And this is how we intuit change as well, irrespective of whether it makes more analytical sense to understand change in terms of time or time in terms of change. There is also no doubt that the concept of time itself, if there is such an autonomous concept, differs to the way we *experience* it. This discrepancy can be and has been explained in a variety of ways, which are not always compatible with each other, covering a wide range of theories of consciousness. Kant explained the unity of consciousness and the meaningfulness of representations in terms of the connections between events that are brought together into a whole with the agent's transcendental imagination (Kant 1998; Lloyd 1993). Phenomenology explained time only through perceptions and the *a priori* rules governing them (E. Husserl 1991). Lévinas explained time fully relationally with reference to the Other (Lévinas 1987). In Freudian psychoanalytic theory there is a wealth of ways in which time has been theorized, ranging from the timelessness of the unconscious to the temporal multidirectionality of dreams and primal phantasies (Green 2002). All this does not necessarily prove the 'unreality' of time, nor does it constitute an extreme fragmentation and relativization of the concept of time. It merely proves that the perception of time is *one* of the constitutive factors of the consciousness of the agent or the identity of a social system.

It is along similar lines that my analysis moves, but I approach the issue from a specifically legal philosophical point of view. I have already shown by way of a general analysis of the foundations of the legal that each legal community develops a specific way of envisaging itself in the world in general. Legal communities create *nomoi*, which are the result of the interplay of their normative bonds and their collective intuitions about the world, that is, what I have called the shared normative experience of the participants in those communities. This idea can now be specified in relation to time. The law's chronology refers to the assumption shared by the participants in those legal communities of the possibility to grasp and control time, to synchronize the imaginary temporality of the normative world with the time of the real world. Not only is this a shared and tacit assumption as

6 It should be noted here that the debate on time and tense is rather complicated and directly related to the A- and B-series theories.

to the nature, form and structure of time and the way it determines or, at least, affects the ontology of the community, but also an assumption as to the way that normativity is placed in time.

The law's chronology refers firstly to the ability to define the temporal limits of the (legal) community. The constitutive instance of jurisgenesis, as Cover described it, or Ost's Promethean time, are not merely the placement of a legal community in time as a continuous sequence of events. The temporal parameters of a jurisgenerative instant are constitutive of the law in a much more substantive and pervasive way. The emergence of a legal order is not simply a historical event. It marks the consolidation of the participants' shared understanding of the normative maintenance of the historicity of their links and the merging of that with the teleology of their existence in common, their shared aspirations and their aims. Imagery of genesis, evolution and demise, metaphors of parenthood (the Motherland, the Founding Fathers), images of birth and death of a community signify the, again metaphoric, emergence of a new consciousness as well as a new sub-conscious, one which is social, shared, but is still determined by its experience of time, whichever content we decide to give it.[7]

But the chronology of the legal is also manifested within norms themselves. Let me explain this by using examples drawn from law, as we know it, that is from State sanctioned law irrespective of the particular jurisdiction. As I explained in Chapter 6, my use of examples from State law squares with my thesis from legal pluralism for three reasons. First, as I have already repeatedly said in this book, the best place to start from is intuitions available at home. Secondly, State law provides a *prima facie* legal order, in the sense that it claims to comprise rules instantiating the idea of rightness in a particular community even if it may turn out that it does not do so in a genuine manner. Secondly, showing that the law of the State misrepresents its jurisgenerative instance, it allows itself to raise an unwarranted claim to universality, thus even collapsing the boundaries between the legal and the moral. Thus, it commits the violence of silencing other legalities, as Cover so insightfully pointed out.

Let us use an example from English jurisprudence with implications both for tort law and legal philosophy, namely *McLoughlin v. O'Brian*,[8] a case used by Dworkin too to illustrate his theory of law-as-integrity (Dworkin 1986). The facts of the case are these: Mrs McLoughlin's husband and three children were involved in a road accident at about 4 pm on 19 October 1973, when their car collided with a lorry driven by one of the defendants. Mrs McLoughlin's youngest daughter was killed in the collision, while her husband and other children suffered severe injuries and were taken to hospital. The claimant learned about the accident and saw her family two hours later, when she was notified about it by a neighbour. The same neighbour also drove her to hospital. She alleged that the impact of what she heard and saw caused her severe shock resulting in psychiatric illness. The court of first instance

7 For the significance of metaphor in law, see Winter 2001.

8 [1983] 1 AC 410 [HL]

found that the defendants did not owe a duty to care to Mrs McLoughlin, as the temporal interval between the accident and her gaining knowledge of it made the psychological harm inflicted on her unforeseeable. The Court of Appeal dismissed Mrs McLoughlin's appeal but on different grounds. They held that, although it was foreseeable that the claimant would be psychologically harmed (it as, after all, her husband and children that were injured and of course she would rush to hospital to see them), the consequences of upholding the appeal would open the floodgates and broaden the scope of compensation for psychological injury far too much. The claimant appealed to the House of Lords. One of the problems that all the courts had to tackle was that in all previous cases bearing a similarity to the one at hand, the claimant was either present at the scene of the accident or went there immediately after. In Mrs McLoughlin's case, how could the foreseeability of the injury and the justification of damages after a two-hour delay be established?

Their Lordships rejected the reasoning employed by the Court of Appeal. They ruled that reasons of principle enjoy priority over reasons of policy and it would therefore be inappropriate to reject a meritorious claim, simply in order to prevent a wave of litigation from breaking out. As Dworkin puts it: 'Once it is conceded that the damage to a mother in the hospital hours after an accident is reasonably foreseeable to a careless driver, then no difference in moral principle can be found between the two cases' (Dworkin 1986, 28).

Dworkin uses the case as an example of his rights thesis as well as his central thesis of law-as-integrity. He focuses on the reasoning employed by the judges. He tells us that despite the fact that neither decision could pass the test of 'fit', as there was no precedent and no clear rule that could have justified either granting or denying damages to Mrs McLoughlin, the substantive test of justification could only yield a favourable result for her. It is only thus that the decision would fall into place in the seamless web of (moral-come-legal) principles permeating or rather constituting the legal system. Dworkin looks for coherence between all the *prima facie* reasons for action: using the facts of the case described as an identifiable event as a starting point, we then proceed to classify that event under the relevant principle.

But what this approach fails to ask is what it is that makes the event description immune to problematization or, to be more precise, what it is that makes the possibility of describing the event in law in the first place immune to problematization. This is not only a question concerning the meaningfulness of history, that is, our faculty to come to conclusions as to whether a certain event took place or not. It is also not merely a question of the normative relevance of the circumstances of events and the limits of that relevance. What is crucial is to ask what are the conditions making event individuation in law possible in the first place, as well as what facilitates the calculability of the event in norms and principles. I would suggest that what lends coherence to the way such cases are treated is the background of a shared normative experience.

And *McLoughlin v. O'Brian* is particularly helpful, because it can be used to illustrate the law's chronology. The case revolves around the temporal relation between two events: the accident and the instant at which Mrs McLoughlin gains knowledge of the event and its consequences. In order for us to grasp what the law exactly does in this case, it does not suffice to understand the convention by reference to which the time interval was calculated, describe the event and then examine whether the event meets the conditions of activation of a principle, whichever way this principle is to be determined. There is nothing *within* the general principle prescribing something along the lines of 'the infliction of harm gives rise to a claim to compensation', which can determine the move from the generality of that principle to the factual specificity of the rule in which it will be incorporated. Even after having determined the principle, there are at least two questions that remain outstanding. In the McLoughlin case these questions can be illustrated as: first, what is it that determines that a two-hour period can still justify foreseeability whereas a longer delay would not? Secondly, and more importantly, what is it that allows this kind of discourse concerning the normative relevance of time intervals to take place?

Even if we accept for now that the first question can be answered convincingly or, at least, plausibly, with reference to some conception of normative coherence, such as Dworkinian integrity, the latter question still poses many more problems. As I have argued, the answer to it does not form part of the normative discourse itself, as this would lead to infinite regress. It can also not be discussed merely empirically, as it does not simply ask whether it is possible to find a common measure for temporal gaps between events. I argue that the only way of the rule or principle being applicable to the situation is against the background of the tacit assumption concerning the translatability of time intervals into normative language. It is only because of that pre-existing commitment to the possibility of normatively grasping, controlling and transforming time and therefore finding a normative meaning to the time difference between the two central events in *McLoughlin* that it is possible to reconcile with the crippling contingency of the decision to attach some normative importance to it and instantiate the relevant rule.

So it appears that the answer to the first question, namely the temporal dimension of foreseeability, and the idea of normative coherence depends directly on this substratum of shared normative experiences after all. Note, for example, how the question of time is mediated by the familial relationship in the case of *McLoughlin v. O'Brian*. The Court of Appeal more or less said that time stands still when you experience a tragedy that has befallen your loved ones (a sentiment often experienced by many of us and found expressed in art and popular culture). It simply would not have been the same had the claimant been a distant relative, let alone a complete stranger to Mr McLoughlin and his children. Thus the court already shapes the normative significance of time in a way that is hardly objective or built into the very concept of time, thus instantiating the normative experiences underpinning the law. Whether it does so, or indeed can do so at all, in a manner that does justice to the commitments of the participants in law is another question, which I will discuss a little later on in this chapter.

The point can be illustrated, perhaps even more clearly, by another example taken from State law, which ties in with my argument in Chapter 5.[9] Take sentencing and, in particular, imprisonment. In England and Wales theft carries a maximum penalty of seven years in prison.[10] The questions that I asked above about the decision in *McLoughlin* can be adjusted appropriately: firstly, how can we explain away the contingency in setting the maximum penalty to seven years and not more or less? One answer, as I suggested above, could perhaps come from an argument from normative coherence. Some crimes carry a greater moral demerit than others, for they deny values that are considered more important. On that level, offences are commensurable. Let us assume as a working hypothesis that this holds, as it is indeed not plausible, at least intuitively, to suggest that murder, for example, is just as reprehensible as theft. So this is how this line of reasoning goes: since our legal practices are guided by the requirements of fairness and justice, then, punishment ought to be meted out in the light of proportionality, both cardinal, which sets upper limits to the punishment that can be imposed, and ordinal, which prioritizes and ranks offences and the prescribed penalties in relation to each other. So, if a legal order is mapped out as a coherent system of norms and principles, which is in turn underpinned by a set of meta-principles, then it is possible to justify the differences in punishing various offences with imprisonment of varying duration. Thus time becomes quantifiable, calculable and it can be related to the moral demerit of acts and our legal response to them.

As I have shown, most legal theories leave the discussion there and they rest content that the connection of law and time has been adequately addressed. But the pressing question is how the discourse concerning issues such as cardinal and ordinal proportionality, the justifiability of punishing crimes by imprisonment of varying duration but also, and perhaps more importantly, the temporalization of freedom, can become possible in the first place. There is nothing within that discourse itself that can explain the connection of time and normativity, the possibility of calculating the moral demerit of an act in time units. The justificatory legal reasoning can only begin after the shared normative experience of the participants has been formed. It is on this level that a shared perception of time is consolidated, not merely as an epistemological presupposition but also in its conjunction with legal normativity. This tacit chronology of the legal answers the very question of the calculability of time in norms at a foundational level, at the very jurisgenerative moment of the emergence of the legal system. A legal system which is not reducible, or at least not necessarily so, to the political formation of the State, but can rather only be made sense of and be demarcated from other

9 I should emphasize here that the same argument can be illustrated with reference to any legal rule, which invokes time for its operationalization, whether implicitly or explicitly.

10 The England and Wales Theft Act 1968 s. 7 provides the following: 'A person guilty of theft shall on conviction on indictment be liable to imprisonment for a term not exceeding seven years.'

normative, regulatory or, indeed, legal phenomena with reference to the shared normative experiences that underpin it. Different conceptions of the way that time is tied up to normativity, of course, with the other aspects of a legal community's shared normative experience constitute the institutional boundaries of that legal order. It is therefore possible, and indeed the suspicion that this is the case is rather strong, that State law is either one among many co-existing legal orders within the territory that it marks itself and *for* itself or that, indeed, it is not a legal order at all, because it does not hinge on a *shared* normative experience.

It should by now have become clearer why I am reluctant wholesale to buy into Ost's idea of the temporal contract. In order for the connection of time and law and therefore for anyone fully to grasp the law, we should be turning our attention not to the expression of that temporal contract but rather the conditions of its possibility. It will then be constantly open to interperspectival reproblematization and critique.

And this is precisely what State law does not and cannot do. Let us consider what claim English law raises when it sets the maximum penalty for the offence of theft to seven years or when it sets the temporal dimensions of foreseeability. Or perhaps it is easier to answer this question by reversing it. How can one argue before a court that the penalty of seven years in prison or the temporalization of the conditions of psychological harm are not applicable to her, because the very calculation of the normative response to her situation in time units is impossible? In the case of theft, even if one agrees that the loss of freedom is an appropriate response to crime, how can one argue that this loss does not have to be extended over time, but a momentary deprivation would suffice in the way that shaming and the loss of one's dignity, say, is effective momentarily? Any such argument before a court would ring absurd. This is because it would turn against the presupposition of the shared normative experience, if any, underpinning the law of the State; presuppositions that set the epistemological limits of the normative reach of the law. But this does not mean that the case of the defendant who denies the calculability of her offence and her freedom in time units will be admissible by the court. The law of the State extends its dominion over the same territory and host of people that the State claims sovereignty over rather than with reference to the way that the people experience their shared normative experiences.

It does so by claiming normative universality. The law of the State purports to treat like cases alike and to apply the same normative standards by classifying the particular circumstances of a case under principles and rules that are context-neutral. This is strikingly obvious in *McLoughlin v O'Brian*. The court decides to make its decision on foreseeability a matter of principle rather than policy (giving Dworkin his cue in the process). But if we look more closely, we will see that the distinction is difficult to sustain for very long. To be sure, the policy argument of preventing congestion in courts is rejected because it would not deliver justice in the instant case. However, the principle which finally decided the case already relies on fixed presuppositions concerning the normative significance of the world, the outer limits of which cannot be put into question from within State legal discourse.[11] In other words, principles serve State law's general policy of maintaining certainty in the face of contingency and pluralism.[12]

This is corroborated by State law's claim to epistemological universality. The conditions of applicability of State law are set with a claim to objectivity, which is usually a (mis)reading of the teachings of science, which is purported to speak the language of objectivity and provide the only true knowledge of the natural world. Thus time becomes calculable and provides the yardstick for calculating the differences between cases. State law radically separates normativity and experience. By not recognizing that it itself can be nothing more than this combination, it transcends its boundaries and abilities and represents itself as an objective order. Objectivity goes hand in hand with exclusivity and exclusivity necessarily leads to a violent monism. That is how violence is done to those that cannot make sense of why and how their freedom or actions can be calculable in time units, because they have different legal commitments which rest on a different normative experience.

Is State law unique in raising this violent claim to exclusivity in the way time or, indeed, any other epistemological condition is relevant normatively? No. Any legal order operating in the same way, that is, by safeguarding its systemic closure and by fixing meaning as a way of guaranteeing certainty and predictability, would commit the same injustice because it would be unable to pay any attention to its own conditions of existence in any manner, let alone a self-critical one. But State law enjoys a special status in that its remit is to subsume all normativity, either by sanctioning it or by rejecting it as irrelevant.

Very worryingly, this is reflected in the way mainstream legal theories treat State law. In the light of that State-centred legal monism, it becomes easier to make sense of the way the same legal philosophical strands theorize the connection of law and time. The two fundamental assumptions are: firstly, that there is only one way to understand time and that is the commonsensical, (pseudo)scientific, therefore definitive, representation of time as a linear, dynamic sequence of events; secondly, the law is epistemologically neutral, in that its existence and distinctness does not depend on its association with a specific form of life and understanding of the world but rather on the distinctness of the State or other political formation to which it is bound. Therefore, the law exists as an identifiable object in time and interacts with the latter but is not determined by it. The law has its own history, which more often than not coincides with the history of the specific political

---

11 I make the argument concerning the inability of State law to universalize in time in Melissaris 2006a.

12 Dworkin argues of course that this is not what the law does but simply how positivism reads the law. For him, principles maintain sufficient flexibility to adapt appropriately to various combinations of facts. I contest this view by arguing that principles as well as rules always hinge on a specific experience of the world, which is exclusive of other alternatives. So, Dworkin's argument can be sustained only if it is admitted that principles the way he imagines them are thin to the point of being vacuous. But this already clearly backfires and undermines his whole view of the law.

formation which it is tied to, but that has no bearing on its normative content. The combination of all these assumptions is what enables the, unique and exclusive, law of the State to raise a claim to objectivity as far as the prescription of action in time is concerned.

Notes on Legal Topology

Living in a Park

Japan's homeless population has been steadily and rapidly increasing over the last 15 years, largely as a result of the country's economic recession. Amongst Japanese cities, Osaka has Japan's largest homeless population, estimated to rise up to perhaps 10,000 people. Many of the Osaka homeless live in makeshift tents in the city's parks. Attempts at evicting them have resulted in violent clashes with the homeless and citizens supporting them.[13]

In 2006, Mr Yamauchi, one of Osaka's homeless, applied to a court to have the park recognized as his legal address. Without a permanent address, he could not join the national health service or be eligible to vote. In the first instance the court granted him permission, but the City Office appealed against the decision, arguing that the tent, made of tarpaulin and wood, did not meet the requirements of a residence as a matter of 'conventional wisdom'. The City was also worried that Mr Yamauchi's case would open the floodgates and encourage even more homeless people to move into parks. The High Court overruled the first instance court's decision and denied the respondent the right to use the park as a legal address. A representative of the Homeless Human Rights Resources Centre in Tokyo regretted the decision, arguing that granting the right to use parks as a legal address would empower homeless people and help them return to normality and independence.[14]

Perhaps the most obvious way of reading Mr Yamauchi's case is as a clash between goods. On the one hand, there is granting homeless people the opportunity to change their lives by gaining some legal recognition. On the other, there is the opportunity of the rest of the people of Osaka to enjoy the parks and perhaps even aesthetically preserving the city image. But this superficial utilitarian calculation is underpinned by something deeper. On a first reading, the clash is between conceptions of the public and the private. Osaka City Office and the High Court seemed to have no doubt that parks belong in the public realm and converting them into legally recognized private settlements would unreasonably disturb the balance between the public and the private. In apportioning the city's geography between

13 <http://news.bbc.co.uk/1/hi/world/asia-pacific/4661152.stm> (last accessed 12 July 2008).

14 <http://uk.reuters.com/article/oddlyEnoughNews/idUKT15021020070123> (last accessed 12 July 2008); *The Pavement*, February 2007, 4.

the public and the private, the law opts for a very specific way of individuating its subjects and understanding them as such. In parks, the legal subject's individuality is tempered and constrained in favour of some conception of a community of anonymous bodies. It is in her own private realm that the individual is identified and fully flourishes as such. Note that the question in Mr Yamauchi's case is not whether he was entitled to sleep in the park but whether he can use the park as his legal address. So it is not just about whether he was being a nuisance to others but rather how he could be identified as a citizen of Osaka and Japan.

This already points to the close interconnection of law and normative conceptions of space. The law constructs space by prescribing it. This is not just an ideological construct, it is utterly real (Ford 2001). Boundaries, borders, gates, but also everything that is contained within them, is given meaning by the law. Surely, this is no news to anyone. But what is less well understood is that this is a two-way relation. Not only does the law construct space but space and its conception also shapes the law. Social constructionist arguments in law often assume that the latter is simply a system of meaning or simply a discourse, which comes and hinges itself on the world. If we cease to view the law as removed from our very experience of the world and begin to understand it as the merging of the normative with the sensible, we will begin to find the law all over, in all our interactions with and in space. This already spells out a critique of State law, which sees space as objective and uniformly perceived by all, and purports to attach to it a normative meaning which is separated from reality and is again objective and accessible to all in the same way. Reconnecting law and space in such an integral manner is, I believe, the most productive reading of Mr Yamauchi's case, because it helps him (and of course others) to reclaim both the law and space.

Travelling and Trespassing

Before the 2005 general election in the United Kingdom, Mr Michael Howard, the then leader of the Conservative Party (which eventually lost the election and as a result their manifesto was never implemented) pledged that trespassing by travellers would become a criminal offence. Backed by tabloid newspapers, Mr Howard stated firmly that he did not believe in 'special rules for special interest groups'. He went on to argue that:

> People realise that there are too many [people] in Britain today who hide behind so-called human rights to justify doing the wrong thing. 'I've got my rights' has become the verbal equivalent of two fingers to authority. The rights culture has blurred the difference between right and wrong and it's taking Britain in the wrong direction.[15]

15 <http://www.guardian.co.uk/politics/2005/mar/21/uk.race> (last accessed 17 July 2008).

The truth of the matter is that there has only been one case brought before the Court of Appeal in which Article 8 of the Convention for the Protection of Human Rights and Fundamental Freedoms protecting private and family life was invoked in order to allow travellers to remain in a settlement site. In *First Secretary of State and others v Chichester Borough Council*,[16] the Court of Appeal ruling revolved around the issue of proportionality:

> The defendants' right to respect for their homes was, accordingly, subject to legitimate attack from the state, providing such interference by the implementation of enforcement notices was a proportionate response to the identified objective of planning control. In the circumstances, it had been manifestly open to the inspector to have found, as he had, that the effects of enforcement had been disproportionate because the harm to the defendants' extended family group would be increasingly serious, whereas the harm to the environment would not be so great.

There are many ways of making sense of the debate. The easiest one is perhaps to view it as a manifestation of the fact that human rights are still a politically contested issue. This would go some way towards explaining the political revulsion exhibited by Michael Howard and other Conservatives towards human rights legislation. Or perhaps the very fact that there was a debate at all only shows that the culture of human rights had not yet fully developed in the United Kingdom at that stage. Seen through the lens of dominant legality, their attitude can only be perceived as disrespect or disregard for those on whose property they might be trespassing, as well as the institution of property, which is even supposed to play a part in constituting the very personality of proprietors. In this light travellers are nothing more than outsiders, who refuse to accept the purportedly universally accepted norms regulating property and the public–private divide.

Thankfully, human rights have enabled us to view such cases more charitably. But are they enough? In *First Secretary of State and others v Chichester Borough Council*, Article 8 of the European Convention of Human Rights enabled the Court of Appeal to privilege consequentialist arguments in order to balance public and private interests and rights (on balancing, see Alexy 2002a; 2003). At various stages, this proportionality test hinges on factual calculations, which are seen as divorced from, though interlinked with, normative questions. In other words, courts ask themselves what factual impact their eventual decision and setting of boundaries of Article 8 rights will have. Such a separation presupposes a strict dichotomy between constative and performative as well as the absolute objectivity of the domain of facts *and* the objectivity of legal norms (either as generally accepted conventions or, somehow, as part of the fabric of nature). The latter then ascribes legal meaning to the former. But, as I have been arguing in this book, this disjunction is artificial. The balancing entailed by the application of Article 8 is

16 [2004] EWCA Civ 1248.

already firmly embedded within a *nomos* heavily prescribing and foreclosing the possibility of meaning while being represented as objective to all. This is the only way in which State law can operate, it is the only way in which it can make the travellers' claim translatable into the rights of site owners or the 'public interest'. In doing so, it remains blind to the particular conditions of emergence of other *nomoi*, the shared normative experiences constituting them. It misrepresents these conditions and, as a result, the *nomos* of the travellers is crushed.

So I would suggest that the issue should be seen in a different light. What appears to me to be revealed in the case of trespassing travellers is a clash between two different *nomoi* rather than simply a clash of interpretations motivated by political or economic interests. Travelling communities seem to have an understanding of space and its normative significance that is quite different from that which Michael Howard represents. The concept of trespass presupposes a very strong conception of and commitment to property as permanent separation and domination over space and things (however a thing may be understood). This appears to clash with the normative significance that space holds for the travelling community and the place it occupies in their experience of normativity.[17]

'Inside' and 'Outside' the Law

The law is itself often perceived as a territory with its own geography. We speak of 'areas of law', one can be 'inside' or 'outside' the law and so forth. Perhaps the most famous story of the law as space, at least in legal scholarship, is Lon Fuller's tale of the speluncean explorers (Fuller 1949), which is of course based on the real case of *Dudley and Stephens*.[18] The 'facts' of the case are well known: a group of amateur speluncean explorers got trapped in a cave when large boulders blocked any known opening to the cave. After 23 days of confinement, one of them suggested that the only way of not starving and surviving would be to kill and eat a member of group. Who the unlucky one would be should be decided by the throw of dice. They agreed on the plan but the same person who made the suggestion tried to pull out just before the dice were thrown. The group would not have any of that and someone else threw the dice on his behalf. He lost, was killed and got eaten.

The story raises a vast range of questions but what I want to focus on is its relevance for legal topology. One of Fuller's fictional judges opined that the explorers should not be held criminally liable, as they had left the state of law and were in a state of nature. Another judge was in disagreement:

> As I analyze the opinion just rendered by my brother Foster, I find that it is shot through with contradictions and fallacies. Let us begin with his first proposition:

17 For a mapping of the legal arrangements in travelling communities, see Weyrauch and Bell 1993.

18 [1884] 14 QBD 273 DC.

> these men were not subject to our law because they were not in a 'state of civil society' but in a 'state of nature.' I am not clear why this is so, whether it is because of the thickness of the rock that imprisoned them, or because they were hungry, or because they had set up a 'new charter of government' by which the usual rules of law were to be supplanted by a throw of the dice. Other difficulties intrude themselves. If these men passed from the jurisdiction of our law to that of 'the law of nature,' at what moment did this occur? Was it when the entrance to the cave was blocked, or when the threat of starvation reached a certain undefined degree of intensity, or when the agreement for the throwing of the dice was made? (Fuller 1949, 70)

A similar question is raised in *Dudley and Stephens*: does the criminal law lose its applicability altogether mid-sea? Was the cabin boy who was killed and eaten by his fellow sailors not murdered but simply killed (Blomley 2001)? It is important to note that the question is not whether the cave and sea cannibals had some excuse or justification for the killings. And it is also not a jurisdictional question, that is, whether the law of this or that country is applicable. It is rather a question of whether *any* law had *any* bearing on their situation at all.

On one reading from the perspective of legal topology, the law of the State seems not to be confined within spatial boundaries. The physical distance from the usual realm of association between legal subjects, the real isolation imposed by the ocean or the boulders blocking the cave entrance, are the law's physical boundaries. Legal normativity occupies a *topos* and this is what makes jurisdictions possible. But in extreme circumstances, such as those that the cave explorers and the seamen found themselves in, the space of the law runs out, the finitude of the legal universe is revealed. But can this really be the case? Can the law *ever* run out? My argument in this book is that it cannot, that the law is ubiquitous temporally and spatially. This is why I suggest that we can make better sense of the cases of the speluncean explorers and *Dudley and Stephens* not by asking whether and, if so, how or when they exited the state of law and entered the state of nature, but rather how legality was transformed in and through the physical environment, how the normative self-understandings of the confined cannibals were shaped. It is only by looking closely at how the law *did* operate, rather than how State law *did not* or *could not*, that we will be able to grasp what may have happened in that cave and on that boat.

Mainstream legal theory treats space just as I argued earlier that it treats time. However, there is some, although by no means much or even enough, legal scholarship on the mutual constitution of law and space (see Blomley 2001; 2004; Manderson 2005; Fitzpatrick and Tuitt 2004). I would suggest that the study of legal topology must take centre stage alongside the study of all shared normative experiences, not as the study of the impact of State law on people's perceptions of space but rather as an enquiry into the very heart of legality through such topological perceptions.

Conclusion

In this, final, chapter I pursued the idea that the shared normative experiences which, as I argued in this book, constitute the law are determined by a temporal and a spatial dimension roughly paralleling the intuitions that make possible all our experiencing of the world. I showed both how perceptions of space and time are built into the sense of law and also that this interplay is played down or altogether ignored by traditional legal theory. And I believe that we can only gain knowledge and an understanding of the legal if we turn our attention to such shared normative experiences framed by perceptions of time and space and their normative significance in co-operation and interperspectival dialogue with all those sharing such experiences and vesting them with their commitment.

Conclusion

This book was motivated by an unease as to the way that the very idea of the law is generally understood. Surprisingly, a thread runs through most legal theories (as well as folk conceptions of the law) despite their fundamental differences in all other aspects. This thread is a view of the law as necessarily associated with the modern State. This is complemented by the assumption that the law is addressed by some parts of the populace (usually a minority) to others without it even being necessary that the group of law-givers enjoy democratic legitimacy or anything of the sort. It is true of course that these legal theories' attitudes to this one-way relationship differ greatly. For some, the picture of the law as deriving from a single source and addressed to others in a way that is beyond problematization can only be a good thing, because it reduces normative complexity, thus allowing people to regulate their affairs in a predictable and certain manner, and it also demystifies the law, opening it up to critique. This is typical of positivist theories of law. However, even substantivist ones, especially Dworkin's interpretivism, do not depart a great deal from this ideal in that they see centralization as valuable, albeit building critique into the very concept of legality. On the other hand, critical legal theories, and here I include most theories of legal pluralism too, see predictability and certainty as rigidity. Some take an even more critical tack and focus on the closure of meaning that State law imposes and the violence that it does in silencing other normative self-understandings. At the same time though, they do not seem very interested in providing an account of the differentiation of the legal from other normative orders or a way in which all these dispersed normative self-understandings will be able to make sense of each other.

So it seems that we find ourselves tangled up in an antinomy: either we have law but we are not free or we have no law and we risk being *too* free. But why should this be an antinomy at all? Why should the law not be understood as enabling rather than constraining, as empowering rather than coercive? Why should there not be some way of reconciling freedom with law? Such antinomic thinking seems to be motivated by fear. Fear that moral preferences are impossible to co-ordinate, because they are so bound to the subject. Or fear that we may collectively get it wrong, as has happened at many historical junctions with tragic consequences. What is even more surprising is that this latter kind of anxiety is displayed by those who otherwise have faith in humanity and its ability to reason practically and peacefully to order its affairs. But once this fear is overcome, once we accept the possibility of autonomously and, at the same time, collectively imposing normative constraints onto ourselves and restore our faith in our abilities while arming ourselves against moral attitudes that can lead to atrocities, then the possibility of decentring and reclaiming the law will open itself up to us.

The aim of this book was to find a way of making sense of legal polycentricity in a productive way. My argument was both methodological and substantive, although I am aware of the difficulty in drawing clear lines between method and substance. The first step was to put to the test the way that the question of the law has been asked by various legal theoretical strands. This enquiry led me to the conclusion that all legal theory relies too heavily on the assumption that the law is necessarily associated with the State (an assumption of both ontological and normative shades) and that it is a one-way relationship between addressors and addressees. This goes hand in hand with the way that legal theory has developed as a modern expert culture, thus alienating those whose very commitments and experiences constitute the law. I thus counter-proposed that legal theory take an interperspectival turn, that it re-democratize itself by instigating a two-way, self-reflexive, critical dialogue with *prima facie* legal discourses.

Such a dialogue would not be possible without some sense of law, which must be under-prescriptive, always open and defeasible. Working with Robert Cover's ideas, I proposed that we understand the law in terms of people's shared normative experiences, that is, the way their normative commitments shape and are shaped by their experience of the world. Such a sense of law can kickstart and inform interperspectival discourse, but it also imposes some constraints to this discourse. Substantive constraints stem from normativity itself and its sources. At the same time, the requirement of commonality, as well as the merging of the constative and the performative entailed in this sense of law, sufficiently differentiate it from other normative orders. But it should be noted that this understanding of law does not presuppose full identification of members of a community with each other. It is meant to reflect the fragmentation of our normative commitments and experiences and, at the same time, provide a way of reconciling them. At the same time, such a sense of law is clearly more expansive than the orthodox centralized model of law. But this should not cause any fear precisely because the law has been reclaimed and the task of drawing its boundaries has been entrusted to those whose commitments constitute it.

So I see the law as ubiquitous because its sources are to be found in all instances and contexts of people's association with each other without anyone being able to prescribe in advance where it will emerge. At the same time, it is ubiquitous because it governs almost all instances of our lives. But, and this is worth repeating, not in a coercive, heteronomous way, but rather collectively, autonomously and responsibly.

Every time I shared my ideas I was presented with the same question, namely how a view of the law as decentred, independent of dissociated experts and reliant on everyone's practical and theoretical reason is to be operationalized, what purchase it has in the real world. It is true that this book does not provide an answer to this. The reason, however, is not the tired excuse of time and space. It is mainly because any attempt at constructing a model of operationalization of my understanding of the law from such a context would go against the very premise of the book, namely that the communication and co-ordination of various legalities can only be done in a particular and context-sensitive way in view of the participants' commitments. It is true that this presupposes a radical rethinking of what counts as law and what everyone's part and responsibility in shaping the law is.

Given the current conditions and the overwhelming prevalence of State law, does this mean that it is all reduced to a therapeutic utopia? If one takes a maximalistic tack, then perhaps so, especially in light of the fact that a basic premise of the book is that State law inevitably remains closed to meaning outside its own institutional boundaries, as I argued in Chapters 5 and 6. Nevertheless, a new conception of the law can still help broaden the horizons of State law and at least make it aware of its own limitations. This can have a bearing on a range of issues, from the way that alternative legal commitments are treated in State legal proceedings to the composition of the judiciary. With respect to the latter, the usual rebuttal of any argument in favour of expanding the pool of people from which judges are selected and for encouraging, if not favouring, people from various disenfranchised communities to join the judiciary, has been that it matters not who the judge is since it is the objective and all-inclusive law that does all the work. I hope that understanding the law in terms of shared normative experiences helps both dispel this myth and highlight the value of diversity. And I hope that it does so not by emphasizing the obvious possibility of bias, which distorts the objective meaning of law, but rather by highlighting that this objective meaning is so thin that it can only be determined in real contexts. To be sure, even if this is registered, State law can only respond and act in a formalistic manner by defining what counts as a disenfranchised community and taking formal measures of inclusion. This is clearly far from the vision of the law which I offered in this book. Nonetheless, it would certainly be a welcome first step.

Crucially, I see this as a contribution to the shift in the research programme of legal theory. As I emphasized repeatedly throughout the book, the sharp distinctions between the philosophical and the sociological study of the law or between normative and descriptive argument in law are artificial and unsustainable. Unfortunately, these distinctions are also so deeply entrenched that they often lead to counterproductive debates as to which approach is epistemologically superior. I say these binaries are artificial because, as I have shown in this book, the question of the law cannot be asked solely philosophically or solely sociologically. A social theory of law must always be informed by a universal sense of law, while such philosophical thinking can only acquire content in real contexts in light of people's experiences. So the study of the law is not *either* philosophical *or* sociological. It is *necessarily both*. And the results of that enquiry are always open to thematization and never offer complete closure. However, the constant open-endedness of enquiry into the legal will not disable us. In fact, quite the opposite: open-endedness makes action possible, because it allows space for critique. What I tried to do in this book was to show how the multiple facets of the law must be reflected in the way we think about it. I also sought to provide a platform that will enable the fruitful communication and integration between legal philosophy and social theory, so as to make possible the study of the legal in a truly interdisciplinary way.

I said earlier that much legal theory seems to be driven by fear. Perhaps this fear is also partly responsible for the monopolization of the question of the law by the expert culture of academic legal theory, which in a sense reflects the monopolization of the practice of law by the specialist caste of lawyers. The fear seems to be that people cannot be trusted to reach an agreement concerning the limitations of their freedom. The corollary of this mistrust is the promotion of coercion as the main motivating force in law. I feel that this attitude needs to be addressed and changed urgently. Legal theory must abandon the expert perspective and democratize itself by opening up the dialogue concerning the law to all the participants in legality, whichever form this may take or in whichever context it may emerge. Only then will it be doing justice both to these participants and also to itself. It will then become able to rediscover and reclaim its genuine critical character and move away both from being the legitimating apologist of the monopolization of legality and violence, and also from the disabling despair that the law is and can only be violent; a despair which goes hand in hand with the yearning for an inaccessible transcendental order as the only one able to do justice. The challenge, I feel, is to detranscendentalize this possibility of justice while reconciling with the possibility of error; it is to reclaim the law, to regain control over it by becoming conscious of its interdependence with our real experiences in the here and now.

Bibliography

Aarnio, A., Paulson, S.L., Weinberger, O., von Wright, G.H. and Wyduckel, D. (eds) (1993), *Rechtsnorm und Rechtswirklichkeit; Festschrift für W. Krawietz zum 60. Geburtstag* (Berlin: Duncker und Humblot).

Abbott, A.D. (1988), *The System of Professions: An Essay on the Division of Expert Labor* (Chicago: University of Chicago Press).

Abel, T. (1977), 'The Operation Called Verstehen', in Dallmayr and McCarthy (eds).

Alexy, R. (1989a), *A Theory of Legal Argumentation: The Theory of Rational Discourse as Theory of Legal Justification* (translated by R. Adler and D.N. MacCormick) (Oxford: Clarendon Press).

Alexy, R. (1989b), 'On the Necessary Relations between Law and Morality', *Ratio Juris* 2:2, 167–83.

Alexy, R. (1992), *Begriff und Geltung des Rechts* (Alber-Reihe). Edition in English: (2002) *The Argument from Injustice: A Reply to Legal Positivism* (translated by Bonnie Litschewski Paulson and Stanley L. Paulson) (Oxford: Clarendon).

Alexy, R. (1997), 'Bulygins Kritik des Richtigkeitsargument', in Garzón Valdés (ed.).

Alexy, R. (1999), 'The Special Case Thesis', *Ratio Juris* 12:4, 374–84.

Alexy, R. (2000a), 'Law and Correctness', in Freeman, M.D.A. (ed.).

Alexy, R. (2000b), 'On the Thesis of a Necessary Connection between Law and Morality: Bulygin's Critique', *Ratio Juris* 13:2, 138–47.

Alexy, R. (2002a), *A Theory of Constitutional Rights* (translated by J. Rivers) (Oxford: Oxford University Press).

Alexy, R. (2002b), *The Argument from Injustice: A Reply to Legal Positivism* (translated by B. Litschewski Paulson and S.L. Paulson) (Oxford: Clarendon).

Alexy, R. (2003), 'Constitutional Rights, Balancing and Rationality', *Ratio Juris* 16:2, 131–40.

Alexy, R. (2007), 'An Answer to Joseph Raz', in Pavlakos (ed.) (2007b).

Allott, A.N. and Woodman, G.R. (eds) (1985), *People's Law and State Law: The Bellagio Papers* (Dordrecht: Foris Publications).

Alston, W.P. (1996), *A Realist Conception of Truth* (Ithaca, NY and London: Cornell University Press).

Arnaud, A.J. (1998), 'From Limited Realism to Plural Law. Normative Approach *versus* Cultural Perspective', *Ratio Juris* 11:3, 246–58.

Arthurs, H.W. (1985), *Without the Law: Administrative Justice and Legal Pluralism in Nineteenth Century England* (Toronto: University of Toronto Press).

Ashworth, A.J. (1992), *Sentencing and Criminal Justice* (London: Weidenfeld and Nicholson).

Auerbach, J.S. (1976), *Unequal Justice: Lawyers and Social Change in Modern America* (New York: Oxford University Press).

Austin, J. (1996), *The Province of Jurisprudence Determined* (with an introduction by W. Morison) (Brookfield, VT: Dartmouth).

Austin, J.L. (1962), *How to Do Things with Words: The William James Lectures Delivered at Harvard University in 1955* (ed. J.O. Urmson) (Oxford: Clarendon Press).

Austin, J.L. ([1956] 1979), 'A Plea for Excuses', Proceedings of the Aristotelian Society 1956–57, reprinted in J.L. Austin, *Philosophical Papers* (Oxford: Clarendon).

Banakar, R. and Travers, M. (eds) (2002), *An Introduction to Law and Social Theory* (Oxford: Hart).

Bankowski, Z. and MacLean, J. (eds) (2006), *The Universal and the Particular in Legal Reasoning* (Aldershot and Burlington, VT: Ashgate).

Bankowski, Z. (1981), 'The Value of Truth: Fact-Skepticism Revisited', *Legal Studies* 1, 257–66.

Bankowski, Z. and Mungham, R. (1976), *Images of Law* (London: Routledge and Kegan Paul).

Bauman, Z. (1987), *Legislators and Interpreters: On Modernity, Post-modernity, and Intellectuals* (Cambridge: Polity Press).

Bereiter, C. and Scardamalia, M. (1993), *Surpassing Ourselves: An Inquiry into the Nature and Implications of Expertise* (Chicago: Open Court).

Berman, P.S. (2005), 'From International Law to Law and Globalization', *Columbia Journal of Transnational Law* 43, 485–556.

Bjarup, J. and Blegvad, M. (eds) (1995), *Time, Law and Society, Archiv für Rechts- und Sozialphilosophie Beiheft* 64 (Franz Steiner Verlag).

Blomley, N. (2001), 'Introduction', in Blomley, Delaney and Ford (eds).

Blomley, N.K. (2004), *Unsettling the City: Urban Land and the Politics of Property* (New York: Routledge).

Blomley, N., Delaney, D. and Ford, R.T. (eds) (2001), *The Legal Geographies Reader* (Oxford: Blackwell Publishers).

Bohman, J. (2001), 'Participants, Observers, and Critics: Practical Knowledge, Social Perspectives, and Critical Pluralism', in Rehg and Bohman (eds).

Brand-Ballard, J. (1996), 'Kelsen's Unstable Alternative to Natural Law: Recent Critiques', *American Journal of Jurisprudence* 41, 133–64.

Brewer, S. (1998), 'Scientific Expert Testimony and Intellectual Due Process', *Yale Law Journal* 107, 1535–1681.

Bulygin, E. (1993), 'Alexy und das Richtigkeitsargument', in Aarnio, Paulson, Weinberger, von Wright and Wyduckel (eds).

Bulygin, E. (2000), 'Alexy's Thesis on the Necessary Connection between Law and Morality', *Ratio Juris* 13:2, 133–7.

Carbonnier, J. (1983), *Flexible droit: textes pour une sociologie du droit sans rigeur* (Paris: Librairie générale de droit et de jurisprudence).

Chiba, M. (1998), 'Other Phases of Legal Pluralism in the Contemporary World', *Ratio Juris* 11:3, 228–45.
Christodoulidis, E. (2004), 'End of History Jurisprudence; Dworkin in South Africa', *Acta Juridica*, Jubilee Edition, 64–85.
Christodoulidis, E. and Veitch, S. (eds) (2001), *Lethe's Law: Justice, Law and Ethics in Reconciliation* (Oxford and Portland, Oregon: Hart Publishing).
Coleman, J. (ed.) (2001), *Hart's Postscript: Essays on the Postscript to the Concept of Law* (Oxford: Oxford University Press).
Cooke, M. (1994), *Language and Reason: A Study of Habermas' Pragmatics* (Cambridge, MA: MIT Press).
Cornell, D., Rosenfeld, M. and Carlson, D.G. (eds) (1992), *Deconstruction and the Possibility of Justice* (London: Routledge).
Cotterrell, R. (1984), *The Sociology of Law: An Introduction* (Oxford: Butterworths).
Cotterrell, R. (1995), *Law's Community; Legal Theory in Sociological Perspective* (Oxford: Clarendon Press).
Cover, R. (1983), 'Nomos and Narrative', *Harvard Law Review* 97, 4–68.
Cover, R. (1986), 'Violence and the Word', *Yale Law Journal* 95, 1601–29.
Coyle, S. (2002), 'Hart, Raz and the Concept of a Legal System', *Law and Philosophy* 21, 275–304.
Coyle, S. (2007), *From Positivism to Idealism: A Study of the Moral Dimensions of Legality* (Aldershot and Burlington, VT: Ashgate).
Coyle, S. and Pavlakos, G. (eds) (2005), *Jurisprudence or Legal Science?* (Oxford and Portland, Oregon: Hart Publishing).
Czarnota, A. (2001), 'Law As Mnemosyne and As Lethe: Quasi-Judicial Institutions and Collective Memories', in Christodoulidis and Veitch (eds).
Dallmayr, F.R. and McCarthy, T.A. (eds) (1977), *Understanding and Social Inquiry* (Notre Dame: University of Notre Dame Press).
Dascal, M. (1994), 'Speech Act Theory and Gricean Pragmatics: Some Differences of Detail that Make a Difference', in Tsohatzidis (ed.).
Davidson, D. (1973), 'On the Very Idea of a Conceptual Scheme', *Proceedings and Addresses of the American Philosophical Association* 47, 5–20.
Davies, M. (2005), 'The Ethos of Pluralism', *Sydney Law Review* 27:4, 87–112.
de Sousa Santos, B. (1995), *Toward a New Common Sense: Law, Science and Politics in the Paradigmatic Transition* (London: Routledge).
de Sousa Santos, B. (2001), 'Toward an Epistemology of Blindness: Why the New Forms of 'Ceremonial Adequacy' Neither Regulate nor Emancipate', *European Journal of Social Theory* 4:3, 251–79.
Derber, C., Schwartz W.A. and Magrass Y. (1990), *Power in the Highest Degree: Professionals and the Rise of a New Mandarin Order* (New York: Oxford University Press).
Derrida, J. (1992), 'Force of Law: The Mystical Foundations of Authority', in Cornell, Rosenfeld and Carlson (eds).
Douzinas, C. (2005), 'Oubliez Critique', *Law and Critique* 16:1, 47–69.

Duxbury, N. (1995), *Patterns of American Jurisprudence* (Oxford: Clarendon Press).
Duxbury, N. (2005), 'English Jurisprudence Between Austin and Hart', *Virginia Law Review* 91:1, 1–90.
Duxbury, N. (2008), 'Kelsen's Endgame', *Cambridge Law Journal* 67:1, 51–61.
Dworkin, R. (1977), *Taking Rights Seriously* (London: Duckworth).
Dworkin, R. (1986), *Law's Empire* (London: Fontana).
Dworkin, R. (1996), 'Objectivity and Truth: You'd Better Believe It', *Philosophy and Public Affairs* 25:2, 87–139.
Dworkin, R. (2004), 'Hart's Postscript and the Character of Political Philosophy', *Oxford Journal of Legal Studies* 24:1, 1–37.
Eberhard, C. (2001), 'Towards an Intercultural Legal Theory: The Dialogical Challenge', *Social and Legal Studies* 10:2, 171–201.
Ehrlich, E. (1936), *Fundamental Principles of the Sociology of Law* (Cambridge, MA: Harvard University Press).
Endicott, T. (2001), 'Herbert Hart and the Semantic Sting', in Coleman (ed.).
Evans-Pritchard, E.E. (1940), 'The Nuer of the Southern Sudan', in Fortes and Evans-Pritchard (eds).
Ewing, S. (1987), 'Formal Justice and the Spirit of Capitalism: Max Weber's Sociology of Law', *Law and Society Review* 21:3, 487–512.
Falk-Moore, S. (1973), 'Law and Social Change: The Semi-Autonomous Social Field as an Appropriate Subject of Study', *Law and Society Review* 7:4, 719–46.
Finnis, J. (2007), 'On Hart's Ways: Law as Reason and as Fact', *American Journal of Jurisprudence* 52, 25–53.
Fitzpatrick, P. (1984), 'Law and Societies', *Osgoode Hall Law Journal* 22, 115–38.
Fitzpatrick, P. and Tuitt, P. (2004), *Critical Beings: Law, Nation and the Global Subject* (Aldershot and Burlington, VT: Ashgate).
Flood, R. and Lockwood, M. (eds) (1986), *The Nature of Time* (London: Blackwell).
Follesdal, A. and Hix, S. (2006), 'Why There is a Democratic Deficit in the EU: A Response to Majone and Moravcsik', *Journal of Common Market Studies* 44:3, 533–62.
Ford, R.T. (2001), 'Law's Territory (A History of Jurisdiction)', in Blomley, Delaney and Ford (eds).
Fortes, M. and Evans-Pritchard, E.E. (eds) (1940), *African Political Systems* (London: Oxford University Press).
Frank, J. (1949a), *Law and the Modern Mind* (London: Stevens).
Frank, J. (1949b), 'The Place of the Expert in a Democratic Society', *Philosophy of Science* 16:1, 3–24.
Frank, J. (1949c), *Courts on Trial: Myth and Reality in American Justice* (Princeton: Princeton University Press).
Freeman, M.D.A. (2000), *Current Legal Problems* 51 (Oxford: Oxford University Press).

Fuller, L.L. (1949), 'The Case of the Speluncean Explorers', *Harvard Law Review* 62:4, 65–79.

Fuller, L.L. (1964), *The Morality of Law* (New Haven: Yale University Press).

Galanter, M. (1981), 'Justice in Many Rooms: Courts, Private Ordering, and Indigenous Law', *Journal of Legal Pluralism* 19, 1–47.

Gale, R.E. (ed.) (1968), *The Philosophy of Time: A Collection of Essays* (London: Macmillan).

Garzón Valdés, E. (ed.) (1997), *Normative Systems in Legal and Moral Theory: Festschrift für E. Alchourrón and E. Bulygin* (Berlin: Duncker and Humblot).

Geertz, C. (1983), *Local Knowledge: Further Essays in Interpretive Anthropology* (New York: Basic Books).

Geuss, R. (2001), *History and Illusion in Politics* (New York: Cambridge University Press).

Giddens, A. (1990), *The Consequences of Modernity* (Cambridge Press: Polity, in association with Blackwell).

Goodrich, P. (1990), *Languages of Law: From Logics of Memory to Nomadic Masks* (London: Weidenfeld and Nicolson).

Goodrich, P. (1999), 'The Critic's Love of the Law: Intimate Observations on an Insular Jurisdiction', *Law and Critique* 10:3, 343–60.

Green, A. (2002), *Time in Psychoanalysis: Some Contradictory Aspects* (translated by Andrew Weller) (London: Free Association Books).

Grice, P. (1992), *Studies in the Way of Words* (Cambridge, MA: Harvard University Press).

Griffiths, A. (2002), 'Legal Pluralism', in Banakar and Travers (eds).

Griffiths, J. (1986), 'What is Legal Pluralism?', *Journal of Legal Pluralism* 24, 2–55.

Günther, K. (1993a), *The Sense of Appropriateness: Application Discourses in Morality and Law* (translated by John Farrell) (Albany: State University of New York Press).

Günther, K. (1993b), 'Critical Remarks on Alexy's "Special Case Thesis"', *Ratio Juris* 6:2, 143–56.

Günther, K. (2001), 'Rechtspluralismus und universaler Code der Legalität: Globalisierung als rechtstheoretisches Problem' in Wingert and Günther (eds), 539–67.

Gurvitch, G. (1935), *L'Expérience Juridique et la Philosophie Pluraliste du Droit* (Paris: A. Pedone).

Habermas, J. (1995), *Vorstudien und Ergänzungen zur Theorie des Kommunikativen Handelns* (Frankfurt-am-Main: Suhrkamp).

Habermas, J. (1987), *The Theory of Communicative Action: Lifeworld and System; a Critique of Functionalist Reason* (3rd corrected edition, translated by T. McCarthy) (Boston and Cambridge: Polity Press).

Habermas, J. (1993), *Justification and Application: Remarks on Discourse Ethics* (Cambridge: Polity Press).

Habermas, J. (1996), *Between Facts and Norms: Contributions to a Discourse Theory of Law and Democracy* (translated by William Rehg) (Oxford: Polity Press).

Habermas, J. (2001), 'Reflections on the Detranscendentalised Use of Reason', in Rehg and Bohman (eds).

Habermas, J. and Luhmann, N. (1971), *Theorie der Gesellschaft oder Sozialtechnologie: Was leistet die Systemforschung?* (Frankfurt-am-Main: Suhrkamp).

Hacker, P.M.S. (1996), 'On Davidson's Idea of a Conceptual Scheme', *The Philosophical Quarterly* 46:184, 289–307.

Hart, H.L.A. (1970), *Punishment and Responsibility: Essays in the Philosophy of Law* (Oxford: Clarendon Press).

Hart, H.L.A. (1994), *The Concept of Law* (2nd edition with a postscript by Penelope Bulloch and Joseph Raz) (Oxford: Clarendon Press).

Hart, H.L.A. and Honoré, T. (1985), *Causation in the Law* (2nd edition) (Oxford: Clarendon Press).

Haslanger, S. (2005), 'What Are We Talking About? The Semantics and Politics of Social Kinds', *Hypatia* 20:4, 10–26.

Haslanger, S. (2006), 'What Good Are Our Intuitions: Philosophical Analysis and Social Kinds', *Proceedings of the Aristotelian Society Supplementary Volume* 80:1, 89–118.

Heidemann, C. (1999), 'Norms, Facts, and Judgments. A Reply to S.L. Paulson', *Oxford Journal of Legal Studies* 19:2, 345–50.

Heidemann, C. (2004), 'Hans Kelsen and the Transcendental Method', *Northern Ireland Legal Quarterly* 55:4, 358–77.

Heidemann, C. (2005), 'Law's Claim to Correctness', in Coyle and Pavlakos (eds).

Honderich, T. (1969), *Punishment: The Supposed Justifications* (London: Hutchinson).

Hudson, B.A. (1996), *Understanding Justice: An Introduction to Ideas, Perspectives and Controversies in Modern Penal Theory* (Buckingham: Open University Press).

Husserl, E. (1991), *On the Phenomenology of the Consciousness of Internal Time (1893–1917)* (translated by John Barnett Brough) (Dordrecht and Boston: Kluwer Academic Publishers).

Husserl, G. (1955), *Recht und Zeit: Fünf rechtsphilosophische Essays* (Frankfurt am Main: Vittorio Klostermann).

Jackson, B.S. (1988), *Law, Fact and Narrative Coherence* (Liverpool: Deborah Charles Publications).

Jackson, F. (1998), *From Metaphysics to Ethics: A Defence of Conceptual Analysis* (Oxford: Clarendon).

Jackson, S. (2006), 'Legal Pluralism Between Islam and the Nation-State: Romantic Medievalism or Pragmatic Modernity?', *Fordham International Law Journal* 30, 158–76.

Kant, I. (1998), *Critique of Pure Reason* (the Cambridge edition of the works of Immanuel Kant) (Cambridge: Cambridge University Press).

Kelsen, H. (1992), *Introduction to the Problems of Legal Theory* (translated by B. Litschewski Paulson and S.L. Paulson) (Oxford: Clarendon Press).

Kevelson, R. (ed.) (1990), *Law and Semiotics Vol. 3* (New York: Plenum).

Kleinhans, M.M and MacDonald, R.A. (1998), 'What is Critical Legal Pluralism?', *Canadian Journal of Law and Society* 12, 25–46.

Korsgaard, C.M. (1996), *The Sources of Normativity* (Cambridge and New York: Cambridge University Press).

Kress, K. (1987), 'The Interpretive Turn', *Ethics* 97:4, 834–60.

Kripke, S. (1972), *Naming and Necessity* (Oxford: Blackwell).

Kronman, A. (1983), *Max Weber* (Stanford, CA: Edward Arnold).

Lacey, N. (1988), *State Punishment: Political Principles and Community Values* (London: Routledge).

Lacey, N. (2004), *A Life of H.L.A. Hart: The Nightmare and the Noble Dream* (Oxford: Oxford University Press).

Le Poidevin, R. and MacBeath, M. (eds) (1993), *The Philosophy of Time* (Oxford: Oxford University Press).

Leith, P. and Morison, J. (2005), 'Can Jurisprudence Without Empiricism Ever be Science?' in Coyle and Pavlakos (eds).

Lévinas, E. (1987), *Time and the Other* (Pittsburgh, PA: Duquesne University Press).

Levison, A.B. (1986), 'Clipping Time's Wings', *Mind* 95:378, 233–7.

Lewis, D.K. (1969), *Convention: A Philosophical Study* (Cambridge, MA: Harvard University Press).

Llewellyn, K.N. (1931), 'Some Realism about Realism: Responding to Dean Pound', *Harvard Law Review* 44:8, 1222–64.

Lloyd, G. (1993), *Being in Time: Selves and Narrators in Philosophy and Literature* (London and New York: Routledge).

Luhmann, N. (1985), *A Sociological Theory of Law* (London: Routledge and Kegan Paul).

Luhmann, N. (1988a), 'Closure and Openness: On Reality in the World of Law', in Teubner (ed.).

Luhmann, N. (1988b), 'The Unity of the Legal System', in Teubner (ed.).

Luhmann, N. (1995a), *Social Systems* (Palo Alto, CA: Stanford University Press).

Luhmann, N. (1995b), 'Legal Argumentation: An Analysis of its Form', *Modern Law Review* 58:3, 285–98.

Lynch, M.P. (1998), *Truth in Context: An Essay on Pluralism and Objectivity* (Cambridge, MA: MIT Press).

Lyotard, J-F. (1984), *The Postmodern Condition: A Report on Knowledge* (translated by G. Bennington and B. Massumi) (Manchester: Manchester University Press).

Lyotard, J-F. (1988), *The Différend: Phrases in Dispute* (translated by G. Van Den Abbeele) (Manchester: Manchester University Press).
MacCormick, D.N. (1978), *Legal Reasoning and Legal Theory* (Oxford: Clarendon Press).
MacCormick, D.N. (1980), 'The Coherence of a Case and the Reasonableness of Doubt', *Liverpool Law Review* 2, 45–50.
MacCormick, D.N. (1981), *H.L.A. Hart* (Stanford, CA: Edward Arnold).
MacCormick, D.N. (1991), 'Notes on Narrativity and the Normative Syllogism', *International Journal for the Semiotics of Law* 4:2, 163–74.
MacCormick, D.N. (1995), 'Time, Narratives and Law', in Bjarup and Blegvad (eds).
MacCormick, D.N. (1999), *Questioning Sovereignty: Law, State, and Nation in the European Commonwealth* (Oxford: Oxford University Press).
MacCormick, D.N. and Weinberger, O. (1986), *An Institutional Theory of Law: New Approaches to Legal Positivism* (Dordrecht and Lancaster: Reidel).
MacDonald, R.A. (1998), 'Metaphors of Multiplicity: Civil Society, Regimes and Legal Pluralism', *Arizona Journal of International and Comparative Law* 15, 69–91.
MacDonald, R.A. (2002), *Lessons of Everyday Law/Le droit du quotidien* (Montreal: McGill-Queen's University Press).
MacTaggart, J.E. (1908), 'The Unreality of Time', *Mind* 17, 456–73.
Majone, G. (1993), 'The European Community Between Social Policy and Social Regulation', *Journal of Common Market Studies* 31:2, 153–70.
Majone, G. (1994), 'The Rise of the Regulatory State in Europe', *West European Politics* 17:3, 78–102.
Majone, G. (1996), *Regulating Europe* (London: Routledge).
Majone, G. (2002), 'The European Commission: The Limits of Centralization and the Perils of Parliamentarization', *Governance* 15:3, 375–92.
Manderson, D. (1996), 'Beyond the Provincial: Space, Aesthetics and Modernist Legal Theory', *Melbourne University Law Review* 20, 1048–71.
Manderson, D. (ed.) (2005), *Legal Spaces: Law, Text, Culture Special Issue* 9.
Manji, A.S. (1999), 'Imagining Women's "Legal World": Towards a Feminist Theory of Legal Pluralism in Africa', *Social and Legal Studies* 8:4, 435–55.
Marcuse, H. (1991), *One-Dimensional Man: Studies in the Ideology of Advanced Industrial Society* (2nd edition with a new introduction by Douglas Kellner) (London: Routledge).
Marmor, A. (1996). 'On Convention', *Synthese* 107, 349–71.
Marmor, A. (2001), 'Legal Conventionalism', in Coleman (ed.).
Marmor, A. (2007), 'Deep Conventions', *Philosophy and Phenomenological Research* 74, 586–610.
Martin, B. (1991), *Strip the Experts* (London: Freedom Press).
Melissaris, E. (2004), 'The More the Merrier? A New Take on Legal Pluralism', *Social and Legal Studies* 13:1, 57–79.

Melissaris, E. (2005a), 'The Chronology of the Legal', *McGill Law Journal* 50:4, 839–61.

Melissaris, E. (2005b), 'The Limits of Institutionalised Legal Discourse', *Ratio Juris* 18:4, 464–83.

Melissaris, E. (2006a), 'Diachronic Universalization and the Law', in Bankowski and MacLean (eds).

Melissaris, E. (2006b), 'Perspective, Critique, and Pluralism in Legal Theory', *Northern Ireland Legal Quarterly* 57:4, 597–609.

Mellor, D. (1981), *Real Time* (Cambridge and New York: Cambridge University Press).

Menski, W. (2006), *Comparative Law in a Global Context: The Legal Systems of Asia and Africa* (Cambridge and New York: Cambridge University Press).

Merry, S.E. (1988), 'Legal Pluralism', *Law and Society Review* 22, 869–96.

Minow, M., Ryan, M. and Sarat, A. (eds) (1995), *Narrative, Violence, and the Law: The Essays of Robert Cover* (Ann Arbor: University of Michigan Press).

Moravcsik, A. (2002), 'In Defense of the "Democratic Deficit": Reassessing the Legitimacy of the European Union', *Journal of Common Market Studies* 40:4, 603–34.

Moravcsik, A. (2004), 'Is There a "Democratic Deficit" in World Politics? A Framework for Analysis', *Government and Opposition* 39:2, 336–63.

Morris, H. (1968), 'Persons and Punishment', *The Monist* 52:4, 31–63.

Murphy, J.G. (1970), 'Violence and the Rule of Law', *Ethics* 80:4, 319–21.

Murphy, J.G. (1971), 'Three Mistakes about Retributivism', *Analysis* 31:5, 166–9.

Newton-Smith, W.H. (1980), *The Structure of Time* (Henley-on-Thames: Routledge and Kegan Paul).

Newton-Smith, W.H. (1986), 'Space, Time and Space-Time: A Philosopher's View', in Flood and Lockwood (eds).

Norrie, A. (1991), *Law, Ideology and Punishment: Retrieval and Critique of the Liberal Ideal of Criminal Justice* (Dordrecht and Boston: Kluwer).

Nousiainen, K. (1995), 'Time of Law – Time of Experience', in Bjarup and Blegvad (eds).

Ost, F. (1999), *Le Temps du Droit* (Paris: Editions Odile Jacob).

Pardo, M.S. (2005), 'The Field of Evidence and the Field of Knowledge', *Law and Philosophy* 24:4, 321–92.

Paulson, S.L. (1998), 'Four Phases in Kelsen's Legal Theory? Reflections on a Periodization: A Review of Carsten Heidemann, Die Norm als Tatsache. Zur Normentheorie Hans Kelsens ("The Norm as Fact. On Hans Kelsen's Theory of Norms") (Baden-Baden: Nomos, 1997)', *Oxford Journal of Legal Studies* 18:1, 153–66.

Paulson, S.L. (1999), 'Introduction' to Kelsen, H. (1992), *Introduction to the Problems of Legal Theory* (translated by B. Litschewski Paulson and S.L. Paulson) (Oxford: Clarendon).

Paulson, S.L. (2001), 'Hans Kelsen's Theory of Imputation', *Ratio Juris* 14:1, 47–63.

Pavlakos, G. (2005), 'On the Necessity of the Interconnection between Law and Morality', *Ratio Juris* 18:1, 64–83.

Pavlakos, G. (2007a), *Our Knowledge of the Law: Objectivity and Practice in Legal Theory* (Oxford and Portland, Oregon: Hart Publishing).

Pavlakos, G. (ed.) (2007b), *Law, Rights and Discourse: The Legal Philosophy of Robert Alexy* (Oxford and Portland, Oregon: Hart Publishing).

Penner, J. (2002), 'The Current Debate: The Semantic Sting: "Soft Positivism", and the Authority of the Law According to Raz', in Penner, Schiff and Nobles (eds).

Penner, J., Schiff, D. and Nobles, R. (eds) (2002), *Jurisprudence and Legal Theory: Commentary and Materials* (London: Butterworths).

Perelman, C. (1980), *Justice, Law, and Argument: Essays on Moral and Legal Reasoning* (Dordrecht and Boston: Reidel).

Perry, S. (2001), 'Hart's Methodological Positivism', in Coleman (ed.).

Pospisil, L. (1971), *The Anthropology of Law: A Comparative Theory of Law* (New York: Harper and Row).

Postema, G. (1986), *Bentham and the Common Law Tradition* (Oxford: Clarendon Press).

Postema, G. (2004), 'Melody and the Law's Mindfulness of Time', *Ratio Juris* 17:2, 203–26.

Prior, A.N. (1968), *Papers on Time and Tense* (Oxford: Clarendon).

Putnam, H. (1973), 'Meaning and Reference', *The Journal of Philosophy* 70:19, Seventieth Annual Meeting of the American Philosophical Association Eastern Division, 699–711.

Quine, W.V.O. (1951), 'Two Dogmas of Empiricism', *Philosophical Review* 60, 20–43.

Rakoff, T.D. (2002), *A Time for Every Purpose: Law and the Balance of Time* (Cambridge, MA and London: Harvard University Press).

Rankin, K. (1981), 'MacTaggart's Paradox: Two Parodies', *Philosophy* 56:217, 333–48.

Rawls, J. (1971), *A Theory of Justice* (Cambridge, MA: Belknap Press).

Raz, J. (1979), *The Authority of Law: Essays on Law and Morality* (Oxford: Clarendon Press).

Raz, J. (1986), 'Dworkin: A New Link in the Chain', *California Law Review* 74:3, 1103–19.

Raz, J. (2007), 'The Argument from Justice: How Not to Reply to Legal Positivism', in Pavlakos (ed.) (2007a).

Reed, M.I. (1996), 'Expert Power and Control in Late Modernity: An Empirical Review and Theoretical Synthesis', *Organization Studies* 17:4, 573–97.

Rehg, W. and Bohman, J. (eds) (2001), *Pluralism and the Pragmatic Turn: The Transformation of Critical Theory (Essays in Honour of Thomas McCarthy)* (Cambridge, MA: MIT Press).

Rescher, N. (1993), *Pluralism: Against the Demand for Consensus* (Oxford: Clarendon).

Rodriguez-Blanco, V. (2005), 'Method in Law: Revision and Description', in Coyle and Pavlakos (eds).

Rodriguez-Blanco, V. (2006), 'The Methodological Problem in Legal Theory: Normative and Descriptive Jurisprudence Revisited', *Ratio Juris* 19:1, 26–54.

Ruskola, T. (2002), 'Legal Orientalism', *Michigan Law Review* 101:1, 179–234.

Ryan, M. (1995), 'Meaning and Alternity', in Minow, Ryan and Sarat (eds).

Sacco, R. (1995), 'Mute Law', *American Journal of Comparative Law* 43:3, 455–67.

Sarat, A. and Kearns, T.R. (1992), 'Making Peace with Violence', in Sarat and Kearns (eds).

Sarat, A. and Kearns, T.R. (eds) (1992), *Law's Violence* (Ann Arbor: University of Michigan Press).

Schlessinger, G. (1982), 'How Time Flies', *Mind* 91:364, 501–23.

Schlessinger, G. (1983), 'Reconstructing MacTaggart's Argument', *Philosophy* 58:226, 541–3.

Schneiderman, D. (2006), 'Pluralism, Disagreement, and Globalization: A Comment on Webber's "Legal Pluralism and Human Agency"', *Osgoode Hall Law Journal* 44:1, 199–209.

Searle, J.G. (1969), *Speech Acts: An Essay in the Philosophy of Language* (Cambridge: Cambridge University Press).

Shah, P. (2005), *Legal Pluralism in Conflict: Coping With Cultural Diversity in Law* (London: Routledge Cavendish).

Shapiro, M. (2005), '"Deliberative", "Independent" Technocracy v. Democratic Politics: Will the Globe Echo the EU?', *Law and Contemporary Problems* 68:3–4, 341–56.

Sherover, C.M. (ed.) (1975), *The Human Experience of Time: The Development of its Philosophic Meaning* (Evanston, Illinois: Northwestern University Press).

Singer, P. (1972), 'Moral Experts', *Analysis* 32:4, 115–17.

Sperber, D. and Wilson, D. (1995), *Relevance: Communication and Cognition* (Oxford: Blackwell).

St Augustine (1912), *Confessions, Book XI* (London: Loeb Classical Library).

Stavropoulos, N. (1996), *Objectivity in Law* (Oxford and New York: Clarendon).

Stavropoulos, N. (2001), 'Hart's Semantics', in Coleman (ed.).

Stavropoulos, N. (2003), 'Interpretivist Theories of Law', in E.N. Zalta (ed.), *The Stanford Encyclopedia of Philosophy* (Winter 2003 Edition) <http://plato.stanford.edu/entries/law-interpretivist/>.

Stroud, B. (1968), 'Transcendental Arguments', *The Journal of Philosophy* 15:9, 241–56.

Tamanaha, B. (1993), 'The Folly of the Social-Scientific Concept of Legal Pluralism', *Journal of Law and Society* 20:2, 192–217.

Tamanaha, B. (1997), *Realistic Socio-Legal Theory: Pragmatism and a Social Theory of Law* (Oxford: Clarendon Press).

Tamanaha, B. (2000), 'A Non-Essentialist Version of Legal Pluralism', *Journal of Law and Society* 27:2, 296–321.

Tamanaha, B. (2001), *A General Jurisprudence of Law and Society* (New York: Oxford University Press).

Teichmann, R. (1995), *The Concept of Time* (New York: Macmillan).

Teubner, G. (1983), 'Substantive and Reflexive Elements in Modern Law', *Law and Society Review* 17:2, 239–85.

Teubner, G. (ed.) (1988), *Autopoietic Law: A New Approach to Law and Society* (Berlin: Walter de Gruyter).

Teubner, G. (1992), 'The Two Faces of Janus: Rethinking Legal Pluralism', *Cardozo Law Review* 13, 1443–62.

Tie, W. (1999), *Legal Pluralism: Toward a Multicultural Conception of Law* (Aldershot: Ashgate).

Tsohatzidis, S.L. (ed.) (1994), *Foundations of Speech Act Theory: Philosophical and Linguistic Perspectives* (London: Routledge).

Tur, R. (2002), 'Time and Law', *Oxford Journal of Legal Studies* 22:3, 463–88.

Turner, S.P. (2003), *Liberal Democracy 3.0: Civil Society in an Age of Experts* (London: Sage).

Twining, W. (2000), *Globalisation and Legal Theory* (Oxford: Butterworths).

Van de Kerchove, M. and Ost, F. (1993), *The Legal System between Order and Disorder* (translated by Iain Stewart) (Oxford: Clarendon; New York: Oxford University Press).

Varga, C. (1981), 'Law Application and its Theoretical Conception', *Archiv für Rechts- und Sozialphilosophie* LXVII:4, 462–79.

Varga, C. (1990), 'The Fact and its Approach in Philosophy and in Law', in Kevelson (ed.).

Varga, C. (1995), *Theory of the Judicial Process: The Establishment of Facts* (Budapest: Akadémiai Kiadó).

von Benda-Beckmann, F. (1988), 'Comment on Merry', *Law and Society Review* 22:5, 897–901.

von Hirsch, A. (1976), *Doing Justice: The Choice of Punishment* (New York: Hill and Wang).

von Hirsch, A. and Ashworth, A. (eds) (1992), *Principled Sentencing* (Edinburgh: Edinburgh University Press).

Waismann, F. (1968), *How I See Philosophy* (London: Macmillan).

Walker, N. (1991), *Why Punish: Theories of Punishment Reassessed* (Oxford: Oxford University Press).

Walker, N. and Padfield, N. (1983), *Sentencing: Theory, Law and Practice* (London: Weidenfeld and Nicholson).

Walzer, M. (1994), *Thick and Thin: Moral Argument Home and Abroad* (Notre Dame: University of Notre Dame Press).

Ward, T. (2006), 'English Law's Epistemology of Expert Testimony', *Journal of Law and Society* 33:4, 572–95.

Webber, J. (2006), 'Legal Pluralism and Human Agency', *Osgoode Hall Law Journal* 44:1, 167–98.

Weber, M. (1968), *Economy and Society* (New York: Bedminster Press).

Weyrauch, W.O. and Bell, M.A. (1993), 'Autonomous Lawmaking: The Case of the "Gypsies"', *Yale Law Journal* 103:2, 323–99.
Wingert L. and Günther K. (eds) (2001), *Die Öffentlichkeit der Vernunft und die Vernunft der Öffentlichkeit, Festschrift für Jürgen Habermas* (Frankfurt am Main: Suhrkamp).
Winter, S. (2001), *A Clearing in the Forest: Law, Life, and Mind* (Chicago: University of Chicago Press).
Wittgenstein, L. (1967), *Philosophical Investigations* (translated by G.E.M. Anscombe) (Oxford: Blackwell).
Wolff, R.P. (1969), 'On Violence', *The Journal of Philosophy* 66:19, 601–16.

List of Websites

http://news.bbc.co.uk/go/pr/fr/-/2/hi/uk_news/7239283.stm (last accessed 30 June 2008).
http://news.bbc.co.uk/go/pr/fr/-/2/hi/uk_news/7239596.stm (last accessed 30 June 2008).
http://news.bbc.co.uk/go/pr/fr/-/2/hi/uk_news/politics/7264740.stm (last accessed 30 June 2008).
http://news.bbc.co.uk/go/pr/fr/-/2/hi/uk_news/7239567.stm (last accessed 30 June 2008).
http://www.guardian.co.uk/society/2005/jun/29/childrensservices.NHS (last accessed 5 March 2008).
http://news.bbc.co.uk/1/hi/health/1682321.stm (last accessed 17 July 2008).
http://news.bbc.co.uk/1/hi/world/asia-pacific/4661152.stm (last accessed 12 July 2008).
http://uk.reuters.com/article/oddlyEnoughNews/idUKT15021020070123 (last accessed 12 July 2008); *The Pavement*, February 2007, 4.
http://www.guardian.co.uk/politics/2005/mar/21/uk.race (last accessed 17 July 2008).

List of Cases

Dudley and Stephens [1884] 14 QBD 273 DC.
First Secretary of State and others v Chichester Borough Council [2004] EWCA Civ 1248.
The Queen on the Application of Mrs Diane Pretty v. Director of Public Prosecutions and Secretary of State for the Home Department [2001] UKHL 61.
McLoughlin v O'Brian [1983] 1 AC 410.

Index